William McKinley versus
William Jennings Bryan

William McKinley versus William Jennings Bryan

The Great Political Rivalry of the Turn of the 20th Century

JOHN M. PAFFORD

McFarland & Company, Inc., Publishers
Jefferson, North Carolina

LIBRARY OF CONGRESS CATALOGUING-IN-PUBLICATION DATA

Names: Pafford, John M. (John Monroe), author.
Title: William McKinley versus William Jennings Bryan :
    the great political rivalry of the turn of the 20th century /
    John M. Pafford.
Other titles: Great political rivalry of the turn of the 20th century
Description: Jefferson, North Carolina : McFarland & Company, Inc.,
    Publishers, 2020 | Includes bibliographical references and index.
Identifiers: LCCN 2020011066 | ISBN 9780786499755 (paperback :
    acid free paper) ∞
    ISBN 9781476639352 (ebook)
Subjects: LCSH: McKinley, William, 1843-1901. | Bryan, William Jennings,
    1860-1925. | Presidents—United States—Election—1896. | Presidents—
    United States—Election—1900. | United States—Politics and government—
    1893-1897. | United States—Politics and government—1897-1901. |
    Political campaigns—United States—History—19th century.
Classification: LCC E710 .P34 2020 | DDC 973.8/8092—dc23
LC record available at https://lccn.loc.gov/2020011066

BRITISH LIBRARY CATALOGUING DATA ARE AVAILABLE

ISBN (print) 978-0-7864-9975-5
ISBN (ebook) 978-1-4766-3935-2

Front cover images: *left to right* William Jennings Bryan
and William McKinley (Library of Congress)

Printed in the United States of America

McFarland & Company, Inc., Publishers
    Box 611, Jefferson, North Carolina 28640
    www.mcfarlandpub.com

To the memory of two flawed men who
had the vision of a country rooted
in Christian verities striving to be a beacon
of order, justice, and freedom.

Table of Contents

Preface

For most of the 19th century, the foreign policy focus of the United States was on trade with other countries, but our projection of power was substantially more limited. There were border disputes to our north with the British in Canada and to our south with Spanish Mexico and later with the independent Mexico. There was little support from the American public, though, for the acquisition of territory beyond the northern hemisphere until the last decade of the century. By then, the United States was well established in the front rank of countries as far as economic strength and population were concerned, but our ability to protect our interests with armed forces had not kept up with that growth. The army was limited in size, concerned with coast defense and frontier security against Indians. Its growth in size and power would not come until 1898. By the mid–1880s during Chester Alan Arthur's Administration, the navy began its slow revival from the doldrums of the post–Civil War years; during those years, it had sunk from being second only to the British navy during our Civil War to being of limited significance even as a coast defense force and of virtually no use in protecting American interests and citizens beyond our shores. The growth in our population and wealth spurred determination to protect better our interests and citizens along with a developing focus on doing our part to expand for people in other parts of the world the order, justice, and freedom so vital to us. There was a slowly growing recognition that as this country grew stronger, there was a concomitant responsibility to help others learn and grow. As the century ended, the United States possessed a powerful navy, an army which had grown quickly in size and capability, and an impressive expansion of its power worldwide, now occupying territories of both strategic and economic significance. We now were too wealthy, too big in population, too strategically located in a world more interconnected to stand apart from overseas events even if we wanted to.

Preface

The key period lying ahead in most of the coming pages is the 1890s, a decade beyond the memories of readers, but not too far removed since many of us have known people whose recollections go back to the years of William McKinley and William Jennings Bryan. Almost we can touch this time.

Introduction

The 1890s were one of the most dramatic decades in American history, one which marked the rapid rise of the United States onto the world stage as a country with powerful armed forces and a significant empire beyond our borders primarily as a result of our victory over Spain in 1898. The American economy, already impressive, continued to grow. Although there were abuses which needed correction, the freedom in the economy produced more and more wealth improving the lives of most of our people and attracting immigrants in large numbers.

The 1896 and 1900 clashes between William McKinley and William Jennings Bryan rank among the most exciting and definitive in the history of American presidential campaigns. The differences between the conservative McKinley, nominee of the Republican Party, and the liberal Bryan, who burst suddenly on the national stage as the Democratic Party choice, were sharp, more pronounced than in preceding post–Civil War elections when neither major party candidate was a big government, high tax, high spending liberal. Both men were devout Christians but drew substantially different conclusions concerning the domestic and foreign policy beliefs they based on that faith. Their personalities also were distinctly different; Bryan one of the most charismatic candidates in our political history, McKinley experienced and solid, but not exciting.

By the mid–1890s, each man was the major figure in his party. McKinley was governor of Ohio after serving seven terms in the U.S. House of Representatives. During the Civil War, he had demonstrated initiative, courage, and leadership, rising to the rank of major by the age of 22. He was committed to the gold standard, believed in limited government and led more from behind the scenes than did the flamboyant Bryan who surged to control of the Democratic Party in 1896, both leading and riding the wave of discontent which swept aside the Cleveland conservatives who had led it until then. Under Grover Cleveland, the Democratic Party

3

had been somewhat more conservative than the Republicans. The major depression of 1893 shook the confidence of many Democrats. When that was combined with Cleveland's being a lame duck as his second presidential term neared its end and Bryan's charisma, the way was opened for the party to shift course radically.

A former two-term member of the U.S. House of Representatives and a defeated candidate for the U.S. Senate in 1894, the 36-year-old Bryan was hardly a household name, but he was driven by a sense of destiny and by personal ambition. He came to the 1896 Democratic Party convention convinced that he would be their presidential nominee. His dramatic "Cross of Gold" speech galvanized the delegates, culminating with his soaring conclusion: "You shall not press down upon the brow of labor this crown of thorns; you shall not crucify mankind upon a cross of gold." From relative obscurity, he shot to prominence, winning the nomination on the fifth ballot. Any possibility for a reasoned defense of the gold standard at the convention was swept away by the flood of enthusiasm for Bryan.

Back in 1892, liberals had faced the bleak prospect of choosing between two conservative alternatives for president, incumbent Benjamin Harrison and Grover Cleveland mounting a comeback. Out of this quandary came the People's Party, also known as the Populist Party. In the general election that year, they carried four states and one electoral vote in another. They were ambitious to become a major party, but Bryan stole much of their left-wing thunder in 1896. He had refused to join them, convinced that he could lead the Democrats to a left of center promised land. Most of the Populists swallowed hard and nominated Bryan who, after all, did support key parts of their agenda. As a face-saving gesture, they chose their own separate running mate for him. This could have been a problem, but Republican McKinley won a clear majority of the Electoral College.

The Cleveland conservatives, numbering barely one-third of the 1896 convention delegates, were inundated by the Bryan tidal wave. Many of these conservatives held a convention in Indianapolis and nominated a ticket of Senator John Palmer of Illinois, 79 years old, and former governor Simon Bolivar Buckner of Kentucky, 73 years in age. These strong gold standard conservatives hoped to unite North and South since Palmer had been a general in the United States army during the Civil War and Buckner had been a Confederate general. Elderly but vigorous, they mounted a spirited campaign, but convinced only slightly over 133,000 voters to support them. Most conservative Democrats, aghast at the thought of

Bryan as President, voted for Republican William McKinley as the far better alternative. The Republicans now were the sound money, pro-business party.

As the Republican presidential nominee, McKinley conducted a then standard "front porch" campaign from his home in Canton, Ohio, speaking to an estimated 750,000 people who traveled there. The energetic Bryan mounted a campaign more familiar to people today. Over 100 days, he covered 16,000 miles and gave 600 speeches before about 5,000,000 people. Theodore Roosevelt, still in his 30s and in the early stages of his spectacular rise to the presidency, demonstrated similar verve as he covered a wide swath of the country in his support of McKinley and stirred the enthusiasm of those who heard him. Audiences resounded with cheers, seeing him as the future of the Republican Party. Although considering McKinley "an upright and honorable man, of very considerable ability and good record as a soldier and in Congress," Roosevelt questioned the nominee's firmness and largeness of vision, but he had no doubt that Bryan was a dangerous radical who would be a disaster as president. With these dynamic young men, a new generation which grew up after the Civil War was moving to the top in both parties.

McKinley won a solid victory, gaining a substantial number of Democratic votes and losing few Republican votes to Bryan. The Republicans again controlled the presidency. Since Abraham Lincoln won in 1860, only Grover Cleveland had broken their run of success.

The year 1896 marked the beginning of the left's control of the national Democratic Party, a control which would slip in 1904 and in 1924, but only somewhat and only for a short time. Never again would the Democrats be the more conservative of the major parties as they had been during the Cleveland years.

Initially, McKinley sought to avoid the Spanish-American War of 1898, but came to see it as an opportunity for the United States to spread our principles of order, justice, and freedom. Bryan too supported the war, an exception to his pacifist convictions, because of his staunch opposition to the brutality of Spanish colonialism. He served as a colonel commanding a volunteer regiment, although he and his unit never left Florida. Theodore Roosevelt's combat leadership now made him a national figure and catapulted him to the governorship of New York in November of that year.

The United States won the Spanish-American War, acquiring Puerto Rico, the Philippines, and Guam plus freeing Cuba from Spain while retaining Guantanamo Bay as a major naval base. Furthermore, in separate transactions, Hawaii in 1898 and the eastern part of Samoa in 1899 also became American.

But by no means was Bryan finished as the key figure in the Democratic Party. The 1900 election was a rematch of 1896, with McKinley slightly increasing his margin of victory, Theodore Roosevelt now his vice president. The assassination of McKinley in 1901 ended this chapter in American history. A brief summary of Bryan's remaining years (1908 presidential nominee, secretary of state under Woodrow Wilson, the Scopes Trial) will conclude the book.

1

McKinley: The Road to the White House

Early Years

William McKinley was born on January 29, 1843, in Niles, Ohio, the seventh of nine children. His father, William Sr., of Scottish Highlander lineage, was part owner of a moderately successful iron foundry. His mother, Nancy Allison McKinley, a devout Methodist from an English Puritan family, raised the children lovingly but firmly. Although neither parent had much formal education, both encouraged their children to learn. Among the modest number of books in their home were, in addition to the Bible, Gibbon's *History of the Decline and Fall of the Roman Empire* plus works by Shakespeare and Dickens. Undergirding all was faithful attendance at church and Sunday School.

A normal, healthy boy, young William enjoyed outdoor activities such as swimming and fishing. It was his determination to learn, to progress educationally that marked him as more than ordinary. Wanting his children to have better schooling than was available in Niles, the older William moved his family to Poland, about 15 miles distant, where the children could attend Poland Academy. William Sr., continued his business in Niles, rejoining his family on weekends in Poland. Here they lived in a large white house shaded by maple trees, the yard surrounded by a white picket fence. While living in Poland, McKinley formally professed his Christian faith and joined the Methodist Church, beginning a lifelong affiliation. Here too he developed his debating skill, exhibiting the ability to make points and win without antagonizing his opponents.

In 1860, McKinley graduated from Poland Academy at the age of 17 and enrolled in Allegheny College across the state line in Meadville, Pennsylvania. During the winter, he dropped out, perhaps due to illness or because of financial problems—it is not clear which. Returning home, he took a teaching position, walking three miles each way.

But the quiet life of a teacher was not to be his. The election of Abraham Lincoln as president in November 1860 spurred the South to secede and form the Confederate States of America. For a time, many on both sides of the border nurtured hope that somehow there would be a peaceful resolution and a coming back together. It was not to be.

Civil War Service

On April 12, 1861, Confederate artillery opened fire on Union-held Fort Sumter in the harbor of Charleston, South Carolina, igniting the Civil War. In June, McKinley, patriotic and anti-slavery, enlisted in the Poland Guards, the local volunteer unit. On June 11, they were sworn into federal service as a company in the 23rd Ohio Volunteer Infantry, a regiment in the rapidly expanding United States army. The regiment initially was commanded by Colonel, later General, William S. Rosecrans with future president of the United States Rutherford B. Hayes serving as a major. Hayes later would command the 23rd Ohio and end the war as a major general. Swearing in the men at their camp near Columbus was General John Charles Fremont, famous as an explorer, soldier during the war with Mexico, U.S. Senator from California, and the first presidential candidate of the Republican Party. McKinley was thrilled by being so close to such a famous, heroic figure of whom he had heard so much. Of this encounter, the awestruck McKinley later said that "I remember he pounded my chest and looked square into my eyes, and finally pronounced me fit for a soldier."[1]

Fremont's prominence led Lincoln to make him a major general in command of the Department of the West comprising Illinois and encompassing the states from Missouri westward to the Rocky Mountains. Within a matter of weeks, he clashed with Lincoln by proclaiming martial law, freeing the slaves in his area of command, and confiscating the property of those in Missouri who supported the Confederacy. Lincoln was determined to end slavery, but at his pace, first ensuring that the Union would survive.

Removed from the Department of the West, Fremont's prominence and popularity moved Lincoln to give him a new assignment, the Mountain Department, which brought together western Virginia, eastern Kentucky, and a slice of eastern Tennessee. Taking over command in late March, Fremont lasted only until June, having been outmaneuvered and befuddled by Confederate general Thomas "Stonewall" Jackson. It was then that Lincoln, still seeking successful generals in the war to preserve the Union, created the Army of Virginia under General John Pope with Fremont one of three division commanders. This Fremont rejected, ending his active service. McKinley, nevertheless, never forgot the hero of his youth even though he did come to see his shortcomings as a general and the wisdom of Lincoln's wanting to preserve the Union first, then move to abolish slavery.[2]

Completing the few weeks of training they would get, in June the 23rd Ohio moved into the western part of Virginia which was pro Union and soon would become the separate state of West Virginia. They were to secure the area from Confederate guerrillas. McKinley was assigned to the brigade quartermaster unit. On September 10, he had his first combat experience, a skirmish at Carnifex Ferry with a Confederate force commanded by General John B. Floyd. Outnumbered, the Confederates withdrew quickly, leaving behind a quantity of supplies and personal effects and boosting the morale of the raw Union soldiers. Soon after, military operations wound down as both sides went into winter quarters.

The new campaign season opened in April 1862 with the 23rd Ohio assigned again to anti-guerrilla operations. That same month, McKinley was promoted to commissary sergeant, assigned to providing supplies and horses for the men plus all the attendant paperwork. His ability and efficiency caught the eye of Major Hayes who wrote of him, "We soon found that in business, in executive ability, young McKinley was a man of rare capacity, especially for a boy of his age."[3]

McKinley, still a teenager, would find 1862 exciting and challenging with opportunities to show more dramatically his initiative and courage. As the year opened, both sides now realized that there would be no quick victory, that a lengthy war with bitter fighting lay ahead. The primary theater of operations was in northern Virginia between Richmond and Washington, the two national capitals. Here the Union forces under General George McClellan grew stronger in numbers and morale, while staying inactive. McClellan was an excellent planner and organizer but lacked the daring and battlefield skill of his soon-to-be opponent, Robert E. Lee.[4]

In the middle of March, McClellan moved his Army of the Potomac by sea to the peninsula between the York and James Rivers southeast of Richmond. This was an excellent plan, attacking from a less expected direction rather than from the north. The implementation of the plan, though, was dilatory even though McClellan's army initially outnumbered the Confederates under General Joseph E. Johnston, a capable defensive commander who lacked Lee's aggressiveness. When Johnston was wounded, Lee replaced him in command of the Army of Northern Virginia. Lee continued Johnston's skillful withdrawal toward Richmond, looking for an opportunity for a sharp riposte even though McClellan's army outnumbered his about 105,000 to 85,000. Seeing his opening, Lee struck, halting McClellan's attack and driving back the Union forces in a series of battles during July leading to the decision by the North to abandon the campaign.

Disillusioned by McClellan's lack of drive, Lincoln summoned General John Pope, who had built a winning record in the Western theater of operations, to command the newly created Army of Virginia. Pope saw himself as a great leader who would humble Lee, showing the Union army in the East how to fight and win. Now, though, he encountered the crème de la crème of the Confederate military—the Army of Northern Virginia commanded by Lee, ably assisted by generals such as Jackson and James Longstreet. Lee determined to attack Pope before McClellan and the Army of the Potomac could withdraw from the failed Peninsula Campaign. In late August, Lee did so, routing him in the Second Battle of Bull Run. At this stage, Pope was removed, sent back west, and his Army of Virginia combined with the Army of the Potomac. Lincoln, in spite of his misgivings about McClellan, turned again to him, recognizing his morale-building and defensive skills.

Following his victory at Second Bull Run, Lee turned northward, invading Maryland with several objectives. This move would bring the war to the North where the Confederates could find horses and food in abundance. Also, a victory here might bring Maryland, a border state with some Southern sympathies, into the Confederacy. Finally, a triumph on Union soil might lead to European recognition and so discourage the North as to bring about an acceptance of Southern independence.

It came close to happening, but a Confederate staff officer dropped a copy of Lee's plans which were brought to McClellan. Knowing now of Lee's intentions, he moved to crush the invaders. On September 17, the two armies clashed at Antietam. Although the North enjoyed an 87,000 to 40,000 numerical advantage as the battle opened, McClellan was convinced that he was outnumbered and held in reserve about half of his men. This lack of drive combined with Lee's tactical skill led to a draw on the battlefield after a bloody and exhausting day. The next day, both sides held their positions; McClellan still did not bring his superior numbers to bear. The day following, Lee retreated, unmolested, into Virginia permitting the North to claim a strategic victory.

Among the Union reinforcements sent east to augment McClellan's Army of the Potomac was the 23rd Ohio which arrived in time to join General Ambrose Burnside's corps for its attack at South Mountain on September 14. The outnumbered Confederates fought hard there, buying time for Lee, fully aware now that McClellan knew of his plans, to concentrate his army at Antietam Creek near Sharpsburg. In the battle at Antietam on September 17, McKinley made his mark for clear-headedness and courage under fire. At first, as a commissary sergeant, he was behind the front lines. As the battle developed and as the hours passed, McKinley recognized that the men of his regiment needed sustenance. He filled two wagons with supplies, hitched mules to them, ordered two privates to join him, and headed into the cauldron. One wagon lost its mule team, but McKinley got through with his despite coming under heavy infantry and artillery fire. Years after the war, one of the men who saw McKinley in action that day wrote:

> Our Regiment had gone into the fight at daylight, without breakfast or rations of food of any kind, and was the first command to receive the fire of that memorable day. Our regiment became almost completely exhausted from fighting, fatigue, and lack of food and water. While in this condition we saw a wagon, drawn by army mules, coming towards us from the rear at breakneck speed, through a terrific fire of musketry and artillery that seemed to threaten annihilation to everything within its range.
>
> I have many times since thought it a miracle that it and its escort was not utterly destroyed. The wagon, when it arrived, proved to be in charge of Comrade McKinley, and contained a supply of cooked rations, meat, coffee, and hardtack, and was heartily welcomed by our tired and half famished boys.[5]

This action earned McKinley a promotion to lieutenant.

After Antietam, the 23rd Ohio was not engaged in any of the great historical battles which highlighted the last three years of the war, but still saw plenty of action away from the headline grabbing clashes.

At this stage, McKinley and his regiment were sent back to the Shenandoah Valley. Although this was not the primary area of military operations in the East, it was important to both sides. It now would be helpful to have an overview of the war as a whole before returning to McKinley.

Following the Union victory at Antietam, Lincoln issued the Emancipation Proclamation declaring that on January 1, 1863, all slaves in states in rebellion against the United States would be free. Lincoln waited for this time to make the announcement so that it would not appear to be a move of desperation to engender support. This put the war officially on a higher moral level, making it difficult for the British and/or the French to aid a country which retained slavery.[6]

As weeks passed and McClellan still failed to mount an offensive, Lincoln's patience snapped and on November 5 he replaced McClellan with the much more aggressive General Ambrose Burnside. On December 13, Burnside rashly attacked the positions held by Lee's Army of Northern Virginia on the heights above Fredericksburg, Virginia. Although the Army of the Potomac fought bravely, they failed to carry the Confederate positions and suffered heavy losses in defeat. In January, after a futile attempt to turn the Confederate flank, Burnside was replaced by General Joseph "Fighting Joe" Hooker. There would be no more major operations in the East until spring. Overall, 1862 had been a good year for the Confederates in the East.

For the Union, 1862 would be better in the West. The year opened with promise for the Confederates on the far western fringes of their territory with General Henry Hopkins Sibley attacking out of El Paso, Texas, defeating Union troops at Valverde, and invading New Mexico, capturing Albuquerque and Santa Fe. There were Confederate dreams of seizing the gold mines of Colorado and, perhaps, even moving on to California, but Union units would regroup, reinforcements would arrive, and Sibley would then be forced to retreat to El Paso, and the dream ended.

In February, General Ulysses S. Grant led the Union seizures of Fort Henry on the Tennessee River in southwestern Kentucky not far from where it flows into the Mississippi and Fort Donelson about 12 miles east on the Cumberland River. When the defenders of Fort Donelson requested surrender terms, Grant stated in his reply, "No terms except unconditional and immediate surrender can be accepted."[7]

In April, Confederates under General Albert Sidney Johnston struck Union forces under Grant at Shiloh in southwestern Tennessee. Enjoying initial success, Johnston was mortally wounded and the next day the Confederates forced to retreat, giving the Union a well-needed major victory.

On April 25, New Orleans fell to Union admiral David G. Farragut closing that strategic port and marking a key step in gaining control of the Mississippi River thereby cutting the Confederacy in half.

On October 8, a Union army commanded by General Don Carlos

Buell clashed at Perryville, Kentucky, with Confederates under General Braxton Bragg. The battle was a draw, but Bragg's retreat to Tennessee marked another forward step for the Union. Buell, slow to move, was replaced by General William Rosecrans who followed the retreating Confederates. The two armies clashed again December 31–January 2 at Stone's River, a few miles southeast of Nashville. Here Bragg won a narrow advantage on the battlefield, but failing to win a clear victory, the Confederates again retreated slowly to the south toward Chattanooga. Although the Confederates did win some minor victories, as 1862 ended, momentum in the West was with the Union.

The arrival of spring in 1863 opened, as usual, the campaign season. Major combat operations in the East would not be long delayed, both Lee and Hooker being aggressive generals eager for victory on the battlefield. Lee, outnumbered as usual, waited as a counterpunching boxer for Hooker to leave himself open for a knockout punch. This happened. Hooker had a sound enough plan if only Lee would sit still and let it develop. But no, Lee sized up Hooker's intentions and again, as at Second Bull Run, divided his army, thoroughly befuddled Hooker and routed the Army of the Potomac at Chancellorsville over May 1–4. Hooker pulled back quickly, saving his army from annihilation.

Tragically, Jackson was wounded fatally by his own men. After commanding the flank assault which struck the decisive blow, Jackson was shot by mistake as he returned to the Confederate position at dusk. Lee reorganized the Army of Northern Virginia into three corps commanded by Generals James Longstreet, Richard Ewell, and A.P. Hill. They were able men, but Jackson could not be replaced fully.

Within a few weeks of Chancellorsville, Lincoln would face the reality that Hooker would have to go; once again, Lee's generalship and the Army of Northern Virginia had triumphed. Lincoln turned now to General George G. Meade, if not a brilliant general, a steady and reliable one.

Lee now moved north into Pennsylvania for the same reasons which motivated his invasion the previous year, seeking that decisive victory which would ensure the independence of the South. On July 1–3, the armies clashed at Gettysburg in the most significant battle of the war. Lee came close to victory, but the Army of the Potomac did not crack. At the end of the three days of bitter conflict neither side had scored a knockout, but the checking of Lee meant that there would be no Southern victory on Northern soil. It is possible that a Confederate win at Gettysburg could have led to recognition of the Confederate States of America by the

British. This might have led further to action by the Royal Navy to break the blockade of Confederate ports and to attack by the British army in Canada against the bordering states. Also, the United States had objected to French intervention in Mexico. Had the Confederates won at Gettysburg, France too might have taken diplomatic, military, and naval steps to support Southern independence. Finally, a victorious Army of Northern Virginia in the North might have compelled the United States government to give in and accept Southern independence.

There is no way to know if these were illusions or potential reality. On July 4, the two armies held their positions at Gettysburg, then Lee retreated to Virginia just as after Antietam the previous year. The Army of the Potomac was itself too battered to contest the move. Also on July 4, Vicksburg surrendered to Grant and now the Union controlled the Mississippi. There was to be no European intervention.[8]

From the vantage point of historical perspective, it was clear as 1863 ended that the North would win the war and that there was no reason to fear that Lincoln would be defeated in his campaign for reelection in 1864. Yet when one is not on the high ground of historical perspective but rather is bogged down in the present, the big picture can be hard to see. In the Western theater, the 1864 campaign season opened with Union forces under General William Tecumseh Sherman advancing slowly and at heavy cost southward from Chattanooga toward Atlanta, being opposed skillfully at each step by the Confederates under General Joseph E. Johnston. On June 27, the impatient Sherman rashly ordered a direct attack on the Confederate position at Kennesaw Mountain less than 25 miles north of Atlanta. Fed up with time-consuming maneuvering, he was determined to crush his enemy with one blow. Instead, Sherman suffered a bloody repulse, learned his lesson, and returned to the slower albeit more effective use of the flanking moves. But, as summer arrived, there was no Union victory in the West. Still seeking that illusive victory in the key eastern theater, Lincoln promoted Grant, who had enjoyed success against Confederate forces in the West, to command all Union armies. Meade remained in command of the Army of the Potomac; however, since Grant actively took the field, he now was in a subordinate position.

In the spring of 1864, Grant began pushing south for Richmond, but constantly was thwarted by Lee who brilliantly led the Army of Northern Virginia in a series of battles. On May 5–6, they clashed at the Wilderness, the area where Lee had triumphed just one year previously in the Battle of Chancellorsville. After two days of bitter fighting, the result was a draw on the battlefield with Union losses almost twice those suffered by Lee's army—17,000 compared with 9000. In the past, a Union general so bloodied, especially in a non-win, would have pulled back to recover. Not so Grant; he now continued his offensive, moving south around Lee's right flank for Spotsylvania Court House, 10 miles away. Could he get there first, the Army of the Potomac would be between Lee and Richmond, forcing Lee to attack in order to protect the Confederate capital, the result of which most likely would have been a decisive loss for the South. Lee, though, reached Spotsylvania first. On May 11, Grant ordered an assault on the Confederate positions. The result was a bloody failure. Yet again, Grant was not discouraged. Lee was facing a Union general different from any of the others he had encountered; Grant continued to move south toward Richmond.

On June 1 at Cold Harbor just outside Richmond, Grant continued his determined policy to smash Lee, but the outcome he sought still eluded him. An even more bloody repulse was the reality as the day ended. Union losses were about 7000, those of the Confederacy about 1500 and Lee still held his lines. The North, though, could replace their losses, whereas Southern numbers were shrinking as Union forces occupied more of the Confederacy. Still as determined as ever, Grant sent forces to seize Richmond from the south, but Confederate reinforcements arrived just in time to blunt the blow.

In the West, Confederate president Jefferson Davis feared that Johnston would give up Atlanta and replaced him with John Bell Hood, a bold general always looking for an opening to launch an offensive. This he did, charging forward at Sherman's army in three battles just outside Atlanta. After heavy fighting, the Confederates lost all three, and Atlanta was occupied by Sherman on September 2. He now began his famous march to Savannah which fell to him on December 13. The previous month, Admiral David Farragut won the naval battle of Mobile Bay closing Mobile, one of the few remaining significant Confederate ports.

With these victories, the end of the war now was in view and the possibility gone that a war-weary electorate would reject Lincoln's bid for a second term, as had seemed quite possible earlier. On August 23, Lincoln had written that "this morning, as for some days past, it seems exceedingly probable that this Administration will not be reelected."[9] The Democrats had nominated George McClellan for president and had adopted a platform making peace the number one priority even if that meant accepting Southern independence and the continuation of slavery there.

In the November election, Lincoln carried 22 states, losing only Kentucky, Delaware, and New Jersey, and winning 55.02 percent of the popular vote to McClellan's 44.96 percent.

For McKinley, service in the Shenandoah Valley of Virginia had him out of the primary battle zones, but in an area of significance to both sides because of its being a key invasion route; both Hooker and Lee had used it in 1863 to launch what each had hoped would be a knockout blow and Grant's 1864 campaign began there. Also, its being a vital source of food for the South focused the attention of both sides on it. For McKinley, the proximity of the Shenandoah Valley to Ohio made his career there of interest to the people of that state and beneficial to him when he began his political career.

McKinley and the 23rd Ohio were part of the force under General George Crook which on May 9, 1864, defeated outnumbered Confederates at Cloyd's Mountain. They also saw action on July 24 at Winchester. Confederates under General Jubal Early struck the Union lines early in the morning and broke through, driving the Union forces from the field, and winning the day, something by now increasingly rare for the Confederate army. During the battle Hayes, now commanding the brigade of which the 23rd Ohio was one of four regiments, sent McKinley to lead back to Union lines a battalion of the 23rd which had been cut off by the Confederate advance. Hayes later commented that he considered the odds long that McKinley would succeed and live through the mission. He did so, further enhancing the esteem in which he was held by Hayes. There was a deep, mutual respect these warriors had for each other. McKinley wrote of Hayes, "His whole nature seemed to change when in battle. From the sunny, agreeable, the kind, the generous, the gentleman ... he was, when the battle was on ... intense and ferocious."[10]

In September, McKinley, now a captain on Crook's staff, fought at Opequham, again showing courage and a willingness to take responsibility. He demonstrated these qualities even more impressively at Cedar Creek on October 19, carrying messages and seeing to the emplacement of artillery. Here again, Early's Confederates launched an early morning assault and drove back their surprised opponents who did not believe that the Confederates still were capable of such an attack. General Philip Sheridan, given command of Union forces in the Shenandoah Valley, had been summoned to a conference in Washington, and returned just in time to rally his men and score a smashing victory. McKinley witnessed this dramatic intervention and joined in the turning of the tide.[11]

On March 13, 1865, McKinley was promoted to brevet major for his "gallant and meritorious services,"[12] the capstone of a commendable career as a soldier. As spring blossomed, the collapse of the Confederacy was rapid. On April 2, Lee was forced to retreat westward from his position at Petersburg and the same day, the Confederate government abandoned Richmond. Just a few days later, on April 9, Lee surrendered to Grant at Appomattox Court House. The assassination of Lincoln on April 14 cast a pall over the events. Still, the war was almost over and the country again united, so rejoicing over that did mitigate the grief. The final Confederate dominoes soon fell. On April 26, Joseph Johnston surrendered to Sherman near Durham, North Carolina, and one month later, Edmund Kirby Smith ordered the last organized Confederate force to lay down their arms.

After marching in the grand review in Washington, McKinley and the 23rd Ohio traveled to Camp Taylor near Cleveland, Ohio, where they were discharged on July 26. In future years, he did not write or talk a great deal about the war. He often was addressed as "Major" McKinley, something he by no means rejected. His memories of the war did not minimize the danger and suffering, but his support for the twin goals of reuniting the country and ending slavery were paramount. As a consequence, his memories focused more on these outcomes. He did not go out of his way to emphasize this service, letting his record and the words of others remind the public of what he had done.

Into the Political Arena

Now 22 years old, McKinley had developed during the Civil War from a raw teenager to a mature young man who had proven that he could act bravely and lead effectively in the intense pressure situations of war. He had done his duty well without being broken by combat or so hardened by it that he could not function in civilian life as happened to some veterans. Under normal circumstances, McKinley would have been a recent college graduate just beginning his professional life. Briefly he considered staying in the army and making a career of soldiering. This did not progress beyond being a brief consideration. His mother had hopes for his entering the clergy, but, in spite of his strong Christian beliefs, he felt no call to full time ministry. The law emerged clearer and clearer from the mélange of possibilities.

As he pondered his prospects, he wrote Hayes who had been not only his commanding officer, but also a mentor. Hayes had been elected to the U.S. House of Representatives in 1864 but refused to take office until the war ended. He advised McKinley to go west to one of the growing metropolises such as Chicago, St. Louis, Kansas City, Omaha, or Leavenworth and enter into commercial business or railroading. These he considered better options than becoming a lawyer.[13] As much as McKinley appreciated the advice, he determined to pursue the legal profession and later seek public office.

At that time, law school was not mandated for prospective attorneys. It was common for those entering this field to study law privately then take the bar examination. This course McKinley chose. He was a determined young man with the capacity to work hard for long hours to attain his goals. He took his first steps down this path by reading the law in the office of Charles Glidden, the most prominent attorney in Poland. Glidden recognized McKinley's potential and advised him to augment what he could gain in a small Ohio community by attending law school. This counsel he accepted and in September 1866 entered Albany Law School in Albany, New York, a well-regarded institution.

Here he continued his pattern of hard work, often studying past midnight. He did fit in time for social life and attending the theater. McKinley was popular with women, being a handsome, well-built young man with the mystique of having been a combat officer in the late war. He was convivial, but never became a playboy; his Christian faith and his determination to rise professionally and politically kept him from such deviations.

In the spring of 1867, he returned to Ohio and passed the bar examination. It is not clear why he did not remain longer in law school. Perhaps, at 24, he was impatient to begin his career. Regardless of the reason, McKinley now was an attorney. Seeking a larger base from which to launch his practice, he moved a few miles away to Canton where his sister Anne was a schoolteacher and where his brother Abner moved. Canton was the county seat of Stark County, was located in a prosperous farming area, and was anticipating industrial development as the postwar economic boom continued. His practice grew due to his ability as a lawyer augmented by his record as an army officer, his good looks, and his personality.

Soon after he opened his law office, McKinley was embroiled in the politics of Ohio, a state where the two major parties were evenly balanced and contentious. The 1867 Republican nominee for governor was Rutherford Hayes, midway through his second term in the House. On June 19, the Ohio Republican state convention had nominated him, and he had accepted. This year was bad nationally for that party, primarily due to the unpopularity of President Andrew Johnson who came within an eyelash of being removed from office by the Senate after being impeached by the House. Hayes won a narrow victory in his race, but the Democrats took control of the legislature and captured Hayes' old House seat. The new governor began his first two-year term on January 13, 1868. He won a second term, declined to run for a third consecutive time, but did reenter the arena in the 1874 race and won. The Republicans captured both houses of the legislature as well.[14] The extraordinarily dramatic and historically fascinating election of 1876 will remain in the wings for discussion later.

McKinley also supported Grant for the presidency in 1868, organizing Grant clubs and serving as chairman of the Republican Central Committee for Stark County. As an organizer and as a speaker, he impressed people as a young man with a bright future. Grant's victory was easy, a combination of his highly successful war record, the Democrats' disarray, and their nominating a candidate, Horatio Seymour, who stirred little excitement.[15] McKinley began his own climb up the political pyramid with his election in 1869 as prosecuting attorney for Stark County. His reelection bid in 1871 fell short and he returned to building his law practice until the next opportunity moved him to start his climb anew.

There was a bright spot, though, earlier in the year; on January 24, he married Ida Saxton, a daughter within the most prominent of Canton families. Her grandfather had founded and edited the Canton *Repository* and her father was a prosperous banker. The newlyweds shared a deep Christian faith. Furthermore, Ida was thoroughly supportive of her husband's determination to rise politically. She was an educated, independent-minded, attractive young lady who was ambitious for a more exciting, dramatic life than was offered by a small city in Ohio. Also evident in addition to these positive qualities was a precarious mental balance which would lead to emotional problems later in their married life. Throughout their lives together, though, they were devoted to each other. They honeymooned in New York, then returned to Canton, moving into a home which was a gift of her father.

Their first child, Katherine, nicknamed Katie, was born on Christmas, 1871. She became the centerpiece of her parents' home life, growing to be a bright, spirited little girl. A second daughter, named Ida after her mother, arrived on April 1, 1873. Sickly from the beginning, the baby died on August 22. Her parents, especially her mother, grieved deeply and focused much more on Katie. The family's woes multiplied when Katie contracted typhoid fever and died on June 25, 1875. This shattered Ida, distraught that she must have displeased God, that He was punishing her. These deaths weakened her already tenuous grasp on mental stability. Her Christian faith and her love for her husband brought her back from the brink of total collapse, but she remained fragile through the remaining years of their marriage, although she supported his career. McKinley's faith grew through these trying times, sustaining him and strengthening him.[16]

Earlier in 1875, before the death of Katie, McKinley had been a delegate to the Republican state convention which had nominated Rutherford Hayes for a third term as governor. Hayes campaigned vigorously, aided by McKinley's talents as an effective organizer and speaker. When the votes were counted, Hayes was back as governor and the Republicans controlled both houses in the legislature. This success in Ohio, one of the key states for someone aspiring to be president, put Hayes on the short list of prospective 1876 candidates for that office.[17]

This same year, 1876, also marked a significant rise in the political life of William McKinley. In the spring, he represented striking coal miners in the Tuscarawas Valley who had been charged with violently attacking workers hired to replace them and with destruction of property. Governor Hayes, although sympathizing with the miners' plight, would not tolerate the breakdown of law and order and sent the state militia to restore them. Public opinion was with the governor and in opposition to the strikers, making it difficult for them to find an attorney to represent those put on trial. McKinley ably presented the case that the miners suffered from poor working and living conditions. He did not justify their using violence but did argue that the mine owners could have averted the trouble had they been more open to the plight of their employees. He called for the jurors to consider what they would have done had they been the miners. Only one man was found guilty; he was sentenced to three years in prison. McKinley refused compensation for representing the men.

This case evinced both McKinley's belief in the rightness of his action and shrewd calculation of the political benefits. He obviously impressed the miners with his successful defense of them and the labor movement in general with his recognition of their legitimate grievances. On the other hand, he was no revolutionary, but rather a firm believer in Christian civilized order which must be just. His pro-business beliefs were evident, so that he earned the friendship and support of Marcus Alonzo Hanna, better known as Mark Hanna, a prominent mine owner. Although they had been on opposite sides in this case, Hanna was impressed by McKinley's sense of justice and fairness, but above all by the prospects for his rising in politics. He would be a loyal, skillful backer and organizer of McKinley's rise through the political ranks to the presidency. By no means, however, was McKinley a puppet controlled by Hanna.

This year, 1876, would be more memorable for McKinley in that it marked his climb onto the national political stage. He mounted a well-organized campaign for the U.S. House of Representatives. On August 15, the district Republican convention nominated him. Primary elections as the standard way political parties chose their candidates lay in the future. With that victory in hand, he covered his district thoroughly, almost wearing out his voice. When the votes were counted, McKinley had won by a comfortable margin and now began the career in national office which would culminate in his winning the presidency in 1896, but first was the question whether Republican Rutherford Hayes or Democrat Samuel Tilden would be the next president. The year 1876 would also be remembered as one of the most contentious in U.S. electoral history, ranking with those of 1824 and 2000.

As the Republican national convention opened in Cincinnati on June 14, the odds-on favorite to be the party's standard bearer was James G. Blaine of Maine, speaker of the U.S. House of Representatives, an intelligent, dominating leader with a charismatic persona. There were, though, serious questions about his ethical shortcomings in office, especially his profiting from railroads willing to pay for favorable treatment from the government. Also contending for the presidency were Governor Oliver Morton of Indiana, Secretary of the Treasury Benjamin Bristow of Kentucky, Senator Roscoe Conkling of New York, Governor John Hartranft of Pennsylvania, Postmaster General and former governor of Connecticut George Marshall Jewell, and Rutherford Hayes, then in his third term as governor of Ohio. Through six ballots, none of the contenders reached the 379-level needed to secure the nomination, although Blaine was well in the lead with 285 votes followed by Morton with 125, Bristow with 113, Conkling with 99, Hayes 61, Hartranft 58, and Jewell 11. On the second through the fifth ballots, the deadlock continued with only minor changes in individual totals. On the sixth ballot, Blaine's total rose to 308, still short of victory.

At this stage, the anti–Blaine delegates voted to adjourn the convention and met to agree upon the best man to both stop Blaine and bring unity to the party. The mantle fell upon the shoulders of Hayes who was governor of Ohio, the state with the third largest number of electoral votes, who had a distinguished Civil War record, and about whom were no scandals. On the seventh ballot Hayes won with 384 delegates. Selected as his running mate was Representative William Wheeler of New York.

On June 28, the Democrats met in St. Louis and nominated Governor Samuel Tilden of New York. An honest, capable administrator, he favored the gold standard, although his running mate, Thomas Hendricks of Indiana, did not. He further earned plaudits for his breaking the power of the notorious Tweed machine in New York City. This looked to be a tough election campaign with the results very much up in the air. Democrat hopes rose, no longer facing the war-hero Grant and encouraged by reports of scandals in his administration.

Differences between the two major parties were not as great during this period of American political history as they would be in 20 years when Bryan and those who supported him would dramatically alter the nature of the Democratic Party, moving it well to the left of where it was in the days of Tilden and when led by Grover Cleveland from 1884 to 1896.

Intense national interest in the election was indicated by the 81.8 percent turnout on election day, November 7.[18] The Republicans gained 33 seats in the U.S. House of Representatives, closing the gap but still somewhat short of taking control from the Democrats. Hayes carried 18 of 22 states outside the South with 52 percent of the vote.[19] Although less impressive than Grant's two victories, it nevertheless is indicative of the respect and support garnered by Hayes, but the South was solidly Democratic, so as the votes were counted, it appeared that Samuel Tilden would be the next president. Of the 185 electoral votes needed for victory, he had 184 firmly in hand with Hayes trailing at 165. Up in the air, though, were the returns for Florida, South Carolina, and Louisiana, states where Reconstruction had not yet ended completely, meaning that the Democrats were not yet back in control. Also, one electoral vote in Oregon was contested.

When the Electoral College convened on December 6, they did not resolve the problem of clashing vote totals coming in from the Southern states. The Republicans charged the Democrats with suppressing the heavily Republican black vote and the Democrats countered by charging the Republicans with throwing out enough Democratic votes to ensure Republican victory. Both were true, although it cannot be determined positively which party benefited more from the wrongdoing.[20] The impasse could not be resolved by Congress since Republican control of the Senate was checked by the Democratic majority in the House. Both Houses selected committees to get a government working when Grant's term expired in March. The two committees met in January 1877 and created a special 15-man commission—five from the Senate, five from the House, and five from the U.S. Supreme Court. The partisan breakdown was seven Republicans, seven Democrats, and one independent—Justice David Davis of Illinois. Davis, however, accepted election to the U.S. Senate as a Democrat and was replaced by Justice Joseph P. Bradley of New Jersey, a Republican. Eight to seven was how the commission voted to give all the disputed electoral votes to Hayes who now was the winner 185–184. On March 4, just one day later, he was inaugurated.

Hayes agreed to end Reconstruction in the three Southern states, removing occupying troops. In return, the new Democratic Party governments were to respect the rights of blacks. The first was done, the second ignored as segregation was imposed.

McKinley began his Washington career at a most dramatic time. His friendship with Hayes continued, he and his wife being guests at the executive mansion which later commonly would be called the White House. McKinley's rise to leadership in the House of Representatives was steady, not flashy, but demonstrating his mastery of the process and his being ready when opportunities opened before him. His positions on issues marked him as a rather moderate member of the Republican caucus. For example, his stance on monetary policy was between the inflationary pressures coming from the silver and greenback lobbies on one side and the sound money arguments of the gold standard devotees on the other. The first called for increasing the paper money unbacked by either gold or silver. The second side called for paper notes to be redeemable in gold in order to ensure their value and public confidence. McKinley stood in the middle, supporting silver but opposing unbacked paper. He broke with Hayes on monetary policy by supporting the Bland-Allison Act of 1878. This moderately inflationary measure called for the United States government to purchase and mint between $2,000,000 and $4,000,000 worth of silver each month. McKinley supported it as did the Ohio legislature and the newspaper back in Canton owned by his wife's family.[21] Hayes, a determined sound money advocate, vetoed it, but Congress overrode the veto, most members not yet clearly in either the sound money or the inflationary camps. McKinley later would modify his thinking and strongly endorse the gold standard.

McKinley also favored high tariff rates on imports both to protect new business from foreign competition and to keep up the wages of American workers. Democrats, including conservatives such as Grover Cleveland, argued that lower tariff rates benefited the general public by promoting more competition and, hence, lower prices.

McKinley was reelected in 1878 and 1880. His 1882 win was contested. Early in 1884, the House ruled that his opponent, Jonathan H. Wallace, had won. McKinley left Washington but returned after defeating Wallace in their November rematch. At the 1888 Republican National Convention, there was talk of McKinley as a dark horse presidential candidate. He emerged from it with enhanced stature, having impressed favorably most there.

After winning another term in 1888, McKinley tested the water for his prospects to win election as speaker of the House, found that Thomas Reed of Maine had more support, and settled for the number two post, House majority leader. Reed was a domineering man with a sharp intellect and slashing wit; he and McKinley complemented each other and made an effective leadership team.

The piece of legislation for which McKinley is best known is the McKinley Tariff of 1890 which established the highest rates in American history. He was then and remained convinced that high tariff rates in an expanding economy promoted growth and prosperity. This and the gold standard would be key points of contention between McKinley and William Jennings Bryan who soon would break out of Nebraska obscurity.

McKinley lost his 1890 race due to a combination of opposition to his tariff position and, especially, the gerrymandering of his district by the Democratic controlled Ohio legislature. Defeating him was former governor John G. Warwick, an immigrant from Northern Ireland who had served one term as the Ohio chief executive. Defeated for reelection, he was available to challenge McKinley in this targeted district. Warwick did not complete his term, dying of blood poisoning on August 14, 1892. By then McKinley had moved on to a better position from which to launch his presidential campaign.

Nationally, 1890 was a disappointing year for the Republicans. Although the party did retain control of the Senate, their lead shrank and the Democrats regained control of the House of Representatives by a substantial margin, their number of seats shooting from 156 up to 231 while those remaining in Republican hands dropped from 173 to 88. Two years later, Grover Cleveland defeated Benjamin Harrison, becoming the only president to serve two nonconsecutive terms, and the Democrats won the Senate and retained the House. The Republicans now were in even worse shape.

Down only for a short time, the next year McKinley was elected governor of Ohio and shot to the top tier of the Republican Party. In 1892, McKinley again tested the presidential nomination waters; an undeclared candidate, he received 182 votes on the first ballot at the Republican national convention, losing to incumbent President Benjamin Harrison who won handily with 535⅙ votes. At that time, delegates could divide their votes between different candidates if they so wished. By not overtly challenging Harrison, McKinley had not antagonized the party regulars and he had shown his popularity. McKinley's Ohio delegation cast 45 votes for him while he, holding to his pledge of non-candidacy, cast his ballot for Harrison. He was walking the fine line between the Scylla and Charybdis of violating his word that he was not a candidate and formally rejecting any interest in serving as president. Harrison, though, did not believe that McKinley was sincere. He later stated, "No mature man can believe that Ohio voted for him without his consent ... nor that the Governor of Ohio and the head of the Ohio delegation could influence no single vote therein, save his own."[22]

Probably Harrison was too harshly judgmental. At any rate, by not openly challenging him, McKinley had not antagonized party regulars and he had worked loyally for a second Harrison term. Prospects now looked excellent for him in 1896. Harrison's loss to Grover Cleveland in the presidential election weakened his influence and McKinley would enter the contest having served two terms as the governor of an electoral vote rich state vital to the interests of both parties.

The convention over, McKinley did campaign in Harrison's failed re-election run against Grover Cleveland. He then returned to being an effective and popular governor of a key state for anyone who aspires to the presidency. In his immediate future lay a potential political trap—how to deal with the rise of the American Protective Association which had been founded in 1887. It was another of the organizations which periodically spring up to warn the American people of the dangers represented by the Roman Catholic Church which they considered a foreign entity since the Pope administered it from the Vatican. Related to this was APA opposition to immigration since by the time it came into being emigration to the United States increasingly was Roman Catholic, coming from Southern and Eastern Europe, augmenting the earlier Catholic influx from Ireland, still part of the British Empire.

William McKinley versus William Jennings Bryan

As had happened before and would happen again, immigrants seeking to establish themselves and to rise up the socio/economic ladder, generally will work for less than those already settled here. This created tensions and sparked movements to stop the changes. The American Protective Association became the most powerful of these nativistic movements in the latter part of the 19th century. It had much in common with the Native American Party, better known as the "Know-Nothing" Party. That designation came from the common answer given by members of the party when asked about its rather secretive inner workings stated that they "knew nothing."[23] The American Protective Association, quite differently, did not constitute itself as a separate political party, preferring to work through the Republicans.

They peaked in influence during the mid–1890s with, probably, about 100,000 members, although they claimed 2,500,000. Internal dissension weakened it and it went into oblivion in the early 1900s and was dissolved in 1911.[24] Its ideas, though, would resurface periodically under different names in future years.

McKinley did show firm principles and courage in standing up to the organization's attempt to pressure him into firing two Roman Catholic prison guards. His refusal to knuckle under to this bigoted demand went over well with most Ohio voters and was part of his reelection victory in 1893, increasing his margin of two years before.

2

The Rise of Bryan

Early Years

The years of William Jennings Bryan prior to the 1890s were considerably fewer than those of McKinley and far less dramatic. He was born in Salem, Illinois, on March 19, 1860, the son of a successful attorney who had served as a Democrat in the state senate, as a circuit court judge, and was an unsuccessful candidate for the U.S. House of Representatives. Both parents were firmly Christian, his father a Baptist elder, his mother Methodist; after marriage, she attended her husband's church, but refused for 20 years to become a Baptist.[1] At age 13, Bryan attended a revival by a Cumberland Presbyterian minister, accepted Christ as Savior and Lord, and became a lifetime Presbyterian, although through the rest of his life he would attend services in other denominations.

When he was 15, Bryan went to a private school in Jacksonville, Illinois, then on to Illinois College also in Jacksonville. This institution had a Christian orientation, both Presbyterian and Congregationalist. Founded in 1829, its first president was Edward Beecher, son of Lyman Beecher and brother of Harriet Beecher Stowe and Henry Ward Beecher. Bryan did very well academically in the expected 19th-century collegiate program, continuing his study of Greek and Latin, history, classical literature. This, though, did not clash with his intense interest in contemporary matters such as tariffs, race relations, and temperance. Also, he honed the speaking skills later so evident in his political career. He graduated in 1881, valedictorian of his class.[2]

The Rise Begins

His private life too flourished during his time at Illinois College. In 1879, he met Mary Elizabeth Baird, an 18-year-old student at Jacksonville Female Academy. She was attractive and intelligent, and she won Bryan's love at their first meeting. They married once he had his degree, beginning a happy and successful marriage. She supported his political aspirations, raised their children during his frequent absences, and studied law herself, passed the bar examination, and aided him in his rise to prominence.[3]

In 1881, they moved to Chicago where he began the two-year course at Union Law College, later Northwestern University School of Law. Bryan's widowed mother helped by paying his tuition and his working part time at the law office of former Senator Lyman Trumbull enabled them to get by. Chicago did not appeal to him as a place to start a career and raise a family; he saw too much big business power, police corruption, and a Democratic Party organization oriented to its own power.

In 1883, degree in hand, the Bryans moved back to Jacksonville where he began a successful law practice. The economy, however, was not doing well there and, when combined with Republican political domination, led him to look for greener pastures. In 1887, he visited Lincoln, Nebraska, while on a business trip and saw it as a place of opportunity. Lincoln and Nebraska as a whole were growing rapidly economically and in population. The Republican control did not deter him since he saw the large number of European immigrants as potential Democratic votes.

He entered into practice with Adolphus Talbot, a friend from law school days. The pro-business Republican Talbot and the liberal Democrat Bryan formed an effectively symbiotic professional relationship, attracting to their firm a divergent clientele. As an attorney, Bryan continued to hone his oratorical skills. Awakening his wife early one morning, he told her, "Last night I found that I had power over the audience. I could move them as I chose. I have more than usual power as a speaker.... God grant that I may use it wisely."[4] After recounting this to her, he knelt beside the bed and prayed for God to so guide him.

In 1888, Bryan further developed his already formidable abilities as a speaker campaigning for Grover Cleveland who was running for reelection as president against Benjamin Harrison and for J. Sterling Morton, candidate for the U.S. House of Representatives. Both men lost their races. Bryan at that time either had not evolved yet into the leader of the political left he was to become, or he was compromising his beliefs, using Cleveland to further his own rise. Although the answer to that quandary cannot be known with certainty, probably Bryan's political positions had not firmed up at that time. He did write to Cleveland commending him,

2. The Rise of Bryan

"Your position was so wisely and bravely taken that I believe the party will look back to you in after years with gratitude and not reproach."[5]

Bryan then proceeded even more effusively with an almost fawning invitation he must have known would not appeal to a rooted Easterner such as Cleveland: "If you would only move to Nebraska and run in '92 as a Western man with the friends you have in the East, we can elect you. Why not come to Omaha or Lincoln?"[6]

Four years later, Cleveland would win his rematch with Harrison, becoming the only president so far to serve split terms. Morton had served as secretary of Nebraska when it was a territory, briefly was governor, and would be secretary of agriculture in Cleveland's second term. In 1872, he took the lead in the Nebraska establishment of Arbor Day, the first state to do so. Soon Bryan would split with Cleveland and Morton, both conservatives, as Bryan's political views moved progressively to the left.

In 1890, the left was becoming more assertive, drawing support from miners, railroad workers and farmers, although not yet dominant in either major party.[7] The Republicans retained control of the U.S. Senate, but the House was much more volatile. In 1888, elected were 173 Republicans, 156 Democrats, and three others. The 1890 election returned 231 Democrats, 88 Republicans, and 14 others as the Populist Party shot briefly into prominence. That year, Bryan was elected to the U.S. House of Representatives, part of the growing liberal wing which in six years would seize control of the Democratic Party from the Cleveland conservatives. Democrats also won the Nebraska governorship that year and the other two U.S. House seats were won by the People's Independent Party, further to the left than Bryan, although he and they were friendly.

In Congress, Bryan was part of the Democratic mainstream in his support of lower tariffs, but he split with the party leadership with his calls for a graduated income tax as the primary source of government revenue and for inflating the money supply through the unlimited coinage of silver.[8] His positions were opposed by the Cleveland forces still in control of the party, who maintained that the value of money is more important that the quantity of it and that the government should not use the power to tax as the means to redistribute wealth, but growing numbers of people were electrified both by his brilliance as a speaker and by his ideas for dramatically changing the political and economic direction of the country.

In 1892, Bryan's growing political base reinforced his outspokenness from the left of center. He refused to endorse Cleveland's second try for a second term, instead backing James Weaver of the People's or Populist

Party, who ran well to the left of both major parties, carried four states, and garnered 22 electoral votes and 1,041,028 popular votes. Nine Populist members won election to the House of Representatives, a most impressive inaugural for a new party. The Democrats also won control of the Senate and retained their majority in the House.[9]

Bryan began his second House term as increasingly a thorn in the side of the conservative Democrats who still controlled the party, men such as Grover Cleveland and J. Sterling Morton of his own state who saw his positions as wrong for the country and for the Democratic Party. On the other hand, a growing number of people saw him as a rising star who could lead the country into a brighter future.

In 1894, Bryan saw an opportunity to rise higher and declared his candidacy for the U.S. Senate. At this time, members of the Senate still were chosen by state legislatures. He needed both the Democrats and the Populists in order to win. He believed that he had cleared the way for himself by getting the Populists to endorse him as well as the Democrats. Bryan persuaded a majority of the delegates to the Democratic state convention to endorse the Populist candidate for governor and two of their U.S. House candidates. In return, the Populists ran no candidate against him for the Senate. This further angered Morton and the conservative Democrats who walked out and endorsed their own ticket. On election day, the Republicans won control of the legislature and derailed, at least temporarily Bryan's plans, even though he did win a majority in a nonbinding poll.[10] Nationwide the Republicans rode the surge of voter discontent with the Democrats in the wake of the 1893 depression, taking back control of the U.S. House of Representatives as they gained 121 seats.

3

1896 Presidential Campaign

As 1896 dawned, Grover Cleveland, battered but resolute, presided over a country which had passed through the worst of the 1893 Depression, but the aftereffects still were being felt in the Democratic Party. In 1894, the Republicans had won both houses of Congress, a domination which would last until 1910 when the Democrats regained the House of Representatives. The hard times also had encouraged and emboldened the left wing of the Democratic Party as well as those further to the left who backed the Populist Party. Cleveland had won the presidency in 1882, lost it to Harrison in 1888, and had regained it in their 1892 rematch. Under him, the Democrats actually were somewhat more conservative than the Republicans, but those days were coming to an end. Now the liberals who had been kept under control by the personal strength and electoral success of Cleveland were poised to break out and seize control of the party at the national convention in July.

Entering into the 1896 campaign season, Cleveland absolutely ruled out a third term. The two-term tradition, dating back to George Washington, was well respected even though Ulysses Grant had been prepared to push it aside if he could have received the support to do so. Also, the demands of the office had taken their toll even on Cleveland's robust constitution. Furthermore, he did see the changes in his party, although not the full extent of them, and did not expect this to be a good year for the Democrats. Cleveland, though, still was president and would continue to hold office until a new administration replaced his on March 4, 1897. As long as he was president, he would be president.

The Cleveland Administration had achieved moderate success in foreign policy. During his first term, he had acted to block German seizure of Samoa in the southwest Pacific. He successfully supported continued

William McKinley versus William Jennings Bryan

Bryan in 1896 (Library of Congress. William Jennings Bryan, https://www.loc.gov/item/2001697076/).

McKinley in 1896 (Library of Congress. William McKinley, https://www.loc.gov/item/89710626/).

Samoan independence which lasted for a few more years. This was not a good period of history for the independence of small, militarily weak non–European countries which were valuable for trade, for natural resources, or, as in the case of Samoa, for occupying strategic locations. In 1899, the United States prevented Germany's incorporating all Samoa by occupying the eastern part; it continues voluntarily to be American.

In particular, Cleveland opposed the further expansion of European holdings in the Americas; he was determined to have the Western Hemisphere be a sphere of influence for the United States. At the same time, he opposed having this country become an imperial power by taking over other countries, ending their independence. Secretary of State Richard Olney proclaimed what came to be known as the "Olney Corollary" to the Monroe Doctrine, asserting that we would mediate disputes in this hemisphere, barring outside countries from expanding in our backyard. This principle was applied to the border dispute between Venezuela and British Guiana. Cleveland reaffirmed the Monroe Doctrine, that we would not tolerate the expansion of British territory in the Americas. He did, though, extend a hand of friendship to them:

3. 1896 Presidential Campaign

I am, nevertheless, firm in my conviction that while it is a grievous thing to contemplate the two great English-speaking peoples of the world as being otherwise than friendly competitors in the onward march of civilization and strenuous and worthy rivals in all the arts of peace, there is no calamity which a great nation can invite which equals that which follows a supine submission to wrong and injustice and the consequent loss of national self-respect and honor, beneath which are shielded and defended a people's safety and greatness.[1]

Facing American determination, the British backed down and engaged in back-channel negotiations with which resulted in a peaceful resolution in 1899 during McKinley's first term. For the British, facing the growing power and expansion of Germany and Russia, there was little interest in adding the United States to their list of major challenges.

Hawaii and Cuba increasingly were the focus of American attention during the Cleveland years and continued as areas of intense interest into the McKinley terms. Hawaii was an independent monarchy, weak in power but occupying a strategic location. Germany and Britain were very desirous of adding the islands to their empires and by the 1890s Japan too was showing interest. Cleveland was determined to see Hawaii remain independent. This, however, would not be possible in the world of the 19th century; it became American in 1898. The clear reality is that if we had not done so, the islands would have become German or British.

The Cleveland Administration preferred to see Cuba develop more freedom within the Spanish system, concerned that an independent Cuba would not be able to prosper, to stay out of the clutches of expanding powers such as, again, Britain and Germany. Cleveland believed the best course for the United States was a Cuba becoming freer and more prosperous as part of a weak, non-expansionist Spanish empire. This too would alter dramatically during the McKinley years.

McKinley intended to campaign for president on the protective tariff and on his record as an effective governor of a large, diverse state; he was resolute in his ordering the national guard to restore order when a strike and resultant violence by the United Mine Workers accelerated beyond what local authorities could handle and yet he kept good ties with workers based on his reputation for honesty and fairness. He did not believe that monetary policy would be a significant factor in the race. In this he really missed the mark, something unusual for a man who normally had an accurate and shrewd grasp on political reality. In the run-up to the Republican national convention, Mark Hanna showed his brilliance as a political operative, organizing for McKinley without fatally antagonizing the other candidates, but Hanna had no doubt concerning who was in charge. Speaking to a meeting of Republican activists in Canton, he said: "Now don't you fellows fool yourselves by thinking that we will be able to give McKinley instructions as to how to run the campaign. After you have talked with him you will find that he knows more about politics than all of us."[2]

The Republicans chose their ticket first in 1896, gathering in St. Louis from June 16 through the 18th. The platform affirmed the protective tariff, called for annexing Hawaii, favored freedom for Cuba, and supported a bigger navy to protect American interests in the face of expansion by Britain, Germany, Japan, and France, but the most explosive issue before the delegates was the gold standard. Most Republicans supported it. McKinley, recognizing that he could not avoid a firm commitment, came out for the gold standard. He understood that this would cost him in the West but avoiding a forthright stance would cost him more.

Trying to hold back the tide, Senator Henry Teller of Colorado introduced a free coinage of silver plank. A veteran member of the Senate, Teller also had served as secretary of the interior in the administration of Chester Alan Arthur. Knowing that his plank would fail he made an impassioned presentation, stating his willingness to suffer whatever political price his stance might cost him. Fail indeed the proposal did, being routed 818½ to 105½[3]; the gold standard Republicans were firmly in the saddle. Party leaders had been concerned about the number of defections over the gold standard affirmation but only 34 delegates walked out and most of them would later return to the fold. Teller did not, remaining in the Senate as a Democrat. It is interesting to note that a band in the convention hall vainly attempted to relieve the growing animosity by playing "Silver Threads Among the Gold." This love song, dealing with age not monetary matters, has had a remarkable career. Lyrics by Eben E. Rexord and music by Hart Pease Danks, it was copyrighted in 1873. Continuing its popularity well after 1896, it was recorded by Bing Crosby in 1948, by Jerry Lee Lewis in 1956 and 1973, and by Jo Stafford in 1969.[4] After walking out, the silver defectors met briefly with a group of Populist leaders who had come to St. Louis hoping for a break in Republican ranks. There were hopes to bring together Populists, silver Republicans, and silver Democrats with Teller as their presidential nominee. Bryan's "Cross of Gold" speech at the Democratic Party Convention about three weeks later, though, would doom the prospects for anyone else to bring these elements together.

This skirmish provided the only real drama at the convention that year. McKinley had a lock on the nomination, his record as governor of Ohio, as a leader in the House, and his political skill, abetted by the organizing skills of Hanna, propelling him to the top. Back in January, the Indiana Republican state committee had endorsed former president Benjamin Harrison, but he firmly rejected another run. Still, though, hoping for something out of the blue that might give their candidacies life and wanting to show their prominence, other nominees presented themselves. They were men of significance, but none had organized a national campaign as had the McKinley/Hanna team. Placed in nomination were Speaker of the House Thomas Reed of Maine, a strong man who knew how to wield power, but ruffled feathers with his abrasive personality; Senator Matthew Quay of Pennsylvania, a scholarly man who tightly controlled the politics there; Governor Levi Morton of Pennsylvania who had been vice president under Benjamin Harrison; and Senator William Allison of Iowa who had been a favorite son candidate in 1892 and who would decline the vice presidential nomination in 1900 which then went to Theodore Roosevelt.

Again, these were capable, experienced men who by no means were neophytes in the arena of national politics, but they had no success against the McKinley/Hanna team, which out-hustled them, setting up McKinley organizations across the country, controlling the selection of delegates to the national convention. At district and state conventions, the McKinley forces were effective in determining who the delegates would be and how they would vote. These changes plus what would happen soon at the Democratic Party national convention made it evident that a new era had opened in American politics. McKinley won easily on the first ballot with 661½ votes. Left in the dust were Reed with 84½, Quay with 61½, Morton with 58, and Allison with 35½.

As his running mate, McKinley's first choice was Reed, who, having lost the presidential nomination, wanted no part of second place. His second option was Levi Morton, who likewise spurned the opportunity. Knowing that he needed a vice president from the electoral vote rich East, McKinley now turned to Garrett Hobart of New Jersey, a wealthy lawyer who had been both speaker of the state House of Representatives and president of the state Senate. He was a solidly committed gold standard supporter. In his acceptance of the nomination, Hobart commented on the fact that a silver dollar coin contained $.53 worth of silver, and stated, "An honest dollar, worth 100 cents everywhere, cannot be coined out of 53 cents worth of silver plus a legislative fiat. Such a debasement of our cur-

The Republican ticket in 1896: McKinley and Garrett Hobart (Library of Congress, https://www.loc.gov/item/93504458/).

rency would inevitably produce incalculable loss, appalling disaster, and National dishonor."[5]

On September 7, he wrote more extensively to the Notification Committee of the Republican National Convention, affirming that "the money standard of a great nation should be as fixed and permanent as the nation itself.... This necessity has made gold the final standard of all enlightened nations."[6] He was well regarded as a man who could bring people together in the general election campaign. His urbanity and equanimity did prove to be assets. The Republicans were confident and comfortable with their ticket.

The Democrats convened shortly thereafter in Chicago from July 7 to the 11th. Their prospects for 1896 appeared bleak, the party being split between the Cleveland conservatives in the East and the liberal, free coinage of silver devotees who dominated the party in the South, the Midwest, and the West. Bryan was not himself a delegate and was not considered a serious contender for the nomination by most of the delegates. A few, though, knew of him as an outspoken opponent of the conservatives and as an effective speaker who could surprise the party and the country with his ability to captivate people through the force of his personality and his words.

The conservative minority at the convention, recognizing that the liberals who never had accepted Cleveland's beliefs now were in control, resolutely stood their ground, but were swept aside. William C. Whitney, prominent New York attorney and good friend of Cleveland's who had been secretary of the navy in his first term, had arrived before the opening gavel to organize the conservatives, but quickly saw that a massive shift had taken place. The liberals won contest after contest—temporary chairman, permanent chairman, keynote speaker, credential challenges. On the third day, July 9, the two sides clashed over the monetary issue. Senator Ben Tillman of South Carolina opened the fray for the pro-silver majority. He was nicknamed "Pitchfork Ben" for his slashing repudiation of Cleveland, stating, "He is an old bag of beef and I am going to Washington with a pitchfork and prod him in his old fat ribs."[7] The stridency of Tillman's speech, however, proved to be counterproductive.

Countering Tillman's vituperation were three gold standard stalwarts. Taking the podium first was Senator David B. Hill of New York who had risen on Cleveland's coattails to be lieutenant governor and governor, then broken with him to pursue his own course of separate prominence. Now, on this principle, they were back on the same side. In fact, earlier Hill had proposed as at least a gesture of unity the following: "We commend the honesty, economy, courage, and fidelity of the present Democratic National Administration." The overwhelming majority of the delegates, however, interested only in total victory, defeated the motion 564–357 with nine not voting.[8] Hill delivered a solid affirmation of the gold standard, charging that inflating the money supply through free coinage of silver "smacks of Populism and Communism," further stating, "I am a Democrat; but not a revolutionist."[9] Then Senator William Vilas of Wisconsin, Civil War veteran, later postmaster general and secretary of the interior during Cleveland's first term, delivered a lengthy defense of the gold standard which left most delegates unmoved. The last gold standard speaker was former Governor William Russell of Massachusetts, once a powerful force among conservative Democrats, now a shadow of what he had been; frail and voice weak, he would be dead in a few days at 39.

Now came Bryan's turn. A master of timing, he had rejected opportunities to speak earlier and had made a deal with Tillman who wanted more time for his address. Bryan yielded some of his time to Tillman in return for speaking last. At this stage of the convention, most of the delegates were restive, knowing that they on the pro silver side held a substantial numerical advantage; they had endured these gold standard presentations and were champing at the bit for an opportunity to let loose their pent-up enthusiasm. Bryan now moved rapidly from the floor up onto the stage and stood poised to launch into one of the most famous speeches in our history. He had the vocal power to fill the auditorium in this pre electronic amplification era and the eloquence to hold the attention of his audience. The delegate mood, combined with and augmented by those who knew Bryan as an exciting speaker, resulted in enthusiastic applause for him.

Bryan opened with the humble acknowledgment that his youth and relative inexperience stood in marked contrast with the leaders of the party: "Mr. Chairman and Gentlemen of the Convention: I would be presumptuous, indeed, to present myself against the distinguished gentlemen to whom you have listened."[10]

Very quickly that mood of diffidence passed and the Bryan confidence that he was right surfaced: "But this is not a contest between persons. The humblest citizen in all the land, when clad in the armor of a righteous cause, is stronger than all the hosts of error. I come to speak to you in defense of a cause as holy as the cause of liberty—the cause of humanity."[11]

Dramatic, rather hyperbolic rhetoric followed with a clear assertion that the silver forces now controlled the course of the party:

> Never before in the history of this country has there been witnessed such a contest as that through which we have just passed. Never before in the history of American politics has a great issue been fought out as this issue has been, by the voters of a great party. On the fourth of March, 1895, a few Democrats, most of them members of Congress, issued an address to the Democrats of the nation,

asserting that the money question was the paramount issue of the hour; declaring that a majority of the Democratic party had the right to control the action of the party on this paramount issue; and concluding with the request that the believers in the free coinage of silver in the Democratic party should organize, take charge of and control the policy of the Democratic party.[12]

Shortly thereafter, he drove home further the sharp change of direction represented by the convention:

With a zeal approaching the zeal which inspired the crusaders who followed Peter the Hermit, our silver Democrats went forth from victory unto victory, until they are now assembled, not to discuss, not to debate, but to enter up the judgment already rendered by the plain people of this country. In this contest brother has been arrayed against brother, father against son. The warmest ties of love, acquaintance and association have been disregarded; old leaders have been cast aside when they have refused to give expression to the sentiments of those whom they would lead, and new leaders have sprung up to give direction to this cause of truth. Thus has the contest been waged, and we have assembled here under as binding and solemn instructions as were ever imposed upon representatives of the people.[13]

Bryan further asserted his support for a personal income tax and engaged in some humor at the expense of William McKinley:

Mr. McKinley was nominated at St. Louis upon a platform which declared for the maintenance of the gold standard until it can be changed into bimetallism by international agreement. Mr. McKinley was the most popular man among the Republicans, and three months ago everybody in the Republican party prophesied his election. How is it to-day? Why, the man who was once pleased to think that he looked like Napoleon—that man shudders to-day when he remembers that he was nominated on the anniversary of the battle of Waterloo. Not only that, but as he listens he can hear with ever-increasing distinctness the sound of the waves as they beat upon the lonely shores of St. Helena.[14]

Shortly thereafter came the dramatic conclusion ending in the words by which the speech is known:

Having behind us the producing masses of this nation and the world, supported by the commercial interests, the laboring interests, and the toilers everywhere, we will answer their demand for a gold standard by saying to them: You shall not press down upon the brow of labor this crown of thorns; you shall not crucify mankind upon a cross of gold.[15]

For a number of heartbeats, as if stunned, the hall was silent as Bryan left the stage. Then, as the *New York World* reported in its July 10 issue, "the whole face of the convention was broken by the tumult—hills and valleys of shrieking men and women." The mood of enthusiasm, close to hysteria, engulfed most of the delegates for close to 40 minutes. Again, most but not all responded so. The conservative, gold standard, pro Cleveland minority sat silently as the pandemonium swept over them.

The nomination, though, was not yet Bryan's. Key leaders of the party may have shared his silver convictions, but they were not ready to anoint him as their leader. Most prominent among them was Representative Richard P. Bland of Missouri, nicknamed "Silver Dick," who had been elected to the House in 1872, then re-elected each year until he was upset in 1894. He won his seat back in November 1896 and died in office in 1899. Also nominated were Senator Joseph Blackburn of Kentucky, Governor Horace Boies of Iowa, former governor Robert E. Pattison of Pennsylvania, newspaper owner and publisher John R. McLean of Ohio, and Governor Claude Matthews of Indiana. Seven other candidates would win between one and 10 delegates on the five ballots which followed.

After the first ballot, Bland led with 235 votes followed by Bryan with 137, Pattison with 97, Blackburn with 80, Boies with 67, McLean with 54, and Matthews with 37. On the second ballot, Bland moved up to 281, Bryan to 197, and Pattison to 100. Boies dropped to 37 while McLean and Matthews stayed at about the same level on this ballot and on the next two. On the third ballot, Bland hit his high-water mark at 291, Bryan continued to gain delegates, now having 219, and Blackburn and Boies faded to 41 and 37. On the fourth ballot, Bryan passed Bland 280–241. Bland now withdrew in favor of Bryan whose nomination was finalized on the fourth ballot. This rise of a former two-term representative from Nebraska, mid-level in significance in the Democratic Party as the convention opened, and little known across the country, was phenomenal; as a story in a novel, most people would consider it far-fetched.

Bryan did not specify the person he wanted as his running mate as most presidential nominees do and had Nebraska abstain because "as I did not myself take any part in the nomination of the candidate for Vice-President I thought it better that the delegation from Nebraska should also decline to participate, lest the vote of the delegation should be considered an expression of my preference."[16]

At this opening, the names of 16 men were presented, the most prominent of whom were Bland and McLean plus former representative Joseph C. Sibley of Pennsylvania and Arthur Sewall of Maine, a wealthy ship builder, bank president, and railroad tycoon, who did agree with Bryan on silver. On the first ballot, the leaders were Sibley with 163 votes, McLean

The Democratic Party ticket in 1896 (Library of Congress, https://www.loc.gov/item/2001697077/).

111 and Sewall 100. The other 12 were down in double or single digits. On the second ballot, Sibley dropped to 113 and Sewall to 37 while McLean rose to 158 and Bland surged from 62 up to 294. On the third ballot, Sibley faded to 50 votes, McLean rose to 210, and Bland fell to 255. On the fourth ballot, Bland and Sibley had dropped out, McLean rose to 298 but Sewall shot up to 261. On the fifth ballot, Sewall went over the top.[17] The hope was that he would help the ticket by appealing to Eastern voters. Sewall's opposition to the gold standard, though, removed that faint hope in a region where both the gold standard and the Republican Party could not be overcome. Most Eastern Democrats favored gold.

For Democratic Party conservatives, supporting Bryan was absolutely unthinkable. Their opposition to the Republican protective tariff position precluded their joining that party even though they agreed with them now on more than they agreed with their old party. Their Democratic Party heritage combined with the tariff issue to impel them to hold their own convention in Indianapolis early in September as the National Democratic Party and nominate their own ticket, Senator (and former governor) John M. Palmer of Illinois for president and former governor Simon Bolivar Buckner of Kentucky for vice president. Palmer, 79, had served as a Union general during the Civil War and Buckner, a bit younger at 73, had been a general in the Confederate army. These men hoped to symbolize national unity, ending whatever regional bitterness still remained.

Cleveland, having resisted blandishments from his supporters to campaign for the Democratic Party nomination, also resisted attempts to enlist him as the new party's candidate. He did, though, support their cause from behind the scenes. On September 5, he wrote to Senator William Vilas of Wisconsin, a member of his first term cabinet, "I am delighted with the outcome of the Indianapolis Convention and as a Democrat I feel very grateful to those who have relieved the bad political atmosphere with such a delicious infusion of fresh air. Every Democrat, after reading the platform, ought to thank God that the glorious principles of our party have found defenders who will not permit them to be polluted by impure hands."[18]

The National Democratic challengers earned wide respect, such as the support of the *New York Times*; limited government, sound money Democrats saw them as representing the party of Grover Cleveland, the party they had joined and wanted renewed, but McKinley and the Republicans also stood for limited government and the gold standard. Added to that was the reality that the Palmer ticket could not win more conservative votes than that of McKinley which had a stronger organization and more money. As the campaign moved toward election day, it increasingly became evident that either McKinley or Bryan would be the next president. From the perspective of these conservatives, McKinley was troubling as a high tariff rate Republican, but Bryan as the Democratic Party standard bearer and possibly as the next president was catastrophic. For them increasingly it became evident that they had to support McKinley. As the campaign moved to its finale, this reality led Palmer to assure those agreeing with him: "I promise you, my fellow Democrats, I will not consider it any very great fault if you decide next Tuesday to cast your ballot for William McKinley, though you may, if you desire, vote for Palmer and Buckner."[19] The Republicans appreciated the potential for the National Democrats to drain normally Democratic votes from Bryan and also recognized them as prospective Republicans after the election. Many would affiliate, although the Republican protective tariff convictions proved to be a hurdle some could not surmount.[20]

Bryan and the Democrats would have more success with overtures to their left. On July 22, the Populists convened in St. Louis, torn by the quandary of how to respond to Bryan's nomination. He shared their positions on free coinage of silver, redistribution of wealth through increasing taxes on those with wealth, and on calling for more regulation of the economy, but the Democratic platform did not espouse nationalization of railroads, the telegraph and telegraph companies, plus having savings banks run by the post office. The Democrats had moved sharply to the left, but they had not adopted all the Populist planks. Most Populists supported Bryan, although some did not.

This would be the most critical national convention in the short but significant life of the party. Their beginning in 1892, as discussed earlier, had been one of the most auspicious in the history of the new parties. Their presidential nominee in that year, James Weaver and other key party leaders scheduled the Populist convention after the Republicans and the Democrats had written their platforms and nominated their candidates for president. By doing so, the Populists could either fuse with a major party, Democrats most probably if they moved to the left, or they could surge to major party status by drawing in disgruntled Democrats. As oriented as he was to the Populists, Weaver placed the cause of left-wing principles above that of party. Those Populists who wanted to realign the American party system now confronted the dilemma confronting new parties since the Republicans shot to prominence in 1856. Since then until today, new parties with impressive starts have faded for one or both of two reasons: (1) the charismatic leader who led them returned to the two-party system and (2) one of the two major parties shifted to incorporate key positions which had given rise to the new party. The Theodore Roosevelt Progressive Party after 1912 demonstrated the first and the rapid fading of the Populist Party was an example of the second.

As the Populists convened in 1896, there was a clear split between those who were prepared to accept Bryan and the Democratic platform as close enough with the chance to win and those determined to continue their crusade, not going along with the Democrats' usurping the Populist leadership of the left. Would the bulk of the party members be absorbed into the Democratic Party, ending the rise of the Populists? Would this mean a weakening of the left by this dilution or would this strengthen their cause through moving the Democrats leftward? There was a determined minority at the convention who wanted to continue Populist independence and rejected this fusion with the Democrats. Putting off resolving this matter, the delegates voted first for their vice-presidential preference, choosing Thomas Watson of Georgia over the Democratic Party nominee Arthur Sewall. They considered Sewall too business oriented and did want to show some independence rather than being absorbed totally. They next adopted a platform affirming free coinage of silver, postal savings banks, public works projects to combat depression, and nationalization of railroads and telegraphs.

Then came the time to nominate their presidential candidate. James Weaver, who had led the party to their high water mark in 1892, reminded the delegates of his dedication to the party and commended the Populists for being the crucial factor in changing the country by spreading knowledge of their economic agenda which paved the way for the Democrats' turning to Bryan and free silver.[21] The minority which opposed fusion with the Democrats, supported Seymour F. Norton, a veteran greenbacker, as the party nominee, but most of the delegates, as did Weaver, saw Bryan as being with them on key issues and were not dedicated primarily to the need for a new party; they believed they could make the Democrats the party of the left. Weaver now nominated Bryan, reminding the delegates of his dedication to the party. Bryan won handily on the first ballot with 1042 votes easily besting Norton's 321 and 12 scattered. Now, the party faced a new situation with Bryan as the standard bearer of the Democrats.

Along with Weaver, also congratulating Bryan as the Populist nominee was Eugene V. Debs, who later would move further to the left, join the Socialist Party, and be their presidential nominee five times—1900, 1904, 1908, 1912, and 1920. Debs wrote Bryan on July 27 enthusiastically encouraging him:

> With millions of others of your countrymen I congratulate you most heartily upon being the People's standard bearer in the great uprising of the masses against the classes. You are at this hour the hope of the Republic—the central figure of the civilized world. In the arduous campaign before you the millions will rally to your standard and you will lead them to a glorious victory. The people love and trust you—they believe in you as you believe in them, and under your administration the rule of the money power will be broken and the gold barons of Europe will no longer run the American government.[22]

Debs' exuberant optimism was evident as was his conspiratorial assertion that the American government was controlled by "the gold barons of Europe."

Also meeting in St. Louis at this same time were the silver Republicans who proclaimed their rejection of the Republican endorsement of gold and the nomination of McKinley. They noted that gold standard Democrats either were supporting McKinley or were planning to nominate a separate ticket to siphon votes away from Bryan. They determined that their course of action should be to endorse the Bryan-Sewall ticket.[23]

On August 12, Bryan opened his eastern states campaign in New York City speaking to a large crowd in Madison Square Garden. This would be a key test for him since the region was more friendly to the politics of Cleveland and McKinley than to the liberal populism of Bryan. Two key factors cut the ground out from under the limited prospects he had for changing the thinking of most easterners. One was his fault, one was beyond his control.

The mistake Bryan made was reading a prepared text, droning on for close to two hours. Gone was the electrifying spellbinder of the national convention. Apparently, he was determined to dispel concerns that he was a wild-eyed radical. This may have been a reasonable intention but abandoning his stem-winder style made no sense. The far better approach would have been a shorter address, one not read but delivered in his usual style. This was a mistake he would avoid repeating in other parts of the country. Former governor Joseph Foraker of Ohio, shortly to be elected to the Senate, trenchantly stated that "Mr. Bryan made himself by one speech, and now he has unmade himself by one speech."[24] This was clever, but rather overstated. Bryan perhaps could have done somewhat better in the East had he made a stem-winder of a speech, but probably the effect would not have been too different when the votes were counted; he was not the candidate the East wanted.

Exacerbating this bad decision by Bryan was a heat wave of unusual virulence which hit New York City as well as other parts of the East and Midwest, holding the city in its grip from August 4 to the 13th. Temperatures consistently were well into the 90s as were the humidity levels. Worsening the situation was that most tenements had been built to hold the maximum number of people with little concern for alleviating the heat through high ceilings, many windows or other ways to improve air flow. Brick, concrete, and stone buildings made conditions worse as did the asphalt streets which conducted heat three times faster than did soil.[25] On the night of Bryan's speech, conditions in Madison Square Garden were described by those there as "sweltering" and "furnace-like."[26] The combination of a boring address and hot, humid weather doomed any faint hopes Bryan might have had to gain ground in the conservative, Republican dominated East.

On August 19, the political war intensified with another major address in Madison Square Garden, this one by William Bourke Cockran, a pro-gold standard, anti–Bryan Democrat. Cockran had served in the U.S. House of Representatives and was a prominent figure in Tammany Hall. By the time Cockran spoke, the heat wave which had plagued the Bryan event had passed, the high for August 19 being a comfortable 73 degrees.[27] A dynamic, charismatic speaker himself, Cockran skewered Bryan with sarcasm, drawing appreciative laughter and applause from the large crowd. He presented Bryan as an enemy of the working people, suggesting that the free silver cause would hurt their prospects for rising.

> To him we say, in the name of humanity, in the name of progress, "You shall neither place a crown of thorns upon the brow of labor nor lay a scourge upon his back. You shall not rob him of any one advantage which he has gained by long years of steady progress in the skill with which he exercises his craft and by efficient organization among those who work with him at the same bench. You shall not obscure the golden prospect of a future improvement in his condition by a further cheapening in the cost of living, as well as by a future appreciation of the dollar in which his wages are paid."[28]

Here Cockran made the case that a strong dollar backed by gold was beneficial for working people, not the inflationary silver argument propounded by Bryan. In spite of his rejection of Bryan, Cockran refused to join the Republicans, opposing them on the tariff and wanting to reverse the "Bryanization" of the Democrats.

Also capable of exciting crowds was Republican Theodore Roosevelt, a young man on the rise who celebrated his 38th birthday a few days before the election. He had been elected to the New York Assembly in 1881 and served as minority leader in 1882 until his independence of the party leaders led to his losing that role. In 1882, Grover Cleveland had been elected governor, serving as such until he moved into the presidency following the 1884 election. Cleveland and Roosevelt developed a mutual respect, clashed on some issues, but generally worked together for honesty and efficiency in government.

On February 14, 1884, his mother died of typhoid fever and his wife of Bright's disease just two days after giving birth to a daughter, Alice. The baby was raised by her aunt Anna until after her father's second marriage in 1886 when she joined the new and soon growing family.

Roosevelt finished the 1884 legislative session, then moved west to engage in the hard and adventurous life of a rancher and part time lawman in North Dakota. It worked; his sorrow assuaged and his zest for life renewed, he returned to New York City where the Republicans, who normally lost this race, prevailed upon him to be their mayoral candidate in

1886. This fascinating campaign had three strong contenders: Democrat Abram Hewitt, backed by Tammany Hall and much of the business community; independent Henry George, known for his "single tax" proposal, the belief that government could be reformed and supported and wealth redistributed by this tax on land; and Roosevelt. When the results were tallied, Hewitt had won with 90,552 votes followed by George with 68,110, and Roosevelt with 60,435.[29] Fears of George's radicalism caused many Republicans to support Hewitt as the better way to head off a George Administration. Considering the odds against him, Roosevelt's future prospects in politics were by no means diminished.

The election now behind him, on December 2, Roosevelt married Edith Carow, a childhood friend three years younger than he. They would have a happy, successful marriage with five children.

Roosevelt's campaigning for Benjamin Harrison's victory over Grover Cleveland for the presidency in 1888 led to his appointment to the Civil Service Commission. Four years later, Cleveland evened the score by winning back the office. Rather to Roosevelt's surprise, Cleveland asked him to stay on; Cleveland's respect for Roosevelt's integrity and ability dated back to their time in New York state government. He continued to serve until 1895. In November of the previous year, Republican William L. Strong won election as mayor of New York City. Now he offered Roosevelt the opportunity to become president of the Board of Police Commissioners. Here he was as the 1896 campaign shifted into high gear, having again evinced his vigor, courage, and ability.

Before 1896, presidential candidates generally campaigned in a manner more restrained and aloof than the pattern familiar today; they made a few speeches but didn't travel throughout the country selling themselves and their ideas. The idea was to appear more dignified, more presidential. To some extent, Republicans Horace Greeley in 1872 and James G. Blaine in 1884 broke out of that pattern as did Populist James Weaver in his 1892 race. But, in terms of miles travelled, speeches made, and people reached, Bryan completely shattered the established campaign mold. From the first week of August until the November election, he tallied over 18,000 miles by train across 26 states addressing about 5,000,000 people. This pace is especially impressive since most of the time he used regular passenger train service until October 7 when a private car was provided for him by the Democratic Party. This was a brutal pace which did reach many voters, but taxed even the robust Bryan constitution, leaving him barely able to speak.[30] Most of his stops were in the key battleground Great Lakes states.

William McKinley versus William Jennings Bryan

The East was considered Republican country and the South likely would be in the Democratic column. The West did have areas of strength for both parties, but at this time it did not have the electoral vote clout that would come in the next century.

McKinley recognized that he could not challenge Bryan's oratorical dynamism and adopted a campaign mode that maximized his advantages. He spoke from his front porch in Canton, Ohio, welcoming about 750,000 people during the weeks between June 19 and the November 2 election.[31] An effective if not exciting speaker, his warm, friendly personality was effective in this setting. The Republican campaign, brilliantly led by Mark Hanna, organized parties of Republicans to make the trek to Canton.

Another of Hanna's activities was arranging for Republican speakers to counter Bryan's campaigning, especially in the critical Midwest. In mid–August, Roosevelt had headed west for three weeks in his well-loved North Dakota stomping ground. He returned to New York City on September 10, tanned, toughened, and ready to battle Bryan, a man he considered a dangerous left-wing demagogue. Hanna assigned him to follow Bryan through Illinois, Michigan, and Minnesota during the second and third weeks of October. Roosevelt was the match for Bryan in vigor and in stirring the enthusiasm of crowds. As such and as a man with ties to the West, Roosevelt as Bryan's opponent for the presidency would have given the country not only sharp differences in political direction, but also two exciting personalities who had remarkable abilities to stir and motivate crowds. The policy differences were there with McKinley versus Bryan, but not the political theater. And, as we know now since their future has become our past, Roosevelt and Bryan never would do battle for the same office.

On October 15, 13,000 people in the Chicago Coliseum cheered Roosevelt's ideas and his persona. Roosevelt once heard Bryan, standing incognito in the rear of the audience. He was impressed by his oratorical skill, by his ability to dominate a crowd, but the Bryan stances repelled him. He furthermore considered Bryan vain and not very intelligent.[32] Roosevelt extolled the virtues of the gold standard and excoriated Bryan for his support of free silver. On October 8, Roosevelt summed up the overall prospects for the campaign, in particular the dangers of the Bryan movement and why he believed the Republicans would win:

> The change of feeling about free silver has been very great. I have never seen a campaign carried along on a higher plane. The appeal has been made straight out on the grounds of morality and patriotism; and the people generally are responding well. I think we shall carry the East by unprecedented majorities, and the

middle west by large majorities; the Rocky Mountain States and the South will be against us; and along the border line between; Maryland, West Virginia, Kentucky, Nebraska, the Dakotas, and possibly the Pacific coast States will be close, and we probably shall carry some of them.

The Bryanites have more and more dropped free silver as the issue of the campaign; the fight has nothing to do with bimetallism; it is simply a gathering of the forces of social unrest. All the men who pray for anarchy, or who believe in socialism, and all the much larger number who have not formulated their thoughts sufficiently to believe in either, but who want to strike down the well-to-do, and who have been inflamed against the rich until they feel that they are willing to sacrifice their own welfare, if only they can make others less happy, are banded against us. Organized labor in the lowest Unions is hot for Bryan, although the workingman would suffer more than anyone else by free silver; but the higher class, including the immense mass of the railroad employees, are for us.[33]

Earlier on September 11, he had addressed the Commercial Travellers Sound-Money League in New York City, stating of the current controversy, "It is really a fight for honest money and honest currency against the debasement of the currency and the impairment of credit. Free silver is but a step toward fiat money."[34]

There was agreement on this issue by an overwhelming majority of Republicans and by a substantial minority of Democrats, mostly in the East. Even if the Bryan campaign had had as much money as did that of McKinley, that could not have overcome the fears his platform engendered. As great as was Bryan's populist appeal with many, more feared that were his platform put into effect business would suffer as would the workers employed by those businesses. A final and key McKinley advantage was Mark Hanna who proved himself on the national stage as a master of political organization and operation.

A colorful, slashingly effective participant in the political wars was *Puck*, the first successful American magazine of its genre. From 1871 until September 1918, it was cheered and cursed for its political cartoons, caricatures, and editorials which presented a Bourbon Democrat, that is conservative Democrat, viewpoint. The name, Puck, was derived from a character in Shakespeare's *A Midsummer Night's Dream*, a mischievous, sometimes slightly malevolent sprite.

The magazine's publishers considered the Roman Catholic Church a threat to American principles of freedom. The Tammany Hall organization was a particular target since it was both a political machine engaged in corruption to further its power and it was dominated by Roman Catholics of Irish background.

William McKinley versus William Jennings Bryan

Puck's high-water mark in terms of both influence and circulation was 1884 when they assiduously worked to elect Grover Cleveland in his contest against Republican senator James G. Blaine, a former speaker of the House of Representatives and both a past and a future secretary of state. The journal was credited with being a key factor in Cleveland's narrowly winning New York which gave him the margin of victory in the Electoral College. Bryan was absolutely unacceptable to the management of *Puck* in 1896 and in 1900; his liberalism doomed any prospect for them to support his succeeding Cleveland.

During the ensuing years, *Puck* declined in influence, but did come back into the news in 1917 when William Randolph Hearst bought it. He had been irritated over the years by its politics which he now got rid of, altering the focus of the magazine to fine arts and social fads. It was to no avail and the last issue of *Puck* was in September 1918.

Each side warned of the dire consequences were the opposition to win. This so often was effective in stirring up people since the distance between the two sides was greater than in any national election since the slavery differences came to a head in 1860. Finally, November 3 arrived, and the voters decided between clashing visions and clashing fears.

This combination of hope and apprehension motivated people in record numbers to express themselves with ballots. Nationwide, 79.3 percent of eligible citizens voted; in the upper Midwest, the turnout topped 90 percent. McKinley won a substantial but not overwhelming victory. He carried 23 states with 271 electoral votes while Bryan was on top in 22 states with 176 electoral votes. Not yet states were Oklahoma, Arizona, New Mexico, Alaska and Hawaii. As a point of interest, the electoral vote actually could have been startlingly different; with a shifting of 19,250 votes in California, Delaware, Indiana, Kentucky, Oregon, and West Virginia those states would have gone to Bryan which would have given him the Electoral College.

The popular vote was closer, although McKinley's lead was solid with 7,104,779 people choosing him, about 51 percent of the total. Bryan trailed with 6,502,925 votes, close to 47 percent. Far in the rear of the major party candidates were Palmer of the National Democrats with 133,148 votes, and Joshua Levering of the Prohibition Party with 132,007 votes, each just under 1 percent of the ballots cast.[35] The Republican strength was solid in the Northeast and the upper Midwest, strong enough to carry North Dakota, California, and Oregon. While most of the South stayed Democratic, Maryland, Delaware, West Virginia, and Kentucky did go Republican. Staying in the Democratic column were the prairie and mountain states plus Washington on the West Coast.[36]

Six days after winning the election, McKinley wrote to Hanna expressing his appreciation for his loyal and skillful support over the years culminating in the winning of the presidency:

> Your unfaltering and increasing friendship through more than twenty years has been to me an encouragement and a source of strength which I am sure you have never realized, but which I have constantly felt and for which I thank you from the bottom of my heart. The recollection of all those years of uninterrupted loyalty and affection, of mutual confidences and growing regard fill me with emotions too deep for the pen to portray. I want you to know, but I cannot find the right words to tell you, how much I appreciate your friendship and faith. God bless and prosper you and yours is my constant prayer.[37]

Meanwhile, Bryan was disappointed that he lost but by no means was he discouraged; there would be no doubting the rightness of his beliefs, no questioning his continued active leadership of what he and his most ardent followers saw as a crusade. These Bryan supporters saw the presidential contest as a clash between good and evil. One of them wrote that Bryan had lost to the forces of "money, coercion, and the devil."[38] Hardly had the 1896 vote count been completed when Bryan began the next round. He gave up his career as a lawyer and now earned a substantial income speaking and writing. In particular, his campaign memoir, *The First Battle*, sold well, helping to keep him from becoming a figure of the past. Some of his advisers urged him to downplay the monetary issue and focus on making the next contest a class struggle of the poor against the wealthy. For Bryan it must be both. He did favor higher taxes on those who had much and benefit programs for those with less, but also was determined to continue his silver crusade. In his admiring biography of Bryan, Michael Kazin wrote:

> Bryan was the first leader of a major party to argue for permanently expanding the power of the federal government to serve the welfare of ordinary Americans from the working and middle classes. With the backing of his followers, he preached that the national state should counter the overweening power of banks and industrial corporations by legalizing strikes, subsidizing farmers, taxing the rich, banning private campaign spending, and outlawing the "liquor trust."[39]

To further aid the Bryan cause, his younger brother Charles and his wife Mary developed a card file of supporters with information on their religion, jobs, income, and as many other insights as possible on what motivated them. It grew to 200,000 names in 1897 and 500,000 by 1912.[40] This was a boon for Bryan, who was not himself a gifted organizer and was an intriguing foreshadowing of later sophisticated campaign organizations.

For almost four more months Grover Cleveland would be president; the change from March 4 to January 20 would not be in place until the beginning of Franklin Delano Roosevelt's second term in 1937. On December 7, Cleveland delivered his last annual message to Congress. In it, he discussed the deadlock in Cuba; the Spanish army-controlled Havana and the major population centers while the Cuban rebels held the rest of the territory, about two-thirds of the island. Cleveland blamed both sides for abuses and stated that the situation was worsening. He reminded the Spanish that the United States had stayed neutral and had not interfered with Spanish sovereignty, but there was a limit to American desire to avoid conflict. Cleveland warned clearly that if Spain did not undertake serious reforms, we could be forced to conclude that "our obligations to the sovereignty of Spain will be superseded by higher obligations."[41] Cleveland's sense of justice was stronger than his desire to avoid war.

In January, he submitted to the Senate an arbitration with Britain to resolve the still festering Anglo-Venezuelan dispute over the border between British Guiana and Venezuela. The Republican controlled Senate refused to ratify it, for different reasons. Some preferred to wait until McKinley took office since that was only a few weeks in the future. Some pro-silver advocates resented the British because of their resolute support of the gold standard. Still others wanted a more assertive foreign policy and wanted the new administration to handle the dispute.[42] Peaceful resolution in 1899 resulted from the combination of American determination and the greater threats to British interests from the aggressive expansion of German and Russian power. Also, war loomed in South Africa against the Boer republics. The British would win, but it would be a difficult triumph. Facing these challenges, conflict with the United States over territory in South America was not worth the probable cost. The resolute stands of the Cleveland and McKinley administrations led to an American diplomatic triumph.

4

First Term Begins

On March 4, 1897, McKinley was inaugurated as the 25th president on a day which was sunny and mild. On the previous evening, he and Cleveland had a friendly meeting. The two men had been political opponents over the years, but now had come to respect each other. McKinley stated his support of Cleveland's policy concerning Cuba, working to encourage more freedom for the people there without war, and vowed to continue towards that goal. They also discussed the gold standard and the necessity to continue it.

McKinley's faith was evinced at the inaugural ceremony by his opening the Bible to 2 Chronicles 1:10 which quoted part of Solomon's prayer: "Give me now wisdom and knowledge, that I may go out and come in before this people: for who can judge this thy people, that is so great?"[1]

In his inaugural address, McKinley set forth the course he intended his administration to take. He opened with the affirmation, "Our faith teaches that there is no safer reliance than upon the God of our fathers, who has so singularly favored the American people in every national trial, and who will not forsake us so long as we obey his commandments and walk humbly in his footsteps."[2] While in Washington, the McKinleys were regular worshipers at the Metropolitan Methodist Church.

On monetary policy, he took a relatively moderate position, recognizing both the necessity for our monetary system to be based on gold and for there to be enough paper in circulation for healthy economic activity. He did anticipate an improvement in the economy so as to "no longer impose upon the government the necessity of maintaining so large a gold reserve, with its attendant and inevitable temptations to speculation."[3] He fundamentally believed now in the gold standard, but monetary policy still was not his strongest point.

McKinley did understand taxation and spending; he continued to espouse conservative fiscal policy, especially since the economy had not yet recovered fully from the depression of 1893: "If the revenues are to remain as now, the only relief that can come must be from decreased expenditures.... The government should not be permitted to run behind or increase its debt in times like the present."[4]

He firmly rejected debt, making clear that borrowing must not be resorted to in order to close the gap between income and expenditure:

> The government should not be permitted to run behind or increase its debt in times like the present....
> The best way for the government to maintain its credit is to pay as it goes—not by resorting to loans, but by keeping out of debt—through an adequate income secured by a system of taxation.[5]

Most assuredly his focus was not primarily on foreign policy. Certainly, McKinley was well aware of the problems in Cuba, but, as was true of Cleveland, his hope was for more freedom and prosperity for Cubans within the Spanish orbit. In less than a year from inauguration day, domestic policy would take a back seat to war with Spain and the consequent emergence of the United States as a major world power.

McKinley now set about getting his cabinet in place. This would be his administration; he knew the policies he wanted and the men who would implement them. Within that context, there was the reality of political debts to be paid, people to be placated. A warm, genial personality made the path smoother for him, but there still were ruts to avoid and hills to climb before his administration was in place and ready to go. For example, the Senate was a logical source of cabinet nominees, having an array of members who were experienced in both domestic and foreign policy matters as well as being experienced in politics. To be taken into account, though, were considerations of who would replace them in the Senate were they to be chosen for the cabinet and could they be counted on as team players or did they have independent agendas of their own?

At the head of the line was Mark Hanna who had been so brilliantly effective organizing and running the winning campaign. McKinley wanted him as postmaster general, the most significant patronage controlling position in Washington. Hanna, though, wanted a Senate seat, an aspiration that appeared blocked by the reality that two powerful Republicans held the Ohio Senate seats—former governor Joseph Foraker who had just been elected in November and John Sherman, one of the most prominent members of that body. Sherman had been elected to the House of Representatives back in 1854, then seven years later to the Senate. He served as secretary of the treasury during the administration of Rutherford Hayes, after which he returned to the Senate where he still sat in 1897. He had made runs for the Republican presidential nomination in 1880, losing to Garfield, and in 1888, losing to Benjamin Harrison. Since these two influential members of his party blocked his way, Hanna's prospects looked dim, but not for long.

As McKinley moved to form his cabinet, an intriguing opportunity to achieve a couple of goals with one move became clear; nominate John Sherman as secretary of state. Now in his mid–70s, and declining mentally and physically, Sherman saw this, the premier cabinet post, as a fitting culmination to his long career. His moving to this position would open his seat in the Senate. If everything went according to the plan, Ohio governor Asa Bushnell would appoint Hanna to fill the vacancy. Bushnell, though, represented a faction of the Ohio Republican Party not enthusiastic behind the scenes for McKinley or Hanna and he appeared to be plotting ways to get the seat himself. Before long, Bushnell saw that he could not succeed. Encountering McKinley, a better political maneuverer than he and now the president of the United States, Bushnell gave up and appointed Hanna to the Senate vacancy.[6]

Prior to this move, McKinley had heard rumors that Sherman's health, both mental and physical, had declined in recent years. But, at this time early in 1897, McKinley and his close supporters either did not see this for themselves or they believed that Sherman, with able subordinates, would be capable enough to serve as the administration established itself. Appointed as assistant secretary of state was William R. Day, a longtime friend of McKinley who had been both a legal and a political advisor during McKinley's past candidacies. Day later would be secretary of state for several months after Sherman resigned, then would head the American peace commission that negotiated the end of the Spanish-American War the next year. After this, he was a judge on the United States Court of Appeals and ended his career on the United States Supreme Court. Second assistant secretary of state was Alvee A. Adee, who held this position for 38 years until his death on July 4, 1924. In September 1898, he would be acting secretary of state for two weeks after Sherman and Day had left and before John Hay took office.

Joining the cabinet as secretary of the treasury was Lyman J. Gage of Illinois, president of the First National Bank of Chicago. A resolute gold standard advocate, he had left the Republican Party and supported Grover Cleveland's presidencies. The Democrats' nomination of Bryan brought

Gage back to the Republicans. He would be a major force behind the Gold Standard Act of 1900. Gage would hold this office through the McKinley and Theodore Roosevelt terms.

Also part of the McKinley economic team was the brilliant and shrewd Charles Gates Dawes, already at 31 a highly successful entrepreneur who had built a thriving natural gas operation in Chicago and surrounding communities. During the presidential campaign, he had been part of McKinley's inner circle. He was interested in serving as secretary of the treasury but realized that his youth stood in the way. He became comptroller of the currency, a post independent of the treasury department with a five-year term of office. Still ahead for him was service as a general in World War I, winning the Nobel Peace Prize in 1925 for his work to stabilize the German economy ravaged by defeat in World War I, and a term as vice president of the United States.

The secretary of war was Russell A. Alger of Michigan, a lawyer who had distinguished himself as a dashing cavalry leader during the Civil War. After the war, he was successful in lumber and railroad operations and served a term as governor of Michigan. Following his cabinet tenure, he was a member of the United States Senate.

The navy department was headed by John D. Long, an alumnus of Harvard College and Harvard Law School who was elected governor of Massachusetts in 1880 and served one two-year term before returning to the private sector. He then was elected to three terms in the U.S. House of Representatives where he became a friend of McKinley's. As secretary of the navy, Long continued the rebuilding of the navy which had begun back in 1883 during the Arthur Administration. At the end of the Civil War in 1865, the United States navy had grown to a level where only the British navy was more powerful. By 1883, the United States not only trailed the major world powers in naval strength, but even Chile had a fleet stronger than ours.[7]

Cornelius N. Bliss of Massachusetts, a prominent business leader there and in New York City, was secretary of the interior.

Charles Emory Smith was postmaster general. He had been a major newspaper man in New York and Pennsylvania and was the United States minister to Russia in the early 1890s.

Attorney general was Joseph McKenna, born in Pennsylvania, then moved to California. He served four terms in the United States House of Representatives, then was selected by President Benjamin Harrison for the United States Circuit Court of Appeals. After less than a year as attorney general, McKinley named him to the United States Supreme Court in January 1898. He is one of the few people to have served in all three branches of the federal government.

Secretary of Agriculture James Wilson of Iowa, born in Scotland, had been speaker of the Iowa House of Representatives, taught agriculture at what now is Iowa State University, was on the Iowa State Railway Commission, and was elected to the United States House of Representatives. He continued as secretary of agriculture under Theodore Roosevelt and William Howard Taft. His total of 16 years in office marks him as the longest serving cabinet member in American history.

All in all, this was a cabinet of capable, respectable men, but not one ranked among the most exciting and brilliant. McKinley let them run their departments without his intrusion as long as they supported the goals of his administration. On Tuesday and Friday mornings he met with them, listened to them, then announced his decisions. He trusted them with the specifics of their offices, but it was his administration.

The greatest excitement would be engendered by the man chosen to be assistant secretary of the navy—Theodore Roosevelt. Still under 40 years of age, he had marked himself as a man of character, intelligence, ability and ambition in positions of significance just below the top tier and had campaigned vigorously and effectively for McKinley. In early 1897, he was campaigning for the post of assistant secretary of the navy, realizing that his youth and relatively modest resume would not gain him a cabinet post. McKinley was wary of Roosevelt's reputation as a firebrand, but powerful voices were raised in support of him: Senator Henry Cabot Lodge of Massachusetts, John Hay, soon to be ambassador to Britain and later secretary of state, Vice President Hobart, and William Howard Taft, at this time a United States Circuit Court judge. Senator Thomas Platt of New York opposed the appointment, seeing Roosevelt as a threat to his power in New York, but had to back down before the array of those supporting him. On April 6, McKinley acceded to the urgings of such powerful supporters and made the appointment. Also helping McKinley decide to appoint Roosevelt was that doing so was a way to remind the powerful Platt that he, McKinley, controlled the administration. Roosevelt now was on the verge of his dramatic ascent from moderate prominence to national power and world fame.

The United States which McKinley would lead was entering into an especially exciting time in both world and national history. Around the world, European empires were expanding, and Japan rapidly was developing as the first major power to emerge outside of European civilization for several centuries. Here in the United States in addition to the McKinley-Bryan match, the last half of the 1890s was significant and exciting. The massive gold strike of 1897 in the Klondike spurred economic growth and credit expansion. In 1898, the separate municipalities of Manhattan, Brooklyn, the Bronx, and Staten Island combined to form New York City. Its population of 3,400,000 marked it as the second largest city in the world, trailing only London.

During these years as the 19th century in the United States came to a dramatic close and the even more dramatic 20th century dawned, there were a good number of remarkable rises by people lacking inherited wealth and lacking also what some later would consider rights, such as that society owed them what they lacked, that they should be taken care of regardless of what they did. The men here considered, though, supported an economy free of government control which guaranteed nothing except opportunity.

One of the most impressive rises from a low rung on the societal ladder to the top was that of John D. Rockefeller (1839–1937), born into a Richford, New York, family of very limited means. At the age of 14 he started work as a clerk in a commission house—a business which sold the goods of their customers for a commission. He worked diligently, saved, invested, and was an early entrant into the oil refinery business. Soon, the Rockefeller enterprises expanded into pipelines, railroad tank cars, and land acquisition. By 1879, he controlled 90 percent of oil refining in this country before slipping back to a still impressive 80 percent. His Standard Oil Company was a masterpiece of efficiency which lowered the prices to consumers. In 1911, the United States Supreme Court ruled that Standard Oil was in violation of the Sherman Antitrust Act and ordered that the 33 subsidiaries be broken off into separate companies. Rockefeller was a devout Christian whose generosity benefited many organizations and individuals. At the same time, he was attacked for corporate growth and consolidation which limited market freedom.

Another spectacular rise was that of Andrew Carnegie (1835–1919) who was born into a struggling Scottish family which emigrated to the United States when Andrew was 12 years old and settled in Pittsburgh. He went to work in a cotton mill and, determined to rise, taught himself to be a telegraph operator. In 1853, he started as a clerk and telegraph operator with the Pennsylvania Railroad, rising to be a division superintendent. During his years of working for others, Carnegie saved and invested in oil, railroad sleeping cars, and iron. In 1873, he took the lead in starting what would become the largest and the most up-to-date steel mill in the country. Carnegie bought the controlling interest in Henry Clay Frick's coke company and made Frick a key subordinate in his growing empire. In 1901, J.P. Morgan bought out Carnegie Steel in one of the most significant moves in our economic history. One of the richest men in the world, Carnegie devoted much of his retirement time and wealth to funding good works such as libraries and schools.

Rockefeller and Carnegie were the key individuals in the development and growth of modern philanthropy. In *Memoirs*, Rockefeller's grandson David wrote that these two men focused on understanding and eliminating social problems rather than alleviating symptoms.[8] Extending educational opportunities to capable young people in poor families, for example, was high on their lists.

James Pierpont Morgan, more commonly referred to as J.P. Morgan (1837–1913), was born into a successful family, the son of a prosperous banker. After studying at the University of Gottingen in Germany, he returned to the United States and started his own financial business which engaged in marketing bonds. His power grew through financially backing burgeoning businesses such as American Telephone and Telegraph, General Electric, and railroads including the New York Central, the Northern Pacific, and the Baltimore and Ohio.

In 1895, Morgan was instrumental in reviving the American economy in the wake of the major depression of 1893, known as the "Panic of '93," the worst depression experienced by this country prior to the Great Depression which began in 1929. Cleveland's leadership in repealing the inflationary Sherman Silver Purchase Act was key to starting the revival. Problems still persisted, though, as foreign investors worried about the cheap money pressure that remained powerful and they sold off their U.S. government securities; since they were paid off in gold, there was a dramatic fall in gold reserves. The looming crisis was averted when Cleveland turned to private bankers, especially Morgan who led a campaign to avert the looming crisis.

Morgan was genuinely concerned about the economic health of this country and also saw an opportunity to profit. He organized and headed a syndicate which sold 3.5 million ounces of gold coins to the government at $17.80 per ounce, receiving in return $62.3 million in bonds. At that time, gold was selling at $18.60 per ounce; the government received $65.1 million in gold in return for $62.3 million in bonds. These bonds would mature in 30 years, paid 4 percent interest, and could be redeemed in either gold or silver coins, the choice being in the hands of the government. The plan worked to stop the outflow of gold and to start gold flowing back into the United States. The syndicate sold their bonds at a reasonable profit, clearing just under 5 percent, hardly unreasonable considering the crisis confronting the country.[9] The economy revived, but by 1896 the Democratic Party no longer was the conservative party of Grover Cleveland and the Bryan liberals were dominant. This new controlling force in the party could not accept Cleveland's having worked with J.P. Morgan, to them a key example of too much wealth and power being possessed by a few individuals.

The automobile industry began to flourish during the 1890s. The first vehicle to travel without human or animal propulsion was built successfully by Nicolas-Joseph Cugnot of France in 1769. His interest was both in carrying people and in towing heavy artillery. In the 1860s, the American Sylvester Roper invented a steam-powered automobile. Karl Benz and Gottlieb Daimler of Germany invented a gas-powered vehicle. In 1891, William Morrison, another American, built the first successful electric car. That same year, the French Panhard et Levasseur became the first car with a front-mounted engine and with rear-wheel drive.

Especially noteworthy now were American ingenuity and inventiveness. Charles and Frank Duryea marketed in 1893 the first gasoline-powered vehicle to hit the market successfully. In 1897 brothers Francis and Freelan Stanley drove their first steam-powered automobile and were marketing their car the next year.

Both steam and electric cars soon would prove to have serious disadvantages competing with gasoline power. Steam-powered automobiles were heavy and accelerated slowly. Electric cars lacked range, their batteries needing frequent recharging, and they were slower than steam and gas cars. Even though they were clean, quiet, and simple in design, their negatives would cause their rapid decline once gasoline engines hit the market more. In 1899, Albert Pope's Columbia Electric produced over half the automobiles in the country, but by 1905 only a few still were being built.[10]

Henry Ford soon became the dominant force in automobile manufacturing in this country and world-wide. He built a gas engine in 1893 and hit the market with his first vehicle in 1896. By a few years into the 1900s, half the cars sold in the United States would be Fords. In 1899, as McKinley began his first term, it would be no stretch to consider Ford the most promising of the many manufacturers entering this new field.[11]

Also significant during the second half of the 1890s was the progress toward fulfilling the dream of building a heavier-than-air flying machine. The Wright brothers, who would succeed in doing that in 1903, would not enter into this venture until 1900. During the 1890s, Samuel Langley, astronomer, former professor of physics, and secretary of the Smithsonian Institution, seemed to be the most likely person to first do this. He built and successfully flew models in 1896. In December 1898, the War Department agreed to grant him $50,000 to design and build an airplane for military use. He was not ready to test his full-sized craft until 1903 when it twice failed to take off. In December of that year, the Wright brothers became the first to fly successfully in a powered airplane.[12]

Technological advances also were evident in communications. After losing the 1896 election, Bryan telegraphed his congratulations to McKinley, the first time someone in his position had done so. Breaking ground too at this time was motion picture development. McKinley was the first president memorialized by a movie camera.[13]

During the years after the Civil War, the American economy grew rapidly, opening up opportunities for an increasing number of people. As always, there were some who did not rise as rapidly or to as high a level as they wanted. They were open to the pronouncements of Marxists and anarchists who called for destroying the political and economic systems of this country and bringing in a radically new order. Success by these radicals was limited because of economic growth and improved working conditions. Blatant abuses such as children laboring in mines and factories instead of developing themselves in schools were being recognized and corrected. The eight-hour workday was spreading; by 1880, only one person in four still worked a 10-hour day.[14] The overwhelming majority of working-class people who had both ability and ambition chose to rise through the system. As always, though, there were some malcontents who listened to the siren song of those who called for radical change, such as replacing private ownership of business with government ownership of the means of production and distribution.

An example of an organization aiming to do this was the first major labor organization in the United States, the Knights of Labor. It was founded in 1869 as a secret fraternal society bringing together workers, farmers, and shopkeepers. The first key leader was Uriah Stephens, a dedicated utopian socialist. He was replaced in 1879 by Terence Powderly, a railroad worker who three times was elected mayor of Scranton, Pennsylvania on the Greenback-Labor ticket. He ended the organization's secrecy and brought it to its peak membership of 700,000 in 1886. Thereafter, as the radicalism of the Knights of Labor became more evident—abolish private banks, nationalize natural resources, replace market capitalism with workers' cooperatives—they lost public support. Strikes, especially against railroads, resulted in sabotage and death. The organization suffered further from the violence in Haymarket Square, Chicago, when a bomb killed seven policemen and one civilian plus injuring dozens.

As the decline of the Knights of Labor continued into the 1890s, it would be superseded by the American Federation of Labor which was founded in 1896. Led by Samuel Gompers, it was determined to improve the status of workers, but within the American economic system; he was convinced that management and labor could work together. Gompers was born in England in 1850 and emigrated to the United States when he was 13 years old. A hard working, ambitious young man, he joined the Cigar Makers Union, and sought to improve himself by taking courses at Cooper Union, an institution catering to those who had to work full time. Gompers was determined to secure better wages and conditions within the capitalist system, rejecting the socialism espoused by the Knights of Labor and by Eugene Debs. In 1886, he founded the American Federation of Labor which aimed at bringing together craft unions, organizations whose members held the same job. Gompers served as president of the A.F.L. from 1886 to 1894 and again from 1895 until his death in 1924. During these years of his leadership, it grew from 150,000 members to over 3,000,000.[15]

Initially, the American Federation of Labor stayed out of the partisan jungle, not endorsing candidates for political office, although Debs personally supported Bryan in 1896 and in 1900. As will be discussed later, this would change in 1908.

Part and parcel with the expansion of organized labor was the growth of urbanization during the second half of the 19th century. It was a mixed bag with overcrowding, water and sewer problems which worsened as more and more people came to urban areas seeking to better themselves. Improvements did come, but the rapid and continued population surge continued to cause headaches. There was another side to urbanization, especially in major cities such as Boston, New York, and Chicago. Reform came in public health and safety with better water and sewer systems. Public libraries, public transportation, and park systems developed. The fine arts also flourished during these closing decades of the 19th century. The Metropolitan Opera, one of the premier opera companies in the world, opened its doors in 1883. During the years McKinley and Bryan dueled for political power, the Metropolitan already was well established in the top tier of these organizations.

Historian John C. Tenford wrote of the United States at the end of the 19th century that those living in our cities had "as high a standard of public services as any urban residents in the world. Problems persisted, and there were ample grounds for complaint. But in America's cities, the supply of water was the most abundant, the street lights were the most brilliant, the parks the grandest, the libraries the largest, and the public transportation the fastest of any place in the world."[16] Furthermore, it is significant that this progress took in municipalities which were financially sound. Increasing urbanization was a reality with both positive and negative consequences. Our leaders in the private sector and holders of public offices, the best of them anyway, would continue to accentuate the positive aspects and to minimize the negative.

Another significant societal force during the closing years of the 19th century was the burgeoning movement to extend the vote to women. In 1869, Elizabeth Cady Stanton and Susan B. Anthony had formed the National Women's Suffrage Association of which Stanton would be president. During the 1890s, some progress was made. In the 1896 and 1900 elections, women could vote in Wyoming, Utah, Colorado, and Idaho. By the time the 19th Amendment took effect in 1920, 29 states already had enfranchised them.

The McKinley Administration certainly favored American dynamism, the inventiveness and the opportunities which characterized the United States but was leery of those who wanted us to become an imperial power. McKinley intended to focus on domestic policy matters, trade and the monetary system in particular. He was well aware of potential overseas problems for us in the Pacific and in Latin America, but he did not foresee war and the acquisition of an American empire.

Concerning the tariff, McKinley was convinced that protection was good public policy, that it would lead to higher wages for workers and that business would be shielded against imports from lower standard of living countries. In March, he called Congress into special session. A bill introduced by his friend Representative Nelson Dingley of Maine, chairman of the Committee on Ways and Means, passed the House 205–122. The Senate would be more difficult as powerful factions lobbied for higher rates on some items, lower rates on others. Finally, the varied factions got together well enough to pass a bill which was signed by McKinley on July

24. Overall, the Dingley Tariff created the highest rates up to that point in American history. The potential damage to trade, though, was mitigated by three provisions in the bill. First of all, the president was given authorization to negotiate with European countries concerning the rates charged on imports of art, wines, liquors, and certain minor items. Secondly, he could do the same with Latin American countries on tea, tonka, and vanilla beans. The third and most significant point was that he could negotiate with any country mutual tariff reductions of up to 20 percent.[17] It is significant to note that by now McKinley had a deepened understanding of world trade not just in terms of economic considerations. Speaking in the summer of 1897 to the Cincinnati Commercial Club, he stated that "good trade insures good will."[18]

Monetary matters also were focused upon by the new administration. On April 12, McKinley appointed a commission to deal with monetary reform; all the members were bimetallists. He wanted to see developed an international system. The British, however, were committed firmly to the gold standard. As the strongest world power, their weight was significant, strengthening the hands of gold standard advocates in other countries. In October, Japan adopted the gold standard as did Russia in December. By the end of 1897, the move to gold was well on its way worldwide. McKinley shifted from his bimetallic stance to support of the gold standard where he now joined most of the key Republican leaders.

During the post Civil War years opposition to the political spoils system was growing with increasing support for merit-based civil service as the alternative to wholesale changes in government personnel from top to bottom when a new administration took office. When in the House of Representatives, McKinley had supported reform. Now, as president, he was a moderate on the matter, wanting qualified people holding government posts while recognizing the political power of patronage. He did state that Cleveland appointees would not be removed without some reason deeper than their being Democrats.[19]

But it would be foreign policy which soon dominated the attention of the administration and the country in general. In 1894, Hawaii thrust itself more to the forefront of American attention. The islands were visited first by Europeans in 1778 when the British captain James Cook landed there, about 2000 years after intrepid Polynesian seafarers had built their first settlement. The coming of the Europeans initially would be devastating to the native Hawaiians; they lacked natural resistance to diseases brought by the newcomers such as smallpox and measles, resulting in a dramatic falling of the population from an estimated 300,000 in the late 18th century to about 73,000 in the mid–1800s. The strategic location of Hawaii was obvious from both naval and trade perspectives. Until almost the end of the 19th century, the Hawaiians used diplomacy to balance themselves between expanding and competing powers, but a weak country occupying such a vital site could not stay independent indefinitely.

The 1887 Hawaiian Constitution permitted foreigners to vote as long as they met residency requirements. In January 1893, Queen Liliukalani tried to implement a new constitution increasing royal power, a constitution, though, which had been rejected by the Hawaiian legislature and by her own cabinet. At this point, Hawaiian citizens of American background, numbering about 2000, and American business interests in the islands formed a provisional government. They were supported covertly by John Stevens, the American minister to the royal government. Marines and sailors from the U.S.S. *Boston* landed in Honolulu, the capital, ostensibly to protect American lives and property, but also serving to deter opposition to the change in government. As it turned out, there was little Hawaiian opposition to the reality that the islands were going to lose their independence, if not to the United States, then to Britain or Germany with Japan now probing that far eastward in the Pacific. At this time in world history, a militarily weak country occupying a strategic location would not long remain independent.

Initially it seemed as if Hawaii soon would join the United States. Benjamin Harrison favored American annexation with the understanding that this represented the wishes of the Hawaiians, but Grover Cleveland took office in March 1893 and was suspicious that Americans were behind the change of government in Hawaii. He withdrew that treaty from Senate consideration and appointed a special commission to determine the truth. When the report confirmed what Cleveland suspected, he stated flatly that Hawaii would not become American and called for restoring Liliukalani to her throne.

In view of the Cleveland Administration's opposition to annexation, the next year the Republic of Hawaii was organized with Sanford Dole as president. Dole was born in Hawaii to American missionary parents. He attended college in the United States, then returned to Hawaii, practiced law and served in the legislature and as a Hawaiian Supreme Court justice. Liliukalani retired to her Honolulu mansion where she lived until her death in 1917.

By 1897, Cleveland had finished his second term and McKinley had taken the oath of office. In June, he submitted an annexation treaty to the Senate, but the tariff question came ahead of it because of strong interest in the issue and because of a vocal anti-expansionist minority reflecting Cleveland's opinion. In June 1898, Congress passed a joint resolution annexing the islands. By then, the Spanish-American War had led to much more interest in matters beyond our shores and the joint resolution approach required just a simple majority in each House rather than two-thirds majority required for a treaty to be approved by the Senate.

5

War with
Spain Looms

Far and away the most significant event of McKinley's tenure in the presidency was the 1898 war with Spain. During the 1500s, that country had been the greatest military and naval power and had the most extensive empire until the 1600s when the British passed them in naval strength and empire development and France rose to be the number one military power in Europe. From then on, the Spanish decline was slow but continuous. In 1898, their holdings remained extensive, including territory in northwestern Africa, islands in the Atlantic and the Mediterranean plus what they were to lose in 1898: Cuba, Puerto Rico, the Philippines and Guam. This still was an extensive empire and their armed forces looked strong on paper. Many Europeans, accustomed to European prowess and having limited respect for the upstart republic across the Atlantic, would be shocked by the rapid American success and the completeness of the Spanish failure on land and sea. The traditional Spanish courage was evident, but the Americans had it too plus a far superior industrial base, better naval ships, and superior generalship.

Spain, declining but proud, was determined to retain their empire and at least the semblance of major power status. Independence movements in Cuba and in the Philippines were opposed by harsh measures of repression, especially in Cuba. The closeness of Cuba to the United States magnified the impact of the Spanish determination to quash the freedom movement there. Some major American newspapers, looking to increase their circulation, vied with each other in presenting lurid, sometimes erroneous, examples of Spanish cruelty. William Randolph Hearst and Joseph Pulitzer were the key leaders of the pack baying for war. Each was a giant in the highly competitive, often cut-throat newspaper business, Hearst owning the *New York Morning Journal*, Pulitzer the *New York*

World. Hearst was born into a wealthy family, the son of George Hearst, United States senator from California who gave him the *San Francisco Examiner*. After succeeding on the West coast, Hearst crossed the country, in 1895 bought the *New York Journal*, and made it one of the most powerful newspapers in the country. He developed the largest newspaper and magazine empire in the world. Pulitzer, an immigrant from Hungary, fought in the Civil War as a teenager and worked his way up in journalism from reporter to his 1878 purchase of the *St. Louis Dispatch* and the *Evening Post* which he combined into the *St. Louis Post-Dispatch*. In 1883, he moved into the New York market with his purchase of the *New York World*. The dramatic and often lurid war between these giants often ignored precise accuracy in the pursuit of exciting headlines and increased circulation. Their excesses, however, should not obscure the reality that Spanish oppression and the desire for freedom it stirred were real. Hearst and Pulitzer were instrumental in moving much of public opinion beyond sympathy for the Cuban people to favoring our intervention.

In 1492, Christopher Columbus had claimed Cuba for Spain. A few years later, in 1511, the Spanish began settling the island, defeating and enslaving the Indians there ahead of them. Few of the Indians survived conditions of slavery, so Africans were imported to work the increasingly profitable sugar plantations. By 1860, about one-third of the world sugar supply came from the island.

The independence movement which swept through Spanish America in the opening decades of the 19th century bypassed Cuba where the ruling class stayed loyal to Spain because they feared a successful slave uprising without Spanish army presence. During the middle years of the century, many of the Cuban ruling class favored joining the United States as the best way to preserve their way of life. This sentiment was reciprocated by American pro slavery elements in the South who feared the rapid growth in population and economic strength they saw in the anti slavery North and by other Americans who saw the acquisition of Cuba as a way to end Spanish oppression. Spain rejected American offers to purchase Cuba. The American Civil War and continued westward expansion in this country distracted much of our attention, but not all; uprisings in Cuba and the often-brutal Spanish reaction kept at least some American focus on Cuba.

In 1868, the Ten Years' War broke out. It was a movement of poor whites, mulattos, free blacks, and slaves. Their goal was the end of slavery and a free Cuba. It failed, although Spain did agree to some reforms. In the middle of the 19th century, just over 1,000,000 people lived in Cuba—of whom 436,000 were slaves and 153,000 were free blacks. Another rebellion, The Little War, followed in 1879–1880. It too failed. Spain finally ended slavery in 1886.

In 1895, a new war for independence erupted led by Jose Marti, a significant literary figure in both prose and poetry who had lived in the United States from 1881 until 1895. He had been born in Cuba, the son of Spanish parents, "Peninsulares." Marti grew up as one of the "Criollos," Cuban-born white professionals and landowners who supported autonomy for the island, if not full independence. He clashed with his father and with the Spanish authorities, was imprisoned briefly, then traveled to Spain where he completed his education. Briefly tempted to blend into the Spanish intelligencia, he returned to his Cuban-independence origins, and furthered the cause from New York. In 1895, Marti decided that his credibility would be limited unless he returned to Cuba and took the field himself. He was killed in combat on May 11 shortly after fighting broke out that year, but the rebellion picked up steam. The military leader of the rebels was the Dominican Maximo Gomez, an experienced warrior who had been a major in the Spanish army, then fought against them. He now was 72 years old, but still dynamic mentally and physically. Serving under him and commanding in eastern Cuba was Antonio Maceo, the charismatic black general who too had an extensive history fighting Spain. He died in combat in December 1896. The Cuban rebels used classic guerrilla tactics, hitting and fading into the countryside. The Spanish tried to concentrate the Cuban populace into carefully controlled areas, depriving the rebels of support. They also built fortified lines north to south across the island trying to pacify Cuba segment by segment. Both sides, in spite of their ruthlessness, enjoyed only partial success at the cost of widespread suffering.

In February 1896, General Valeriano Weyler took command of the Spanish forces in Cuba. He served as Spanish military attaché to the United States during the Civil War and developed a deep admiration for General William Tecumseh Sherman. By no means a sadistic, unfeeling man, he was absolutely determined to smash the rebellion. To deprive the rebels of supplies and a population into which they could blend, he ordered rural populations and their cattle into designated areas. Theoretically this *reconcentrado* policy provided for the support of these people, but this proved illusory. At least 200,000, more likely 400,000 people died of hunger and disease.[1]

American support for the rebels was extensive with very few people in this country favoring Spain. The key question was what we should do. A number of Americans, such as former president Cleveland and William Jennings Bryan, opposed military intervention by us. McKinley so believed. By no means a pacifist, his memories of Civil War carnage led him to hope for the end of Spanish heavy-handedness and more freedom for Cubans by means short of our going to war. He was well aware of the overseas problems this country faced in the Pacific and in Latin America, but he did not foresee war and the acquisition of an American empire. As 1898 dawned, he and most members of his administration were hopeful that Spain would show restraint and reason, that Cuban autonomy within the Spanish Empire would be preferable to a weak, independent Cuba which could fall prey to expanding European empires; Germany in particular was casting a covetous eye on territory anywhere which was not possessed by one of the major powers. The McKinley Administration also hoped that the Cuban rebels would accept this status short of full independence. Events in the opening months of 1898 dashed any hope for a peaceful, compromise settlement of the conflict.

The American navy which had grown during the Civil War to be second only to that of Britain, went through an equally dramatic reduction, sinking to twelfth place by 1870. By the early 1880s, concern about our inability to protect our interests led to the beginning of revival during the Arthur Administration. In 1891, Congress authorized our first modern battleships, steel-hulled and coal-fired—the *Indiana*, the *Massachusetts*, and the *Oregon*. All would play significant roles in the Spanish-American War. By 1894, the United States navy had grown to number six in the world, trailing those of Britain, France, Italy, Russia, and Germany.[2] Our ships were modern, an advantage of starting just a few years before with a small and mostly out-of-date fleet. Now in 1897 and early 1898, growth was spurred by opposition to Spanish oppression in Cuba and by worries about increasing German imperialism in the Caribbean and in the Pacific. As will be discussed later, the army at this time had not yet begun its growth to major power status. By the end of the century, the U.S. navy had grown to fifth place and early in the new century with Theodore Roosevelt now president, it once again would be surpassed only by the British.[3]

Secretary of the Navy John D. Long of Massachusetts was an honest, intelligent gentleman who respected and liked his assistant secretary, Theodore Roosevelt, although he did have some qualms about his exuberant nature. Their working together proved to be effective, especially since Long looked forward to leaving behind the hot, humid summers of

5. War with Spain Looms

Washington during this time before air conditioning and going north to his country home at Hingham Harbor, Massachusetts. Roosevelt reveled in the opportunity to assume responsibility and to push the preparedness of the navy were war to be the next step in the relations between the United States and Spain. A symbiotic relationship developed with each man getting to do what he wanted. Long, though, was by no means either a weakling or a fool, so Roosevelt wrote him frequently and carefully so as not to arouse any concerns or suspicions. Long too wanted a stronger U.S. navy, as did McKinley, even if his pace of development was not as rapid as Roosevelt wanted; the young assistant secretary was smart enough to avoid pushing too hard, although he did come close.

A good example was an incident in September 1897 when Roosevelt read a letter from Senator William E. Chandler of New Hampshire urging the appointment of Commodore John A. Howell to command American naval forces in the Far East. This prospect filled Roosevelt with misgivings since he believed Howell lacked the strength and determination for such a post, especially if war broke out between the United States and Spain. For this appointment he considered Commodore George Dewey far and away the best choice that could be made. Since Long was at his summer home, Roosevelt acted quickly, meeting with Dewey. He learned that Dewey knew the influential senator Redfield Proctor of Vermont, a friend of McKinley's and a fellow Civil War veteran. Proctor, very much in agreement with Roosevelt concerning expanding American influence, met with Dewey and then spoke with McKinley urging the appointment of Dewey to the Asiatic command.[4] McKinley, knowing of Dewey's record which also dated back to the Civil War and valuing Proctor's opinion, wrote Long calling for Dewey's posting to that command.[5]

This action by the president Long accepted, although he was irritated by Roosevelt, believing that his assistant had pushed the envelope too far. The breach would not be permanent since Long did appreciate Roosevelt's abilities. In a few months, Dewey's success at Manila Bay would ensure that his selection was the right move. In February 1898, while Long was ill, Roosevelt ordered Dewey to move his squadron to Hong Kong, to keep his ships fully coaled, and to prepare for action in the Philippines. He also ordered full readiness for our European and South Atlantic commands.[6]

As 1898 opened, however, prospects for peace appeared brighter. The previous year, a new government took office in Spain headed by Praxedas Mateo Sagasta, a veteran politician who previously had held the post as prime minister. Now, he determined to lessen the tension between his country and the United States by recalling Weyler, replacing him as governor-general with General Ramon Blanco, and promising moves toward Cuban autonomy. Perhaps he was sincere in his willingness to grant Cuba more autonomy within the Spanish Empire, but clearly Spanish pride would tolerate few concessions to American pressure, preferring honorable defeat to giving in to demands by this upstart country on the other side of the Atlantic.

Hoping to further the prospects for peaceful change in Cuba, McKinley ordered the battleship *Maine* to sail from Key West to Havana. On the morning of January 25, she dropped anchor. McKinley's intent was to demonstrate friendship while also reminding the Spanish of American power. Also, German warships were in the Caribbean, a facet of Germany's determination to spread their power throughout the world. At this point, McKinley was not aiming at the establishment of an American empire, but he was determined to prevent the expansion of the German empire into our backyard.

The *Maine* was classified as a second-class battleship. She finally joined the now growing U.S. fleet in 1895, nine years after her funding. The ship was 6,683 tons, 319 feet in length and 57 feet wide, substantially smaller than mid–20th-century battleships. Her main armament was four 10" guns, two forward and two aft, plus six 6" guns and four torpedo tubes. The *Maine* was staffed by 354 officers and enlisted men.[7]

The American consul in Havana was Fitzhugh Lee, nephew of Robert E. Lee and a dashing Confederate cavalry general back in the Civil War years. He later wrote a biography of his uncle and served a term as governor of Virginia. Appointed to his post by Grover Cleveland, Lee had been retained by McKinley as a gesture of national unity and, possibly, to have a Democrat in Havana on whom responsibility could be placed if relations between the United States and Spain soured. Lee opposed Spanish rule in Cuba and favored acquisition by the American government. Now, in early 1898, he did express the possibility that the visit of the Maine might not have a calming effect but could ignite a conflict.[8]

Spanish officials in Cuba were furious with this show of American pressure and power but observed the proprieties. There were some expressions of hostility such as handbills proclaiming: "Death to the Americans! Death to autonomy! Long live Spain! Long live Weyler!"[9] The Spanish population of Havana opposed independence for Cuba because of their patriotic support for the once great empire and also fears of what their place would be in an independent Cuba which might turn on those with close ties to Spain. The Spanish authorities in Havana maintained order; although the chill was palpable, American officers were entertained on shore, such as at the bullring, and Spaniards were received on the *Maine*.

At this very time as relations between the United States and Spain were tense, an indiscretion by the Spanish ambassador, Enrique Dupuy de Lome, added fuel to the growing distaste for Spain. A personal letter written by the ambassador to his friend Don Jose Canalejas, editor of *El Heraldo*, one of the most powerful newspapers in Spain, was stolen by Gustavo Escoto, a secret agent of the Cuban rebels. Cuban overt and covert operations in the United States were effective. Quickly recognizing the significance of what he had taken, Escoto passed it on to those who brought it to the attention of Assistant Secretary of State Day and to the media, in particular William Randolph Hearst's *New York Morning Journal* which published it on February 9. In it, the ambassador wrote: "Besides the natural and inevitable coarseness with which he repeats all that the press and public opinion of Spain have said of Weyler, it shows once more that McKinley is weak and catering to the rabble and, besides, a low politician who desires to leave a door open to himself and to stand well with the jingoes of his party."[10] He proceeded to indicate that the Spanish grant of autonomy to Cuba was a subterfuge to hoodwink the Americans to accept the continuation of Spanish rule over the island.

Recognizing that he had been caught in a major diplomatic indiscretion, Dupuy de Lome wired his resignation to Madrid before the McKinley Administration could demand his recall. The Spanish government issued a rather pro forma apology which was accepted by the U.S. government. Beneath the surface, though, American distrust of Spain grew, and Spanish pride suffered a further blow at having to apologize for what widely was considered an accurate depiction of McKinley and American interference in what was none of their business. The prevailing Spanish attitude was that war, even if lost, was preferable to quiescently yielding to American demands. Cuba probably could not be kept, but even if Spain lost the war, the Americans would be given sharp blows and Spanish honor upheld.

Spanish naval commanders, such as Vice Admiral Pascual Cervera, understood clearly the realities they would face were war with the United States to break out. Too many ships were old, not well maintained, and their crews, although courageous, were not well trained, especially in gunnery. Shortly prior to the outbreak of hostilities, when Cervera was told that he would command the Spanish naval units fighting the Americans in the Atlantic and in the Caribbean, responded, "I shall accept; knowing however that I am going to a Trafalgar," referring to the defeat of a combined French and Spanish fleet by the British commanded by Horatio Nelson in 1805. He stated this loss could not be avoided unless the government allocated the funds for the coal and ammunition needed for extensive practice.[11] Now 59 years old, Cervera had fought for Spain in Asia, in South America, and in civil wars.

So here stood the situation in February 1898. In the United States, there was extensive support for Cuban freedom and for us to develop as a major world power. In Spain, there was reluctance to face the reality that they no longer were a major power and a fatalistic preference to fight and lose rather than to accept peacefully the end of their empire.

6

War

The *Maine* still was moored in Havana harbor as night fell on February 15. At 9:40, an explosion reverberated through the city, bringing down plaster and knocking out lights. At first, there was speculation that the arsenal had blown up. It quickly became evident that the *Maine* had been rent by the blast and was settling to the bottom. She came to rest in about 40 feet of water with her super-structure above the surface. In the maritime tradition, sailors from ships in the harbor, including the Spanish cruiser *Alfonso XII*, the Spanish transport *Legazpi*, and the American *City of Washington*,[1] rescued survivors. Of the 355 sailors and Marines on the *Maine*, 254 died in the blast and eight more died in hospitals shortly after.

Among the survivors were Captain Charles D. Sigsbee and executive officer Lieutenant Commander Richard Wainwright. Sigsbee, a Civil War veteran, later commanded the armored cruiser *St. Paul*, a former ocean liner, in operations off Santiago and was promoted to rear admiral in 1904. Wainwright also served at Santiago, commanding the armed yacht *Gloucester*, which had been owned by J.P. Morgan, in the naval clash on July 3. He too would retire as a rear admiral.

The Spanish authorities were involved in the proprieties of honorably burying the bodies which had been recovered from the *Maine*. They were only 19 in number, most of the dead still being in the wreck. On February 19, the bodies lay in state at the Havana Municipal Palace. That afternoon, they were buried at Colon Cemetery. Captain Sigsbee read the burial service from the Episcopal Book of Common Prayer. Father John P. Chidwick, the *Maine*'s chaplain, conducted the Roman Catholic service together with the bishop of Havana. Leading the dignitaries present was Governor General Ramon Blanco. In December, Captain Sigsbee, now commanding the battleship *Texas*, took charge of the operation to bring the bodies back to the United States for burial at Arlington National Cemetery.[2]

Now began the process of determining officially the cause of the explosion. Many Americans were convinced from the start that Spain was responsible; such was their view of Spanish perfidy that no other reason was conceivable. The Hearst and Pulitzer newspapers enthusiastically fanned these flames. On the other hand, many naval officers understood the danger of coal bunker fires, especially in ships such as the *Maine* where ammunition magazines and coal bunkers were close to each other. Exacerbating the danger was the electrical wiring in the walls near the bunkers. Shortly before, spontaneous fires in the bunkers of the battleship *New York* and the cruiser *Cincinnati* almost spread to their magazines; only narrowly was tragedy averted. The *Washington Evening Star* found most of the naval officers they interviewed believed that the most likely cause of the sinking was an accidental explosion.[3]

Rear Admiral Montgomery Secord, commanding the North Atlantic Squadron, appointed a Court of Inquiry to determine the cause of the disaster. It was headed by Captain William T. Sampson, who commanded the battleship *Iowa*. Lieutenant Commander Adolph Mannix, former executive officer of the *Maine*, was judge advocate. The other members were Captain French E. Chadwick, who had commanded the *New York* and had headed the Office of Naval Intelligence, and Lieutenant Commander William P. Potter, respected for his technical knowledge of ships.

McKinley earnestly wanted to avoid war, his memories of the Civil War carnage still fresh, but he too was determined not to accept passively the continuation of Spanish misrule in Cuba. He hoped ardently that both could be achieved. He did propose that the United States purchase Cuba, but there was little congressional support for the idea. On February 25, he broached the idea that if the Court of Inquiry determined that Spain had caused the sinking of the *Maine*, a cash indemnity could be the best answer. This too failed to gain congressional backing.[4]

As time dragged on, McKinley recognized that Spain had to see with clarity American resolve to fight if necessary, in addition to the American preference for a peaceful settlement. He proposed and Congress approved the spending of $50,000,000 for expanding our armed forces. On March 8, it became law, the House passing it 311–0, the Senate 76–0. Most of the money would be spent on the navy, centering on the building of three battleships, 16 destroyers, and 14 torpedo boats.[5]

The likelihood of American intervention gained momentum on March 17 when Senator Redfield Proctor of Vermont, a friend of McKinley's and a fellow Civil War veteran, addressed the Senate on his recent trip to Cuba. He spoke calmly and dispassionately for over an hour. Since the Court of Inquiry had not yet issued its report, Proctor refrained from commenting on what caused the loss of the *Maine*. He said that he had gone to Cuba as one who wanted the United States to refrain from intervening, but now he was convinced that we could not stand aside. What he saw there was Spanish oppression far beyond what he had imagined, leading him to believe that conditions would not improve until Cuba was free.[6] He said: "To me, the strongest appeal is not the barbarity practiced by Weyler, nor the loss of the *Maine* ... but the spectacle of a million and a half of people, the entire native population of Cuba, struggling for freedom and deliverance from the worst misgovernment of which I ever had knowledge."[7]

The impact of his remarks was profound, although a few, such as Speaker of the House Thomas Reed of Maine, tried to hold back the tide. Reed considered what was happening in Cuba just a local uprising, not Americans' business.

On March 24, Secretary of the Navy Long ordered the peacetime white color of our warships replaced by gray. Step by step, both countries were moving closer to the outbreak of war; in both countries, those who wanted to avoid hostilities were losing control of events.

On March 28, the report by the Court of Inquiry was released to the public. Although there was no direct statement that Spain was behind the sinking of the *Maine*, the report blamed an external device for causing the explosion and stated that no blame or negligence was borne by U.S. naval personnel.[8] Of course, since the ship was sunk in Havana harbor, the implication that Spain was responsible was obvious to all but the most obtuse. The belief in Spanish culpability rapidly was pushing aside suggestions that this might have been an accident. For both sides now, war was a preferred course of action.

As March moved to an end, McKinley continued his efforts to resolve the *Maine* crisis and further justice for Cuba without war. Hope continued that Spain would be reasonable. The American ambassador to Spain, Stewart L. Woodford, was optimistic that these ends were within reach. On April 1, the Spanish accepted most of the American stipulations, but not the call for an armistice; they wanted the rebels to agree first. For many Americans, this refusal was the crossing of the Rubicon; war now was the only course open to us if we were to take seriously our freedom and to do what we could to spread that freedom to others. On April 4, McKinley again postponed his message to Congress when reports came to him that Spain was prepared to make further concessions. When it became evident that

Spain was not serious about any meaningful agreement concerning Cuban freedom, on April 11, McKinley sent a message to Congress wanting authorization for the use of American military force to stop the bloodshed and to bring about freedom for the people of Cuba. Having failed to further justice and freedom peacefully, McKinley now saw war as the better option than abandoning these principles. On October 19, in a speech in Chicago several weeks after the fighting had stopped, McKinley said that "the war with Spain was undertaken, not that the United States should increase its territory, but that oppression at our very doors should be stopped."[9]

On April 19, Congress finalized support for Cuban independence, to be secured by American intervention if necessary. The span of days between the submission of the message and its passage was not due to opposition, although some such as Speaker Reed tried to block it, but rather because so many members wanted to put their remarks on record. The Senate passed the resolution 42–35, the House 310–6. Since members of the House of Representatives are elected every two years, their vote reflected the widespread popular support for action. It is interesting to note that the Roman Catholic community in the dominantly Protestant United States extended little support to Spain even though that country was solidly of their faith. For these American Catholics, such as Archbishop John Ireland of St. Paul, the war demonstrated the superiority of the rising United States over the declining Spain, that this country would be the key future world power.[10] By the 1890s, the Roman Catholic Church was the largest American denomination, though far from constituting a majority of the population. Church leaders did look forward to a future day when the majority of Americans would be Catholic.

There were questions concerning what we should do with Cuba, but the clear consensus was that it should be independent. On April 25, Congress passed the Teller Amendment to make clear that the United States had no intention to annex Cuba.

Spain reacted sharply to what they saw as our sticking our nose into what was none of our business. On April 21, the Spanish government broke diplomatic relations with the United States and on April 24 declared war. The next day, we issued our declaration, backdating it to April 23.[11] Before autumn, the American rise would be astounding as would be the Spanish imperial collapse.

But the outbreak of war came at a time when the United States army was not prepared for serious campaigning, especially overseas. At this time, its strength stood at 2143 officers and 26,040 men. There were 25 regiments of infantry and 10 of cavalry, but the army was not organized into divisions and corps, let alone anything larger. As a Civil War veteran, McKinley remembered well the number of generals in that conflict who had received their rank because of political considerations. Although understanding the necessity to bind the country together through these appointments, he had seen the military cost of doing so and was determined not to have the same thing happen during his presidency. Of 26 major generals in the war with Spain, 19 were regular army men as were 66 of 102 brigadier generals.[12] The most senior officers had served in the Civil War. The two top generals, Nelson Miles and Wesley Merritt, had distinguished themselves as combat leaders in that conflict and would do so in this one. Miles would be passed over for command of the Cuban operation because of concern that he would use such a triumph to run for president in 1900. He did lead the conquest of Puerto Rico since that came after the victory in Cuba had ensured American victory. Merritt would command in the Philippines.

By August, the number of regulars had increased to 56,365 and 200,000 volunteers had been authorized. Secretary of War Alger offered command of one of the new volunteer regiments, the 1st Volunteer Cavalry, soon better known as the "Rough Riders" to Theodore Roosevelt. Although no "shrinking violet," he did realize that he was not yet ready to command a regiment in war and proposed Leonard Wood as colonel with himself as second in command with the rank of lieutenant colonel.[13] This was done. Shortly after the campaign in Cuba began, Wood was promoted to brigadier general and Roosevelt succeeded him in command of the regiment. Wood too was a most remarkable man, a doctor who graduated from Harvard Medical School, won the Medal of Honor fighting the Apaches, and now was McKinley's personal physician as well as being Alger's doctor. He later would command the army and serve as governor general of the Philippines.

The regiment commanded by Wood and Roosevelt established itself as one of the most fascinating in military history during its short life— it was disbanded in September. It drew from the East college graduates who were some of the best athletes in the country, men who had starred in football and polo. From the West came most of the regiment, Indian fighters (as well as some Indians), lawmen, ranchers. They were rugged and used to weapons. Roosevelt said of them, "All-Easterners and Westerners, Northerners and Southerners, officers and men, cowboys and college graduates, wherever they came from, and whatever their social position—possessed in common the traits of hardihood and a thirst for adventure."[14]

The pace of mobilization was more rapid than the system could handle. For most units, tropical uniforms were not available, and they served in Cuba in the summer wearing blue woolen garb. As will be discussed later, Theodore Roosevelt's Rough Riders did secure light weight uniforms, but they were the exception. Still, as will be seen, the American armed forces overcame shortcomings and blazed an impressive record of bravery, initiative and success.

The United States, already a major economic power, was poised to join the ranks of the major world empires. At this time, the British Empire stood head and shoulders above the others, occupying about one-quarter of the world's land and governing about one-quarter of the people. It would so continue until after World War II when the waves of independence swept it into the pages of history. By and large this empire established peace and justice so that their rule was maintained by an army of less than 100,000 British soldiers. Also of significance was the Royal Navy whose 100,000 men and 38 coaling stations around the world greatly enhanced the spread of British power. Throughout this empire spread Christianity plus Western ideas of political and economic freedom.[15] Queen Victoria's Diamond Jubilee in June 1897 provided an opportunity for British power to be exhibited peacefully but with clarity. For the naval review at Spithead, 22 countries had been invited to send ships. This provided an opportunity for the Royal Navy to remind both friend and potential foe of its strength, amassing 21 battleships and 53 cruisers without weakening their overseas commitments.[16]

By 1898, the Americans and the British no longer were rivals facing the prospect of war as had been true not that many years previously, during the American Civil War, for example. Now, the United States saw Spain, Germany, and, just beginning, Japan as greater threats. The British clearly saw Germany as their major danger.

The outbreak of war between the United States and Spain quickly made evident European opinions as to the likely outcome of the fighting. Although there was the recognition that the United States was a country on the rise and that Spain's greatest years lay behind it, there still was the widespread belief by Europeans that the Spanish armed forces would do well. As an example, there was the conviction that the American Asiatic naval forces under then Commodore Dewey would be defeated by the

Spanish ships in the Philippines commanded by Admiral Patricio Montojo, that the Americans were doomed.

Now that war had been declared formally on April 24, Secretary of the Navy Long telegraphed Dewey, who had concentrated his squadron at Hong Kong, that "war has commenced between the United States and Spain. Proceed at once to Philippine Islands. Commence operations at once, particularly against the Spanish fleet. You must capture or destroy. Use utmost endeavors."[17] The aggressive Dewey needed no prodding, just this green light. He was a graduate of the U.S. Naval Academy at Annapolis and had served under Admiral David Farragut during the Civil War. Just hours before receiving these orders, Dewey had moved his ships to nearby and deserted Mirs Bay where he refueled his ships, engaged in gunnery practice, and collected as much intelligence as possible on what lay ahead of him in the Philippines. On April 27, he ordered his ships to sea. As dawn broke April 30, the mountains of Luzon rose above the horizon. Dewey now issued orders to enter Manila Bay after dark and attack the Spanish just after dawn.

Nine ships sallied forth under Dewey, six being involved in the upcoming battle. The flagship and the largest was the protected cruiser *Olympia* of 5,870 tons. Her main armament was four 8" guns backed up by 10 5" guns. She now is a museum ship in Philadelphia. The second largest ship was the cruiser *Baltimore*, 4,413 tons and armed with four 8" guns and six 6" guns. The protected cruisers *Raleigh* and *Boston* were 3,213 and 3,000 tons, the former carrying one 6" gun and 10 5" guns, the latter two 8" guns and six 6" guns. The gunboat *Concord* was 1,710 tons with six 6" guns. The gunboat *Petrel* was the smallest of the U.S. ships engaged, being only 892 tons, but with four 6" guns. The other three vessels, the revenue cutter *McCullough*, the collier *Nanshan*, and the supply ship *Zafiro* were kept back from the clash to come since they carried little in the way of effective armament and they were not armored.

Seven Spanish ships would do battle with Dewey's squadron. The unprotected cruiser *Reina Cristina* was Montojo's flagship, 3,520 tons with six 6.3" guns. The unprotected cruiser *Castilla*, 3,260 tons, had had her 8" guns removed to be used as shore batteries. She had left four 5.9" guns and two 4.7" guns. She remained moored during the upcoming clash because of problems with her propeller shaft. Also unable to maneuver was the unprotected cruiser *Don Antonio du Ulloa*, 1,152 tons. As if that were not problem enough, she carried only four 4.7" guns on her starboard side since her port side guns had been removed to reinforce shore artillery.

Three other small unprotected cruisers saw combat in Manila Bay, the *Don Juan de Austria*, 1,159 tons, four 4.7" guns; the *Isla de Cuba*, 1,045 tons, four 4.7" guns; the *Isla de Luzon*, also 1,045 tons with four 4.7" guns. Last of the Spanish ships was the *Marques del Duero*, a 500-ton gunboat with one 6.3" and two 4.7" guns.[18]

The Spanish armed forces on land were more formidable on paper than in actuality. Their coast artillery around Manila Bay impressed with its numbers more than with its capability. The opening into Manila Bay was only 10 miles wide, divided by the island of Corregidor just two miles south of Bataan Peninsula. Most of the guns on Corregidor and Bataan were old as were the 226 guns covering Manila and its environs. The best were four 9.4" guns at Manila. Unfortunately for Spain, such modern weapons were too few.[19] Making the situation worse for Spain was the rather misguided chivalry of Admiral Montojo. He should have kept his ships close to Manila where they could have been covered by the best of the coast artillery. Instead, he moved his ships six miles south of Manila to Cavite. This spared the city from possible damage from American guns but ensured that Dewey's ships were beyond the range of the Spanish guns. The outcome of the battle probably would not have been different, but Montojo could have played his cards better.

It was here at Cavite that the Americans found the Spanish ships after looking first off Manila. At 5:40 a.m. on May 1, Dewey gave the order to the captain of the *Olympia* Charles V. Gridley, "You may fire when you are ready, Gridley." Gridley, also a graduate of Annapolis and a Civil War veteran, was terminally ill, probably from liver cancer, and had only a few weeks to live, dying June 5. Although weakened by the disease, he rose to the occasion doing his duty bravely and well.

The American victory was overwhelming. By the time the Spanish struck their flag shortly after noon, their squadron had been sunk in battle or so battered that they were scuttled and 381 Spanish died.[20] The American ships were hit 15 times during the battle, but no men were killed and only eight wounded.[21] This overwhelming victory doomed any realistic Spanish prospects for retaining the Philippines. There still remained their 9,500-man garrison in Manila, but increasingly they were hemmed in by the Filipino independence fighters under Emilio Aguinaldo, a charismatic leader of Tagalog and Chinese ancestry just 29 years of age. Born into a plantation-owning family, he had studied law, but did not complete the requirements for a degree. Earlier in the 1890s, he had led the revolt against Spain on Luzon, the largest, most populated, most developed of the Philippine islands, and the site of Manila. On December 14, 1897, he and the other rebel leaders agreed to the Treaty of Biak. According to the terms, the rebels gave up their arms and their leaders, including Aguinaldo, agreed to leave the Philippines. In return, Spain pledged to govern in a milder manner and paid off in cash the leaders now going into exile in Hong Kong.[22]

After the war began, the American consul general in Singapore, E. Spencer Pratt, contacted Aguinaldo to negotiate an alliance against Spain. Pratt informed him that the United States supported "much greater liberty and much more material benefits than the Spaniards ever promised you."[23] This Aguinaldo assumed to mean a promise that the U.S. would back independence for the Philippines. Misunderstandings would not stop there. The Americans transported him back to Manila Bay where he conferred with Dewey on May 19. Out of this meeting too would arise misunderstandings. Dewey insisted that he made no commitments to independence for the islands, obeying his instructions from Secretary of the Navy Long to avoid making any political promises.[24] His main focus was on commanding American naval forces and furthering American interests under increasingly complex and volatile circumstances. Aguinaldo wanted American support for the independence of his country; he believed that he had it. It is not unusual for people to hear and believe what they want to hear and believe. Aguinaldo set up his government at Cavite and in June proclaimed the independence of the Philippines with himself as president.[25] Still, a good number of Americans, such as Oscar Williams, the former American consul in Manila and Rousenville Wildman, American consul in Hong Kong, were convinced that the islanders would welcome having us take over the Philippines from Spain.[26] Complications would grow in June. The Filipinos considered the islands an independent country, the American position had not yet solidified, Spain still controlled Manila, and Germany was starting to probe aggressively into what their leaders thought to be an opportunity to spread their empire.

The first American army units sailed from San Francisco on May 25. On their way, they seized the island of Guam bloodlessly; the Spanish commander there knew nothing of the war.[27] General Wesley Merritt was given command of the new Department of the Pacific and the 8th army corps. He arrived in the Philippines in July with further American forces, including Brigadier General Arthur MacArthur. Merritt had an extensive combat career. He graduated from West Point in 1860, served gallantly in the Civil War reaching the rank of brevet major general, and saw further service in the Indian wars. Now in 1898, he ranked behind only Nelson Miles among American generals.

The coming of significant U.S. army units was important since Germany was becoming more assertive in its interest in taking over the Philippines from Spain, raising the possibility of conflict with the Americans. British, French, and Japanese warships had arrived soon after Dewey's victory of May 1. They acknowledged and respected the formalities of the war between the United States and Spain, especially the legality of the American blockade; they officially reported their presence, anchored where instructed, and did not interfere with American operations. The Germans would be an entirely different matter. At first, German naval ships entering Manila Bay did not report their arrival to Dewey and even sailed by his flagship, ignoring its presence. Dewey overlooked the first German ship which did this, believing this oversight would not be repeated as more senior German officers arrived. When a second German ship entered the bay at 3:00 a.m., he signaled her to identify herself. When his command was ignored, he ordered a shot fired across her bow. This got the attention of the Germans and resulted in their observing proper procedures thereafter.[28]

But the Germans were not through probing for American weakness and opportunities for them to expand their empire. For example, they landed men on Bataan for drill. More significantly, German officers visited the Spanish forces on shore and entertained Spanish officers on their ships. This raised concerns that a deal could be in the works resulting in German acquisition of the Philippines. As is now known, this was not as likely as had been supposed, although Germany certainly was interested and would push until firm resistance were encountered. The German commander, Vice Admiral von Diedrichs, found that the British naval contingent under Captain Chichester fully supported the American control.

On a second occasion, a German ship ignored reporting to the American blockaders until, once again, a shot across her bow induced the captain to respect the formalities.[29] Germany was aggressively pursuing expansion anywhere an opportunity was seen, but the prospect of fighting the Americans who probably would be supported by the British was clearly a bad choice. It is interesting to note, though, that at the close of the 19th century, there were German admiralty plans for a possible war with the United States. This hypothesized Germany's attacking Puerto Rico, defeating the American fleet in the Caribbean, shelling New York, landing army units in New England, and seizing Washington, D.C. Consideration of this farfetched scheme was cancelled officially by Chief of Staff Alfred von Schlieffen in 1903 since it was totally unrealistic unless Germany first dominated Europe and had nothing to fear from the British navy.[30]

Now, as summer began, the Americans firmly held Manila Bay, the city of Manila still was Spanish, and the Filipino independence movement controlled most of the rest, although Aguinaldo was not acknowledged universally beyond Luzon. So the situation in the Philippines would remain tense but relatively stable until the final peace. Cuba shortly would be the primary theater of operations.

After the war began in April, there was a brief scare that Spanish ships would bombard American Atlantic coast cities, but cooler, better informed heads quickly prevailed. Realistically, Spain would have quite enough trouble defending its still extensive empire in the Caribbean and the Pacific. Still, there was uncertainty concerning the destination of the Spanish flotilla which had disappeared from sight after sailing westward from Spain. It could be headed for Puerto Rico or to a base in Cuba—possibly Cienfuegos or Santiago, both on the southern coast. On May 20, firm information arrived in Washington that the ships had anchored at Santiago. The force numbered four cruisers—the *Infanta Maria Teresa*, the *Vizcaya*, the *Cristobal Colon*, and the *Oquendo*—plus the destroyers *Furor* and *Pluton*. The Spanish admiral, Pascual Cevera y Topete, former minister of marine, was an experienced and brave commander, one who saw little hope for victory, but who was determined to do his duty, uphold Spanish honor, and die bravely. Although there may be nobility in this attitude, few victories come forth from a mindset of this nature. He was well aware of that. He also was well aware that the Spanish ships were not well maintained—engines needed overhauling and hulls needed to be scraped to remove weeds and barnacles which cut speed—and their crews not as well trained as the Americans, especially in gunnery. Furthermore, the choice of Santiago was not the best Cevera could have made. Cienfuegos would have been better since it was much closer to Havana, the main center of Spanish military forces and, therefore, easier to reinforce than Santiago which was further to the east. Also making Cevera's decision more questionable was that transportation was less developed in eastern Cuba and guerrilla strength greater, increasing the difficulty of defending that location against a serious assault.

Now that Cevera had been found, the major units of the Spanish navy now were accounted for. The Philippine force had been eliminated, their Caribbean squadron blockaded, and most of their remaining ships defending home waters. Initially, Spain intended to send naval reinforcements to the Philippines but abandoned that idea after Dewey's victory.

The size of the Spanish garrison in Cuba at this time is not certain; the best estimate would seem to be about 140,000 regulars and 80,000 volunteers.[31] They were widely scattered, the Havana garrison of about 32,000 being the largest, with an additional 17,000 men stationed in Matanzas about 100 miles to the east. The Santiago garrison numbered about 9,500 with 24,000 more men stationed elsewhere in the province,[32] but poor roads, strong forces of guerrillas, and American naval supremacy made reinforcing Santiago extremely difficult.

The Cuban campaign would be short but dramatic. American forces landed on June 10 at Guantanamo and on August 12 the armistice ending the fighting on the island was signed. Between those dates were demonstrations of heroism, reputations made or enhanced, and the new reality of American military and naval power made impossible to ignore. There were also, though, initial stumbles in rapidly increasing the size of the army and moving it to foreign lands—Cuba, Puerto Rico, and the Philippines. Providentially, Spain lacked the capability to take advantage of these teething problems and we learned fast.

The war necessitated the organization of the newly expanded army into divisions and corps for the first time since the Civil War. There were senior officers whose service dated back to then, but that was over 30 years in the past. The invasion of Cuba was to be mounted out of Tampa, Florida, which appeared to be a sound choice being on a large, sheltered bay. The development of Florida as a winter vacation destination for Northerners with a distaste for cold weather and the money to assuage that distaste had picked up steam during the preceding decade. During the 1880s, Henry M. Flagler, a Rockefeller associate who had helped organize Standard Oil, focused his attention on Florida. St. Augustine, Palm Beach, and Miami grew in popularity. Georgia industrialist Henry B. Plant was significant in the rise of Tampa. In 1898, it was a rather drab municipality of 26,000 people. Rising almost like a vision from the flat, sandy landscape was the Tampa Bay Hotel. This luxurious extravaganza of Plant's opened in 1891. Moorish in style, it rose five stories, numbered 500 rooms, and was set amidst six acres of gardens. Enjoying the amenities were upper level army and navy officers, newspaper personnel, and various dignitaries both American and foreign. Regimental bands provided a musical background with selections ranging from Strauss waltzes to such popular songs as "After the Ball Is Over" and "Sidewalks of New York."[33] Edith Roosevelt did visit Theodore there, but most of the couple of weeks before the expeditionary forced sailed he spent with his regiment.

As it turned out, the rail system was not adequate for moving in large numbers of men and supplying them. The port facilities were not up to handling well all the roughly 16,000-man expeditionary force which sailed for Cuba on June 13. Their departure had been delayed by false reports of Spanish warships in the Gulf of Mexico.

An often-overlooked point is that the first Americans to invade Cuba were the 650 Marines under Lieutenant Colonel Robert W. Huntington who landed at Guantanamo 40 miles east of Santiago on June 10 in order to establish a coaling base for the navy. After several days of fighting, they secured the position which has continued to be American ever since.

On June 20, the day before the main American landing, General Shafter and Admiral Sampson, commanding the naval units in Cuban waters, met with General Calixto Garcia, the rebel leader in eastern Cuba, to gain more information on the terrain, on the Spanish forces in the area, and to get the cooperation of the Cuban fighters against these forces. The information was useful and the Cubans helpful in harassing Spanish attempts to reinforce Santiago and forcing the dispersion of the Santiago garrison to guard against them.

On June 21, American troops landed at Daiquiri on the southeastern coast of Cuba, 15 miles east of Santiago. Spanish resistance to the landing was light and the few troops stationed there pulled back toward Santiago. The Americans soon had on shore 819 officers and 15,058 enlisted men organized as the 5th corps under Major General William R. Shafter, dashing medal of honor winner during the Civil War, now an aging, corpulent (about 300 pounds) hulk, no longer the inspirational leader of his youth. His courage, experience, and common sense still stood him in good stead, but his bulk, the tropical heat, and malarial fever diminished his prospects for inspirational leadership. Nevertheless, his positive qualities, good subordinates, and the hesitant Spanish command fostered the American triumph.

Under Shafter, the 5th corps consisted of the 1st division of three brigades under Brigadier General David F. Kent; the 2nd division also of three brigades commanded by Brigadier General Henry W. Lawton; and the cavalry division with two brigades led by Major General Joseph Wheeler. The 1st volunteer cavalry regiment, the "Rough Riders," were part of the 2nd brigade commanded by Brigadier General Samuel B.M. Young. The other two regiments in the brigade were regulars—the 1st cavalry and the 10th cavalry, the latter one of two black cavalry regiments. The other, the 9th cavalry, was part of the 1st brigade. In addition, there was an independent brigade under Brigadier General John C. Bates consisting of two regiments of infantry and a squadron of cavalry.[34] Following the Civil War, the 9th and 10th cavalry plus the 38th, 39th, 40th and 41st infantry regiments had been organized as black formations. The cavalry regiments in particular had served well on the Western frontier against the combative Indian tribes who labeled them "buffalo soldiers." This description of them came from the Cheyenne comparison of them to wild buffalos and/or the Comanche use of these words because of their dark skin and their tight, curly hair. A Cheyenne warrior referred to their having "a thick and shaggy mane of hair" and that they "fought like a cornered buffalo."[35] In the three decades since the Civil War, black income and education levels had improved, but there still was prejudice against them, especially in the former Confederate states. Once Southern whites who had served the Confederacy regained the vote and again held office, they stripped away black civil rights, but progress came. In the army, combat experiences drew men together, narrowing the racial divide. When your life has been saved by someone of a different race, prejudice fades. By no means was racial discrimination dead, but slowly a new day was dawning, especially as black soldiers proved themselves in action. Five men in the 10th cavalry regiment were awarded the Congressional Medal of Honor for their gallantry in Cuba and 25 others received Certificate of Merit Medals.[36]

Now ashore and organized, the Americans struck out for Santiago on June 24. The road system in eastern Cuba was not well developed, making moving and supplying the expeditionary force difficult. A short distance inland, the Americans ran into an ambush at las Guasimas. The few Spanish soldiers there, about 1500, could not stop or seriously endanger the 5th corps, but they did provide combat experience for those soldiers who were new to war. In this action, 68 Americans were killed and wounded. Among the eight Rough Riders killed were Sergeant Hamilton Fish II, grandson of Grant's secretary of state, Hamilton Fish, and Captain Allyn Capron, both praised by Theodore Roosevelt who wrote of the impression they made on him as they met the night before the clash: "As we stood around the flickering blaze that night I caught myself admiring the splendid bodily vigor of Capron and Fish—the captain and the sergeant. Their frames seemed of steel, to withstand all fatigue; they were flushed with health; in their eyes shone high resolve and fiery desire. Two finer types of the fighting men, two better representatives of the American soldier, there were not in the whole army."[37]

Pushing back the Spanish covering force, the Americans moved on to Santiago. On July 1, the Spanish were defeated in two sharp battles, San Juan Hill just to the east of the city and El Caney a short distance to the northeast. Seizing El Caney was necessary since it lay on the right flank of any attack on Santiago. Shafter recognized the significance of the position and ordered Lawton to move his 2nd division to seize it. At the same time, the rest of the corps would assault the San Juan Heights, then be joined by Lawton's men once they had secured El Caney, an operation expected to take two or three hours, but the Spanish contingent, 520 men under General Joaquin Vara del Rey, defended the stone fort and wooden block houses there with great valor and skill, holding their position for six hours against 10 times their number. Most of the Spanish, including Vara del Rey, were killed or wounded before Lawton and his division won the day. American casualties numbered 81 killed and 360 wounded.[38]

Meanwhile, a few miles west and south, Kent's 1st division, Wheeler's cavalry division, and Bates' independent brigade waited for news that all was going well at El Caney. As the day wore on and the 2nd division still was delayed there by the resolute Spanish resistance, the decision was made to proceed with the attack on the San Juan Heights. The Rough Riders were on the right flank of the attacking force. They now were led by Theodore Roosevelt after the promotion of Leonard Wood to assume command of Young's brigade after he was laid low by fever.

The Americans swept forward, seizing Kettle Hill and San Juan Hill, suffering significant losses in winning. General Arsenio Linares and after he was wounded, General Jose Toral, failed to concentrate their forces against what obviously was the main American point of attack. Granted, they had an extensive perimeter to defend against the possibility of another American landing and they did have to guard against the Cuban insurgents who controlled the interior, but with better generalship they could have made the American success more difficult and costlier.

Roosevelt's courageous, dynamic, and effective leadership of the Rough Riders ensured his meteoric rise from mid-level political figure to the top. He led his regiment uphill against intense Spanish fire first at Kettle Hill, then at San Juan Hill, moving him and his men into history. Other reputations were made that day, but the colorful nature of the regiment and its commander especially caught the imagination of the country.

As an interesting aside, also distinguishing himself in this battle was an obscure 37-year-old West Point graduate still only a lieutenant, John J. Pershing, who was serving as quartermaster of the 10th cavalry regiment. Soon he would begin his belated but rapid rise to the top of the American army. Here he served gallantly with the 10th Cavalry and was profoundly impressed by their bravery and skill. His nickname, "Black Jack," came from his years with and praise of black soldiers. Pershing praised the courage of those assaulting Kettle Hill, calling attention to the common cause which united men regardless of race or the side for whom they had fought back in the Civil War:

> Each officer or soldier next in rank took charge of the line or group immediately in his front or rear and halting to fire at each good opportunity, taking reasonable advantage of cover, the entire command moved forward as coolly as though the buzzing of bullets was the humming of bees. White regiments, black regiments, regulars and Rough Riders, representing the young manhood of the North and the South, fought soldier to soldier, unmindful of race or color, unmindful of whether commanded by ex-Confederate or not and mindful only of their common duty as Americans.[39]

Racial progress since the Civil War was real, but slow. By 1898, the first blacks had graduated from West Point, but only three of the 12 who had enrolled. The United States Naval Academy at Annapolis had enrolled five black midshipmen, but none had graduated. It was not until 1949 that the first black completed his studies there and was commissioned.[40]

As late as 1941, there were only five black army officers on active duty: Benjamin O. Davis, Sr., who the previous year became the first black general; his son, Benjamin O. Davis, Jr., who was the fourth black to graduate from West Point, became a highly decorated fighter pilot in World War II and Korea, and ended as a four star general; and three chaplains.[41] Benjamin Sr. joined the army July 13, 1898, at the age of 18. He served as a temporary lieutenant in a black unit, the 8th United States Volunteer Infantry Regiment, which stayed in Georgia during the fighting. It was disbanded in 1899. Davis then joined the regular army, was assigned to the 9th Cavalry serving under Charles Young, the third black West Point alumnus. With encouragement from Young, Davis studied for and passed the officer candidate test in 1901. He then shipped out to the Philippines where he saw active duty until the next year. He continued on active duty through World War II.

As had happened previously and would happen again, fighting alongside racially different people generally eradicated racial biases, especially when outstanding courage was demonstrated. As was mentioned earlier, exemplifying this progress was the winning of five Congressional Medals of Honor by men in the 10th Cavalry: Sergeant Major Edward L. Baker and Privates Dennis Bell, Fitz Lee, William H. Thompkins, and George Wanton.[42] Further indicative of the growing appreciation for integrating black citizens into the mainstream of American life were the views expressed by McKinley in the October 1898 speech he delivered at Abraham Lincoln's home in Springfield, Illinois. In it, he said of the president under whom he served in the Civil War:

> He liberated a race—a race which he once said ought to be free because there might come a time when those black men could help keep the jewel of liberty in the family of nations. If any vindication of that act or of that prophecy were needed, it was found when those brave black men ascended the hill of San Juan, Cuba, and charged the enemy at El Caney. They vindicated their own title to liberty on that field, and with other brave soldiers gave the priceless gift of liberty to another suffering race.[43]

McKinley will say more on racial matters as the full political campaign developed.

With the defeats at San Juan Heights and El Caney, with Cuban Guerrillas hampering land reinforcements, and with the naval blockade tight, the Spanish situation was critical. Facing now the possibility that the Spanish ships in Santiago harbor could be lost without a fight, Governor General Ramon Blanco telegraphed from Havana instructions to Admiral Cervera to sally forth with his squadron if the fall of Santiago seemed imminent.[44] On July 3, he did so, convinced that victory over the much stronger Americans was not possible, that death with honor was their best hope. At 9:35 a.m., the American cruiser *Brooklyn* reported that the sortie was beginning.

The main Spanish units were the armored cruisers *Infanta Maria Theresa*, *Vizcaya*, *Cristobal Colon*, and *Oquendo*. The *Cristobal Colon* had seven 6" guns and the other three each mounted two 11" guns and five 5.5" guns. Two modern torpedo boat destroyers also joined in the foray.[45] Their prospects for success were dimmed by their need for maintenance— engine overhaul and cleaning sea growth from their hulls—and by limited crew gunnery training. Furthermore, the narrow harbor opening necessitated their sailing out one at a time.

Confronting them were four American battleships, the *Iowa* mounting four 12" guns and four 8" guns plus the *Indiana*, the *Massachusetts*, and the *Oregon* each carrying four 13" guns and four 8" guns. The *Oregon* had completed an extraordinary 14,700-mile voyage, leaving San Francisco on March 19, circling South America, and arriving on May 24 at Jupiter Inlet, Florida. The amount of time, though, to move from one coast of the United States to the other strengthened interest in a canal across Central America. Also participating in the upcoming battle were the cruiser *Brooklyn* and the armed yachts *Gloucester* and *Vixen*.

As the Spanish ships emerged led by the *Infanta Maria Teresa*, Cervera's flagship, they opened fire on the Americans and turned to the west headed for Cienfuegos, about 300 miles away. Again, as had been true at Manila Bay, the Spanish valor was impressive, but their ships were not as well maintained as were those of the Americans and their gunnery training was at a lower level. Even when the Spanish ships did score some hits, the results did not favor them. For example, the *Iowa* was hit twice by the *Cristobal Colon*, but suffered no casualties. All the Spanish ships were destroyed, either driven ashore or sunk, suffering 323 dead and 151 wounded. One American was killed and one wounded.

Although both the American army and the American navy had won significant victories, disease and the enervating tropical climate caused serious concern. General Shafter, physically and mentally drained, proposed pulling back his forces to higher ground, a bad idea for victorious troops, an idea quickly vetoed by McKinley. Actually, the Spanish were worse off by far. Although better acclimated than the Americans, they had been defeated and were isolated from any prospect for significant relief. Shortly after the Spanish naval defeat, a column under Colonel Federico Escario entered the Spanish perimeter. On June 22, just as the Americans were landing at Daiquiri, the 3752-man force had left Manzanillo to the west. To reach Santiago, they had to fight past Cuban guerrillas for 160 miles through jungles and over mountains. Their arrival, though, could not change what lay ahead for Spain.

It is interesting to note how rapidity of communication had increased during the 1890s. In the White House (although commonly used, the name did not become official until Theodore Roosevelt made it so shortly after he became president in 1901), 25 telephone lines and three telegraph wires gave McKinley the ability to learn quickly what was happening far from Washington and to issue orders which could be received by U.S. army units in Cuba within 20 minutes.[46]

Facing the inevitable, General Toral asked for terms. He proposed that he and his men be permitted to withdraw to Holguin, 75 miles northwest of Santiago. Shafter proposed that these terms be accepted, stating that this would permit the return to the city of the civilians who had fled fearing bombardment, that destruction of property would be prevented, the harbor opened, and his men spared from the ravages of yellow fever which were just beginning.[47] This was rejected sternly by McKinley who responded to Shafter, "What you went to Santiago for was the Spanish army. If you allow it to evacuate with its arms you must meet it some-where else. This is not war."[48] Again, it was made abundantly clear that while McKinley preferred peace to war, once war become the reality then a clear victory was the only course for a major power.

General Nelson A. Miles, army commanding general, had recently arrived. Although more resolute than Shafter, he agreed that the American forces faced serious problems. He cabled Alger that Toral was willing:

> To surrender Santiago province, force, batteries, munitions of war, etc., all except the men and small-arms. Under ordinary circumstances would not advise accep-tance, but this is a great concession and would avoid assaulting intrenching lines with every device for protecting his men and inflicting heavy loss on assault-ing lines. The siege may last many weeks, and they have the provisions for two months. There are 20,000 starving people who have fled the city and were not allowed to take any food.... I concur with General Shafter and the major-generals, and would request that discretion be granted in view of the importance of other immediate operations.... The very serious part of this situation is that there are 100 cases of yellow-fever in this command, and the opinion of the surgeon is that it will spread rapidly.[49]

The Spanish commander, General Arsenio Linares. who had been wounded on July 1, from his hospital bed had a cable sent to the govern-ment in Madrid:

> The situation is fatal; surrender inevitable; we are only prolonging the agony; the sacrifice is useless; the enemy knows it, fully realizing our situation....
> These defenders are not just beginning a campaign, full of enthusiasm and energy; they have been fighting for three years with the climate, privations and fatigue; and now that the most critical time has arrived their courage and physical strength are exhausted, and there are no means for building them up again. The ideal is lacking....
> There is a limit to the honor of arms, and I appeal to the judgement of the gov-ernment and the whole nation....
> If it should be necessary to consummate the sacrifice for reasons of which I ignore, or if there is need of some one to assume the responsibility of the *denoue-ment* anticipated and announced by me in several cablegrams, I offer myself loy-ally on the altar of my country for the one purpose or the other, and I will take it upon myself to perform the act of signing the surrender, for my humble reputa-tion is worth very little when it comes to a question of national interests.[50]

This realistic assessment won out over the stubborn pride so evident in Madrid. A few minor American concessions paved the path for signing what could not be avoided. The Spanish were permitted to have the word "capitulate" used instead of "surrender." The Spanish could not march out with their small arms, but the weapons would be sent back to Spain along with the defeated soldiers.[51] On July 17, the formal surrender took place, the Spanish flag was lowered, and the American flag was raised.

The McKinley Administration soon would be pressured to get the troops home quickly because of malaria and the more deadly yellow fever. At first General Shafter had reported to Washington that the men could be moved by rail about 20 miles inland from Santiago to higher ground where they would be free from the danger. Further investigation showed that the railroad could handle few men each day and the higher ground was not that free of disease danger. On the last day of July, a meeting between Shafter and the senior officers under him developed the plan to have Roosevelt and Wood write letters to Shafter about the disease danger which then would be leaked to the press. This was done, Roosevelt's words stirring more attention. Roosevelt also wrote directly to Secretary of War Alger, stating, "The canned roast beef is worse than a failure as part of the rations, for in effect it amounts to reducing the rations by just so much, as a great majority of the men find it uneatable. It was coarse, stringy, tasteless, and very disagreeable in appearance, and so unpalatable that the effort to eat it made some of the men sick…. Moreover, the water was very bad, and sometimes a cask was struck that was positively undrinkable."[52]

Concerning care of the wounded and sick, he continued his setting forth of shortcomings, writing, "On several occasions I visited the big hospitals in the rear. Their condition was frightful beyond description from lack of supplies, lack of medicine, lack of doctors, nurses, and attendants, and especially from lack of transportation."[53] This embarrassed the administration, especially Russell Alger, but recognition of the severity of the situation and press criticism produced action. Three days later, orders arrived to return the troops to the United States. By mid–August, they were going through the quarantine process at Montauk Point, Long Island, heartened by the cool sea breezes.[54] The war did spur research to learn more about yellow fever, typhoid, and malaria. Mosquitos were not yet recognized as carriers of yellow fever and malaria.

Complaints about corruption and mismanagement were lodged against the War Department, leading to the appointment of a commission headed by railroad tycoon Grenville M. Dodge. The Dodge Commission report found no corruption, but that poor management was all too common. Although no criminal charges were brought against Secretary Alger, his status was much diminished and although he tried to hold onto his office, he was pressured to resign the next year, replaced by Euhu Root.

A few days later on July 21, 3314 men under General Nelson Miles, who, now that most glory had been won, got his chance for active command, sailed from Guantanamo Bay eastward for Puerto Rico to complete the conquest of Spain's empire in the Americas. Smaller than Cuba, it stretched at its greatest extent 111 miles from east to west and 39 miles from north to south. Here Spain did not face a rebellious populace such as they did in Cuba and in the Philippines. In 1897, Puerto Rico had been granted home rule and an elected legislature.

Awaiting the American attack were 8,000 Spanish regulars and 9,000 volunteers, the latter of questionable combat value. The Spanish forces were scattered covering prospective landing sites with their major focus the protection of San Juan, the capital, located on the north coast. The Americans landed at four locations on the south coast, brushed aside weak opposition, consolidated their positions, and brought in reinforcements from the United States, increasing their numbers to about 15,000 by early August. They then began their move northward on San Juan. The American operation was better organized and led than was that in Cuba, partially due to learning from experience, more because Miles was a much better commander than Shafter. There were some sharp skirmishes as the Americans advanced, but no major battles before the armistice on August 12 ended combat operations.

Although there had not been a rebellious populace in Puerto Rico as there had been in Cuba and in the Philippines, there also was not despair at the passing of Spanish rule. Frequently the advancing American troops were welcomed. Absent were the determined independence movements so powerful in the other two territories. Puerto Rico would be integrated into the American system with the people keeping their culture and soon electing their own government as an American territory.

The stalemate in the Philippines—the Americans controlling Manila Bay, the Spanish still holding Manila, and the guerrillas dominant elsewhere—prevailed into August. By then, the Spanish authorities knew of the American military and naval victories in Cuba. Isolated as they were without hope for reinforcement, their options were limited and grim: falling into Filipino hands was unthinkable considering the harsh treatment the Spanish had meted out to those subject to their rule; surrendering to the Americans was humiliating, but survivable. A face-saving arrangement, therefore, was made. The Americans would attack the Manila fortifications, a few shots would be fired, and then the Spanish would surrender, honor intact. The Americans not the Filipinos would occupy the city and the Spanish garrison could return to their homeland. This was done, to the dismay of Aguinaldo and his government who were coming to recognize that they were rid of one occupier but now subject to a new one. A new, more complex, and more prolonged war for the United States was just over the horizon.

For the present, negotiations to end formally the war between the United States and Spain were the primary concern of the McKinley Administration. On April 25, Secretary of State John Sherman had resigned. Slipping into senility and not supporting administration foreign policy, his departure had been desired and was welcomed. Assistant Secretary William Day assumed the office. He would hold the office until August, serving loyally and effectively. His deepest hope for his career in public life was a federal judgeship. This would be his shortly after one more assignment from McKinley.

Day was selected by the president to chair the American commission at the peace talks to be held in Paris during the autumn of 1898. The other members were Republican senator Cushman K. Davis of Minnesota, chairman of the Senate Foreign Relations Committee; Republican senator William P. Frye of Maine, president pro tempore of the Senate; Democratic senator George Gray of Delaware; and Whitelaw Reid, owner of the *New York Tribune*. John Bassett Moore, prominent international lawyer, served as secretary.

Although among the members of the commission were the three positions on the Philippines which separated the general American public—keep the islands, keep part of them, withdraw totally—the majority agreed with McKinley that the first position was right both for the United States and for the Filipinos. Davis, Frye, and Reid supported that policy. Day wanted only an American base in the islands but was loyal to McKinley and open to considering his viewpoint. Gray adamantly maintained that we should withdraw completely.

McKinley, as usual, was in control of policy while ensuring that he was leading in the direction most Americans wished to go. He certainly had convictions but was patient and willing to proceed slowly as public opinion moved in his direction. Historians differ concerning the extent to which he molded these opinions and the extent to which he followed in their wake. Probably he did more molding than was believed by those who saw him as an honest, well-meaning, but weak president. Unfortunately, he did not leave much of a record concerning the formulation of his policy and he was guarded even with those close to him. Still, people on the inside of his campaigns and administrations, people such as Mark Hanna and Charles Dawes, considered him clearly the man in charge.

The commission members had dinner with McKinley at the White House then sailed for France. Negotiations with the Spanish negotiators began in Paris on October 1. The Spanish understood that they were playing a weak hand and dragged out the talks hoping that the Democratic Party would gain control of Congress in the November election. Since key leaders of that party opposed the creation of an American empire, especially favoring Filipino independence, this was the only realistic prospect for mitigating the enormity of the Spanish defeat. This hope, though, was in vain as the public backed McKinley and the Republicans, increased their margin in the Senate, now holding 53 seats to 26 Democrats and 11 outside the major parties. The Republican hold on the House slipped, but still was substantial with their 185 members still a majority over the 163 Democrats and nine others.

Reality now trumped Spanish national pride. The McKinley Administration was determined to control what had been seized and Spain was in no condition to continue the war. To apply some balm to the battered Spanish pride, the United States did pay $20,000,000 for the Philippines. This was far below their value, but Spain was in no position to complain. All things considered, the terms were not draconian.

The Treaty of Paris was signed on December 10. Spain lost Cuba, Puerto Rico, Guam, and the Philippines. In 1902, Cuba was granted independence. Puerto Rico and Guam continue American, voting freely to keep this association. The McKinley Administration did not consider the Philippines ready for the independence demanded by Aguinaldo and his followers. The concern was that with a weak government, the islands would be seized by one of the expansionist powers; Germany and Japan had shown themselves ready to pounce if the United States did not move to solidify its initial gains. As was discussed earlier, the opening of the war with Spain spurred the McKinley Administration to act on the Hawaiian request for annexation. In June 1898, this was done. On January 17, 1899, uninhabited Wake Island, 2000 miles west of Pearl Harbor, was annexed. It would serve as part of the transpacific cable route from San Francisco to Manila, as a stop for the aerial clipper route, and in December 1941 as the site for a heroic defense by the outnumbered Marine Corps garrison against the invading Japanese.

The Treaty of Paris now was submitted to the Senate for ratification. There was no question that a majority favored the treaty, but there were concerns that the requisite two-thirds level of support was there. The opponents, led by Senator George Hoar of Massachusetts, did not want the United States to become an imperial power. They fought hard but fell short; most Americans backed the McKinley Administration. In early February, the Senate approved the treaty 63–29, topping the constitutional two-thirds requirement.

7

The U.S.
a World Power

An American overseas empire now existed in fact if not in name. Since McKinley revealed little of his inner thoughts and since he did not leave behind in writing much to clarify why he acted as he did, historians will continue to differ concerning the extent to which he led or was led. Shortly after the Senate ratified the peace treaty, McKinley gave a speech in Boston on February 16 stating that "the Philippines, like Cuba and Porto Rico, were intrusted to our hands by the war, and to that great trust, under the providence of God and in the name of human progress and civilization, we are committed. It is a trust we have not sought; it is a trust from which we will not flinch."[1]

Later in his address he elaborated on our intentions: "The future of the Philippine Islands is now in the hands of the American people. Until the treaty was ratified or rejected, the Executive Department of this government could only preserve the peace and protect life and property. That treaty now commits the free and enfranchised Filipinos to the guiding hand and the liberalizing influences, the generous sympathies, the uplifting education, not of their American masters, but of their American emancipators."[2]

Among the few Republicans opposing this expansionism was Carl Schurz (1829–1906) who was born in Prussia and studied at the University of Bonn before joining rebel forces in the 1848–1849 uprisings that enjoyed a short-lived run of success in Germany, Austria, and France before being suppressed by the governing powers. He then fled to the United States in 1852, living first in Philadelphia, before moving on to Watertown, Wisconsin. He studied law, passed the bar examination, and practiced law in Milwaukee. One of the early Republicans, Schurz was an unsuccessful candidate for governor, then, after Lincoln's victory in the 1860 election, was selected to serve as ambassador (then designated minister) to Spain. The outbreak of the Civil War led him to resign from that post, return to the United States, and serve in the army, rising to the rank of brigadier general.

After the end of the war, he moved to St. Louis, Missouri, followed a career in journalism, and was elected to the United States Senate in 1868. He did not run for a second term. Not yet finished with political office, Schurz was secretary of the interior during the administration of Rutherford Hayes. He then returned to journalism in New York City. His is another of the remarkable accounts of people moving to the United States, assimilating, and rising to prominence.

Schurz vociferously countered the McKinley policy. In an address at the University of Chicago on January 4, 1899, he set forth reasons for his disagreement, stating of these newly acquired lands that "they are not continental, not contiguous to our present domain, but beyond seas, the Philippines many thousand miles from our coast. They are all situated in the tropics, where people of the northern races, such as Anglo-Saxons, or generally speaking, people of Germanic blood, have never migrated in mass to stay; and they are more or less densely populated, parts of them as densely as Massachusetts."[3]

He went on to express his fears that this expansion would be inimical to American freedom:

> If we [become an imperialist power], we shall transform the government of the people, for the people, and by the people, for which Abraham Lincoln lived, into a government of one part of the people, the strong, over another part, the weak. Such an abandonment of a fundamental principle as a permanent policy may at first seem to bear only upon more or less distant dependencies, but it can hardly fail in its ultimate effects to disturb the rule of the same principle in the conduct of democratic government at home. And I warn the American people that a democracy cannot so deny its faith as to the vital conditions of its being—it cannot long play the king over subject populations without creating within itself ways of thinking and habits of action most dangerous to its own vitality.[4]

Sharp philosophical and policy lines of demarcation clearly were evident between the two sides. The debate over the assertion of American power beyond our shores continues as a topic of current events.

The development of American/Filipino relations give credence to the sincerity of McKinley's words, even though he did not believe that the Filipinos were yet ready to establish and preserve order, justice, and freedom. Ethnically, most Filipinos were of Malay stock. At that time, the total population was over 7,600,000. Close to 7,000,000 of them were Roman Catholics with at least a veneer of European civilization. About 10 percent of the population were educated and part of Spanish culture. Over 640,000 Filipinos were indigenous people, close to half of whom were Muslims. Not yet were the people of the islands ready to establish and to protect their national freedom in a world with powerful, expansionist empires with voracious appetites for territorial gain in Asia, countries such as Germany and Japan. The time for the independence of the Philippines was near by the 1930s, but that day was delayed until 1946, once Germany and Japan had been defeated in World War II and the Filipinos freed from Japanese occupation. In 1898, if the United States had not incorporated the Philippines, another country would have.[5]

The rapid growth of European empires plus those of the United States and Japan was a significant feature of the 19th century. A number of factors led these countries into this expansion. Naval and army bases were acquired by them to protect the territory they held plus to promote further territorial and trade growth. Colonies became sources of raw materials and markets for manufactured products from the home country. There also was a more altruistic concern for the advancement of these subject peoples. The responsibility of the West to further the well-being of the people whose lands they occupied rather than simply exploit them was set forth by Rudyard Kipling. He focused primarily on the British Empire, but also saw the United States as sharing in the duty to improve conditions for people in those parts of the world where oppression, poverty, and disease ruled. He expressed these convictions in "The White Man's Burden," the opening stanza of which proclaims:

> Take up the White Man's burden—
> Send forth the best ye breed—
> Go bind your sons in exile
> To serve your captives' need;
> To wait in heavy harness
> On fluttered folk and wild—
> Your new-caught, sullen peoples,
> Half devil and half child.[6]

To be sure, Kipling did rejoice in the growth of British power, but the sense of service expressed above also was a part of this imperial enthusiasm. Another poem he wrote during this latter part of the 1890s, "Recessional," expressed this same sense of duty. The first and fourth stanzas prayed:

William McKinley versus William Jennings Bryan

God of our fathers, known of old,
Lord of our far-flung battle-line,
Beneath whose awful Hand we hold
Dominion over palm and pine—
Lord God of Hosts, be with us yet,
Lest we forget—lest we forget!
If, drunk with sight of power, we loose
Wild tongues that have not Thee in awe,
Such boastings as the Gentiles use,
Or lesser breeds without the Law—
Lord God of Hosts, be with us yet,
Lest we forget—lest we forget![7]

Although McKinley and Kipling were not friends, as Kipling and Theodore Roosevelt were, McKinley's sense of responsibility to improve the lot of those living in the new American Empire was the same as the principles set forth by Kipling, if less dramatically stated.

Before continuing further, William Jennings Bryan must be brought back into the history of 1898. Although not center stage this year, he still was a force in American politics and dominated the Democratic Party when he chose to assert himself. The outbreak of the war with Spain presented Bryan with a quandary. On the one hand he favored Cuban freedom from Spain; on the other he opposed war, seeing militarism as a tool of the upper classes. Many of his supporters, though, supported the war as a crusade for the freedom of this Cuban people. When combined with the first of Bryan's leanings, this tipped the scale.[8] On May 19, he enlisted in the Nebraska National Guard. Governor Silas Holcomb, a Populist who had supported Bryan's 1896 presidential run, asked him to form a new regiment. Close to 2000 men from all six of Nebraska's congressional districts joined what was designated the 3rd Nebraska. As could be done by volunteer units at this time, the regiment elected Bryan its colonel.[9]

The regiment never saw action, arriving at their camps in northern Florida just two weeks before Spain faced the reality that the war was lost and asked for terms. In September, Bryan went to Washington to request of McKinley that the regiment return home since the fighting in Cuba and Puerto Rico was over and the men suffering from malaria and yellow fever. McKinley was polite but did not order that this be done. It is possible that the president refused the request in order to keep Bryan out of campaigning for Democrats in the November election. Some have so suspected, but the record is not clear. In December, after the peace treaty was signed, Bryan resigned his commission and returned home.[10]

Back in politics, he supported ratification of the treaty by the Senate for several reasons. As a matter of reality, he did not see much hope for defeating what most Americans favored; at best the minority opposing the treaty could be obstructionists. Since many Democrats supported the treaty and U.S. expansion, he hoped to put the matter in the past before he ran again for president in 1900. Additionally, this would bring the troops home. The issue of Philippine independence he would bring up as a separate issue.[11]

8

The Domestic Scene

As 1898 closed, Bryan still was a powerful force in American politics and Theodore Roosevelt, no longer a mid-level public figure, had shot into the top tier. He built on his fame as a war hero and leader with his winning the governorship of New York in November. Senator Thomas Platt, the key Republican in the state, was well aware of Roosevelt's independence, of his not being subservient to the party leaders, but realized also that without the charismatic war hero leading the ticket, the Democrats could take advantage of a weak Republican incumbent with scandals in his administration and win the state. Most Americans were impressed and excited by his rise, but, as will be seen during the next couple of years, many national Republican leaders feared him as a popular, powerful man not controlled by them.

Shortly after the 1898 election, one of the most dramatic storms in our history hit New England. Known as the Portland Gale, it started with the coming together of two low pressure systems in the Atlantic off Virginia. It then moved north, striking New England on November 26 and 27 with hurricane-force velocity. Over 400 people were killed and over 150 vessels were sunk. The key loss was the *Portland*, a steamer with side-mounted paddlewheels which had been built in Bath, Maine, and launched in 1889 to carry passengers and freight between Portland and Boston. She was 2,284 tons, 291 feet in length, and 42 feet wide. On November 26, the *Portland* sailed from Boston heading north for the approximately 130-mile voyage to Portland, Maine. Her captain knew of the storm coming from the south but underestimated its severity and the speed at which it was moving. Shortly after sailing, she was seen by the crews of a couple of vessels heading into Boston to avoid the approaching peril. The *Portland* never again was seen; she went down with 192 passengers and crew. The wreck was identified in 2002 off Gloucester, Massachusetts, in 460 feet of water and first reached by divers in 2008.

8. The Domestic Scene

Monetary policy continued as a divisive matter separating Republicans and Democrats. The question of gold backing for the dollar or silver backing or a combination of both or paper money backed by neither divided people sharply and deeply. This certainly was a vital issue, if rather arcane to many. Initially, McKinley had believed in money backed by both gold and silver but had become convinced that the gold standard was sounder. Bryan continued a devotee of silver. Those who advocated unbacked paper money still were a minority with little power. Although there still were some gold standard Democrats and some pro silver Republicans, the rise of Bryan had brought about a substantial realignment with most gold standard backers now Republicans and most who preferred silver had switched to the Democratic Party. The realignment produced sharp partisan divisions. The time when Grover Cleveland and the limited government, sound money positions controlled the Democratic course had passed. In the Republican ranks, the devotees of inflating the money supply through unlimited coinage of silver had been significant even if they did not control the party. Most of them now had moved to the Democrats. Conversely there was a movement of gold standard Democrats to the Republican side, although a number, such as Senator David Hill, ground their teeth and stayed Democrats. Overall, McKinley saw that the time was getting closer for the administration to move from the halfway house of bimetallism, the dollar defined in terms of both gold and silver and adopt the solid gold standard position.

For the last four decades of the 19th century, the country had been divided between those who believed inflating the money supply would enhance economic prosperity and those convinced that sound, stable money would be preferable. Those favoring inflating the quantity of money in circulation wanted to abolish the requirement that paper money must be backed by gold. Some supported unbacked paper currency, the position that would come into effect later in the next century. In the 19th century, the more powerful inflationary campaign was unlimited minting of silver. The gold standard advocates maintained that money backed by gold would be more beneficial for all in the long run. The Civil War printing of unbacked paper money ceased with the end of the conflict, but there were those, especially debtors, who wanted paper and an inflated money supply so that they could pay what they owed in dollars of increasing number and decreasing value. The sound money people had success in January 1875 with the passage by Congress of the Specie Resumption Act which called for the treasury to redeem paper money, greenbacks, in gold beginning on January 1, 1879.

They, though, did not yet have total victory. The two sides were fairly evenly balanced. Solving problems through printing more paper seemed an easy solution to many voters. The sound money people now were forced into a slow retreat. In 1878, Congress passed, over the veto of President Hayes, the Bland-Allison Act which mandated the minting of between $2,000,000 and $4,000,000 of silver each month. During the administrations of Hayes, Garfield, Arthur, Cleveland, and Harrison, the government opted for the minimum purchase. This, combined with the reality that silver money cannot be pumped out as readily as paper, mitigated the severity of the inflation. The Sherman Silver Purchase Act of 1890 marked an advance by the inflation devotees. It required the minting of 4.5 million ounces of silver per month, substantially increasing the money in circulation.

In 1892, Grover Cleveland returned to the presidency, the only chief executive to win, lose, then win again. Shortly after he was inaugurated on March 4, the country was hit by the depression called the Panic of 1893. Cleveland was convinced that repealing the Sherman Act and restoring the gold standard were the best steps to revive our economy. He stated:

> I want a currency that is stable and safe in the hands of our people. I will not knowingly be implicated in a condition that will justly make me in the least degree answerable to any laborer or farmer in the United States for a shrinkage in the purchasing power he has received for a full dollar's worth of work, or for a good dollar's worth of the product of his toil. I not only want our currency to be of such a character that all kinds of dollars will be of equal purchasing power at home, but I want it to be of such a character as will demonstrate abroad our wisdom and good faith, thus placing us upon a firm foundation and credit among the nations of the earth. I want our financial conditions and the laws relating to our currency safe and reassuring, that those who have money will spend and invest it in business and new enterprises instead of hoarding it. I want good, sound and stable money and a condition of confidence that will keep it in use.[1]

On March 7, 1900, McKinley's signing the Gold Standard Act completed the long struggle for victory of those advocating this path to national prosperity. The United States had returned decisively to sound money. In the Western World, the international gold standard had been gathering momentum since the second decade of the 19th century. Writing of this time, historian John Lukacs stated that

> money continued to be as good as gold, and as solid as the rock of Gibraltar. In 1900 the pound, the dollar, the franc, the florin, the crown, the mark, the lira—

all of these national currencies with their names that reach back to the Middle Ages—were worth, in each other's terms, the same everywhere. They were available in the form of gold pieces (except in the United States during the Civil War), silver coins and bills, freely exchangeable at one's convenience.[2]

McKinley did favor the gradual improvement in the status of black Americans. On December 16, 1898, speaking at Tuskegee Normal and Industrial Institute in Tuskegee, Alabama, he praised the "genius and perseverance" of Booker T. Washington in founding and developing the school, referring to it as a "noble enterprise."[3] He went on to say, "No country, epoch, or race has a monopoly upon knowledge.... But in this great country all can have the opportunity for bettering themselves, provided they exercise intelligence and perseverance, and their motives and conduct are worthy."[4] In general, McKinley was correct, although even cursory study of American history will show that blacks had more obstacles in their paths that had to be overcome than did whites.

Two days later, December 18, he spoke at Georgia Agricultural and Mechanical College, a black institution in Savannah. He emphasized individual responsibility to develop and nurture good character. He went on to laud solid homes, stating, "The home is the foundation of good individual life and of good government."[5] He continued by praising the heroism of the black regiments at San Juan Hill and El Caney during the Cuban campaign. He concluded his remarks by charging his audience to "be patient, be progressive, be determined, be honest, be God-fearing, and you will win, for no effort fails that has a stout, honest, earnest heart behind it."[6] Although these words by McKinley were sincere and although racial progress certainly had been made in the slightly over 30 years since the end of the Civil War, still it is true that improvement all too often was glacial in speed.

9

1900: Rematch

As 1900 dawned, optimism about the future overrode fear and pessimism. There was no ignoring of problems and/or potential problems, but the prevailing sentiment was that Americans would triumph, that the future would be better than the past. With low taxes, especially no income tax, people could keep the overwhelming majority of what they earned. There was much poverty, but the economy was growing with opportunities for the ambitious, talented, and hard-working to rise. The phrase "barefoot millionaires" was used to describe the rich who had risen from humble origins.[1] Health conditions were improving with, for example, more hospitals opening and better standards of cleanliness. Pasteurized milk now was in use.

By no means would this vibrant expanding power be a cultural wasteland. A vital part of this late 19th-century American surge was the expansion of the fine arts. English historian Paul Johnson wrote of this time: "That the United States, lifted up by an extraordinary combination of self-created wealth and natural talent, became a great cultural nation in the second half of the nineteenth century is a fact which the world, and even Americans themselves have been slow to grasp."[2] Especially significant were the opening of the Metropolitan Museum of Art in New York City and of the Boston Museum of Fine Arts, both in 1870. The Metropolitan Opera started in 1883 and moved quickly to the top tier of world opera companies. American literature and painting flourished during these years as did American institutions of higher education. Generous funding for the arts came from private sector wealth, some individuals giving from a sense of noblesse oblige, some because they wanted the fame. Regardless of motivation, the public benefited.

Sports too flourished. In 1900, Bryon Bancroft "Ban" Johnson announced plans for a new major league in baseball, the American League, which would open the still flourishing competition with the National

League. Connie Mack moved his Philadelphia team to the new league. Cy Young and Napoleon Lajoie were established stars and Ty Cobb shortly would burst on the scene. Heavyweight boxing was dominated by James J. Jeffries who won the title in that division by knocking out champion Bob Fitzsimmons in a rematch, then beat former champion James Corbett twice and Tom Sharkey. He retired in 1905.

At this time the United States led the world in mining iron, coal, gold, and silver and in steel production. Actually, American steel and coal output surpassed that of Britain and Germany combined. In world trade, only the British were ahead of us. This surge by the United States caught much of the world by surprise. It would take some time for the major world powers to appreciate fully the rapid growth in American economic and armed forces power. The insightful Frenchman Alexis de Tocqueville in his *Democracy in America*, published a few years after his 1831 visit here, predicted that the United States and Russia would become the greatest of the world powers. Still, most world leaders were surprised in the late 19th and early 20th centuries by the surge of this country to the front rank.[3]

Also in 1900, the Hay-Pauncefote Treaty (John Hay, the U.S. secretary of state, Sir Julian Pauncefote, the British ambassador to the United States) marked another step forward in the closer relationship developing between the United States and the United Kingdom as the British recognized more and more the menace of the aggressively expanding German power and that drawing closer to the United States made sense in terms of world power politics. Reinforcing this conviction were the shared heritage and common values of the two countries. The treaty was signed on February 5. It recognized the right of the United States to build a canal across Central America, to fortify it, and to close it in time of war; in peace it was to be open to the ships of all countries.

The American rise to world power status was made evident by the Boxer Rebellion in China during the summer of 1900. China, a large country with natural resources, a strategic location, good ports, and a market for manufactured goods from the developed countries, was militarily weak, thereby stirring the appetites of European powers and Japan, all of whom seized chunks from this militarily weak giant. The United States sought no territory there and pushed the others to stop their carving up China. Secretary of State John Hay in July stated that American policy was "to seek a solution which may bring about permanent safety and peace to China, preserve Chinese territorial and administrative entity, protect all rights guaranteed to friendly powers by treaty and international law, and safeguard for the world the principle of equal and impartial trade with all parts of the Chinese Empire."[4] This noble sentiment was ignored in practice by the other major powers and before long, the attention of the United States was drawn away from China by more serious crises which culminated in World War I which broke out in just 14 years.

During the 1890s in China, a nationalistic, terroristic organization called the "Righteous and Harmonious Fists," known commonly in the West as the "Boxers," which had developed in opposition to the Manchu Dynasty, now focused on ridding China of foreign influences. They now operated with a wink and a nod from the Dowager Empress and the imperial government who, with a combination of hope and fear, were glad to have the attention off them. Hundreds of Christian Chinese and foreign missionaries were killed. By June, foreigners in Peking (now Beijing) together with a number of Christian Chinese, sought refuge in the legation quarter after the German minister to China was murdered. Here a combined patchwork aggregation of 600 soldiers and armed civilians dug in to fight off a far greater number of Boxers and Chinese army men.

By early August, the relief expedition of 19,000 men struck out from Tientsin some 70 miles away. Troops from eight countries—the United States, Britain, France, Japan, Germany, Austria-Hungary, Russia, and Italy—comprised the attacking force. The 2500 Americans were commanded by Major General Adna Chaffee who led a brigade in the Cuban campaign before being assigned to the Philippines. On August 15, the rescuers broke through into Peking and the siege was over. The Chinese government was forced to give up the fight.[5] In 1901, the Boxer Protocol forced China to pay an indemnity and authorized the victorious countries to keep troops in Peking as well as on the railroad line between Peking and Tientsin.

Of the $333,000,000 reparations figure, the United States demanded only $25,000,000. The American government determined later that this was too much; in 1907 and in 1924, almost $17,000,000 were used to establish a trust fund for educating young Chinese in both the United States and China.[6]

The paths to the Republican and Democratic presidential nominations in 1900 looked straight and smooth for McKinley and Bryan. McKinley faced no threats thanks to victory in war, economic prosperity, and his political skill. Bryan's position atop the Democratic Party continued based on his strong run in 1896, his personal charisma, and the failure of any potential challenger, such as Senator Arthur Gorman of Maryland

and Senator David Hill of New York, to attract enough support to mount a serious assault. Very briefly in the spring, Admiral Dewey nursed hopes for the nomination, but his inexperience and ineptitude in the political jungle plus Bryan's dominance doomed his faint hopes.

The Republican national convention met first, beginning on June 19 in Philadelphia. Although the nomination of McKinley for a second term was a sure thing, the death of Vice President Garrett Hobart on November 21, 1899, led to major administration headaches concerning his successor. The president very much respected Elihu Root but needed him more in the cabinet as secretary of war. Root subsequently would be secretary of state under Theodore Roosevelt and William Howard Taft. Declining the opportunity to be vice president were Senator William Allison of Iowa and Secretary of the Interior Cornelius Bliss. McKinley considered Secretary of the Navy John Long but realized that there was little support in party ranks for him as vice president. He was well aware of the enthusiasm for Roosevelt which was continuing to pick up momentum after his election as governor of New York, then the most populous state in the country. McKinley, though, viewed him as too independent, too little inclined to be a team player. Since he did not get an acceptance from one of his preferences for vice president and since he was leery of Roosevelt, the president determined that the best course was to stand aside and let the convention choose as it wished without administration pressure.

It soon became apparent, however, that a serious complication had arisen, namely the intense antipathy for Roosevelt spewing forth from Mark Hanna, now a U.S. senator from Ohio as well as still being chairman of the Republican National Committee. His reasons for opposing Roosevelt as the vice-presidential nominee were the same as McKinley's but were marked by a vehemence not expressed by the president. To head off Hanna's causing a division in the party, McKinley issued a firm statement that the administration did not have a candidate for vice president, that it would accept the choice of the delegates.[7] Both furious and discouraged, Hanna stood down, ending his efforts to block Roosevelt. He did, though, fulminate, "Don't any of you realize that there's only one life between this madman and the Presidency?"[8] This was a remarkably prescient observation, as would be evident the next year. McKinley respected and liked Hanna, but here gave him another clear reminder concerning who was running the show.

The object of all this controversy, Theodore Roosevelt, had mixed thoughts on the push for his nomination. On the one hand, he recognized the honor and the prestige of his being, on paper, second only to the president. On the other hand, the vice presidency was a post with little power. Of the 26 men who had held this office, only Martin Van Buren had then been elected president. Four other vice presidents had moved up after the death of the president—John Tyler, Millard Fillmore, Andrew Johnson, and Chester Alan Arthur—but not one of them then won the office on his own. All too often, the vice presidency had proven to be a dead-end office for second tier party leaders. Initially, Roosevelt preferred a second term as governor of New York, then a run for the presidency. As it turned out, the strength of the support for his nomination, the enthusiasm of the delegates, became difficult to resist.[9]

For Hanna, there were more headaches to come from the surge of Theodore Roosevelt. Hanna's close ties to McKinley and increased power in the Republican Party had earned him enemies. One of them was Senator Matthew Quay, who controlled the party organization in Pennsylvania. At the convention, he moved that delegates be allocated among the states based on the Republican vote total in each state. Delegates from the Southern states vehemently opposed the motion. In those years, the South was solidly controlled by the Democrats; the black vote was overwhelmingly Republican, but blacks were a minority and a minority increasingly held down by the Democratic majority. Hanna's power in the party depended on the Southern delegates. No stranger to political shenanigans himself, Hanna recognized what was happening and yielded to Quay, agreeing to second Roosevelt's nomination. For Quay, the motivation was partially to support Platt, who wanted Roosevelt out of New York, and partially it was a chance to reduce the stature of Hanna. To look ahead, Hanna would recover, regain his status in the party, manage the victorious McKinley-Roosevelt campaign, and contemplate challenging Roosevelt for the 1904 presidential nomination until his death ended that prospect.[10]

The 1900 convention culminated with the nomination of the McKinley-Roosevelt ticket by the enthusiastic delegates. There were no dissenting votes on McKinley and the only vote against Roosevelt was the one he cast himself—an honorable move or a quixotic gesture, depending on one's viewpoint.

A few days later, on July 4, the Democratic national convention convened. As it began, there were few doubts concerning who dominated the party. As soon as Bryan knew that he had lost to McKinley in 1896, he began campaigning for 1900, convinced that he simply had to bring his

The Republican presidential ticket in 1900 (Library of Congress, https://www.loc.gov/item/93504452/).

message to more people; he had no doubt that most Americans would support him once they understood better what a Bryan presidency would mean for the country. His major rivals in 1896 had faded in strength or had left the political arena. Politically weaker in 1900 were Representative Richard Bland who had been in first place on the first three ballots at the 1896 convention and Governor Horace Boies of Iowa. Conservative gold standard Democrats, such as Senator David Hill of New York, still had strength in the Northeast, but in the rest of the country the liberal Bryan forces increased their dominance of the Democratic Party organization. Indicative of Bryan's firm hold was the unanimous vote by the national committee of the party that silver would be the main issue in the 1900 race. Some more moderate Democrats wanted to soften the stance, to still be supportive of silver, but in a less confrontational manner. Bryan would not compromise.

The Democratic national convention convened in Kansas City on July

4. The weaker conservative faction briefly considered challenging Bryan's again being the presidential nominee, but quickly saw the utter futility of doing so. There was a brief moment of tension over Bryan's demand that the platform again endorse the 1896 call for the free coinage of silver. He made clear to the delegates that he would not be the Democratic standard bearer unless this affirmation were included. The Resolutions Committee did so by a one vote margin. Even some Bryan backers, such as Senator Ben Tillman, were nervous about such a clear statement and wanted to soft-pedal it. Bryan refused to compromise but did realize that the party would stay united better if opposition to overseas expansion were given equal status with inflating the money supply. Opposition to big business (breaking up the trusts) also appealed to the party left-wing enthusiasts.[11]

The convention unanimously nominated Bryan with Adlai Stevenson of Illinois as his running mate, but the unanimous vote for Stevenson was on the second ballot, after some minor drama on the first. David Hill did receive 200 votes as a limited protest against the Bryan steamroller. Several other candidates drew some scattered support. Stevenson easily led the field with 559.5 delegates choosing him. Then, a second unanimous ballot was cast. Stevenson, grandfather of the Adlai Stevenson who lost the 1952 and 1956 presidential elections to Dwight Eisenhower, had been vice president in Cleveland's second term and came from the state with the third largest population in the country at that time. A silver standard devotee, Stevenson had been a sop thrown to the pro silver side by the then in control gold standard Democrats. This time, Bryan adhered to the tradition that major party presidential candidates did not attend the conventions. His presence and Cross of Gold speech in 1896 were explained by his being only a minor candidate as the convention had opened. Now, in 1900, he adhered to tradition and remained at his home. Franklin Delano Roosevelt ended this practice in 1932 when he gave his acceptance speech to the delegates at the Democratic national convention. Although distant, Bryan left nothing to chance, keeping contact with his supporters at the convention through long-distance telephone and a direct telegraph line. A step in the direction of unifying the Democrats was having the conservative, gold-standard Senator David Hill of New York second the nomination. This Hill did, graciously praising Bryan's integrity. There were, however, no meaningful concessions to the conservative wing of the party. Grover Cleveland, in retirement in Princeton, New Jersey, remained unalterably opposed to the "Bryanization" of the Democratic Party.

As far as the two presidential candidates were concerned, 1900 was a replay of 1896. McKinley stayed at home in Canton, Ohio, addressing those who came there, but not challenging Bryan who once more vigorously hit the road to cover as much territory and speak to as many people as possible. His approach to campaigning would be met and surpassed by Theodore Roosevelt who covered over 21,000 miles to Bryan's somewhat over 18,000 and gave 673 speeches, topping Bryan's 600.[12] Bryan actually had covered more miles than he had done in 1896 and still stirred enthusiastic crowds.

As had been evident in 1896, Roosevelt was both intellectually and viscerally opposed to Bryan, a man he still considered a dangerous, left-wing demagogue, a man who would be dangerous as president. In his speech at Military Park in Indianapolis on August 8, Bryan attacked the development of an American empire, labeling it an immoral violation of our values. He considered bogus the administration claim that Americans were bringing others "the blessings of liberty and civilization."[13] Here Bryan was following through on his tactical decision to emphasize more

Mrs. Mary Baird Bryan and Mrs. Ida Saxton McKinley (Library of Congress. Mrs. William Jennings Bryan, https://www.loc.gov/item/2016858225/ Mrs. William McKinley (detail), https://www.loc.gov/item/2003653466/).

his opposition to what he saw as American imperialism even though he still believed as firmly as ever in the path to prosperity through the free coinage of silver. Giving the Democrats a degree of hope was their control of several key city governments—New York, Chicago, Baltimore, Indianapolis, and San Francisco. They also held the Southern states firmly in their control; although the black vote was solidly Republican, their participation in elections was restricted and they were a minority, although a large minority as will be seen, Democratic prospects for adding enough electoral votes outside the South to defeat McKinley were not bright. Support for Bryan represented, to some extent, fears by a segment of the population that wealth was being concentrated into too few hands; a small number of tycoons in banking, business, and industry was controlling too much. Yet the reality was that the overall standard of living was improving. Conflicts so familiar today flared in the McKinley-Bryan clashes.

Also during the 1890s pressure had grown for the election of United States senators by a popular vote rather than by state legislatures. The proposed constitutional amendment to do so easily passed the House of Representatives on July 21, 1894, by 141–50, on January 12, 1898, by 185–11, and on April 13, 1900, by 242–15. On each occasion, though, the Senate blocked any further action.[14] The change to the popular election of senators was instituted in 1913 when the 17th Amendment to the United States Constitution was ratified after the Senate stopped blocking it.

Once again, as in 1896, the Populist Party had to decide whether to support Bryan, a Democrat who shared many of their beliefs, or to emphasize their independent stance to the left of the Democrats. There now in 1900 were far fewer people who identified themselves as Populists since most of those who had supported Bryan four years previously had stayed with him in the Democratic Party. On May 9, the remnant identifying themselves as pro Bryan but still Populist held their convention outside Sioux Falls, South Dakota. They nominated Bryan for president and Charles Towne of Minnesota for vice president. When the Democrats later chose the Bryan-Stevenson ticket, Towne withdrew, and the Populists endorsed Stevenson. This faction believed that endorsing Bryan and still keeping their separate party identity would move the country to the left better than simply joining the Democrats.

The even smaller number of Populists determined to carry on as a totally separate party nominated for president Wharton Baker of Pennsylvania. He had been a company commander in the Union army during the Civil War, then was a banker. For vice president, they chose Ignatius Don-

TAKE YOUR CHOICE OF THE TWO BILLS!

The Republicans advocated sound money based on gold (Library of Congress, https://www.loc.gov/item/2003688942/).

nelly, former lieutenant governor of Minnesota who later served three terms in the U.S. House of Representatives as a Republican. He also was a rather successful writer of science fiction and speculative history. In the second category, Donnelly set forth his conviction that the plays attributed to William Shakespeare actually were written by Francis Bacon and that

Atlantis really did exist as a great civilization which was destroyed, he believed, in the great flood recorded in Genesis.

Eugene Debs continued his migration to the left, moving from the Populist Party and his 1896 endorsement of Bryan to the Socialist Democratic Party, becoming its presidential nominee at the party's Indianapolis convention. Debs rejected the atheistic, violent revolutionary nature of Marxism, seeing socialism as "Christianity in action."[15] While proclaiming his admiration for the American founders and extolling Abraham Lincoln as his favorite person, he did consider capitalism as exploitative and called for its end. He did advocate the end of capitalism and the establishment of socialism through peaceful, democratic means within the American constitutional system. Within months, the Social Democrats would merge with the moderate minority of the Socialist Labor Party to form the Socialist Party. Five times Debs would lead the Socialists in presidential contests, peaking in 1912 with just under 6 percent of the popular vote.

To the left of the Socialist party was the Socialist Labor Party which nominated Joseph F. Malloney of Massachusetts for president and Valentine Remmel of Pennsylvania for vice president. Marxist thinking did dominate the party in the 1890s, but it later did reject the dictatorship of the Soviet Union.

The persistent Prohibition Party nominated John G. Wooley, an Illinois lawyer, with Henry B. Metcalf, a Rhode Island businessman, as his running mate. Their party never made much of a splash in terms of presidential election votes, although it did elect a few candidates to lower offices such as Sidney J. Catts of Florida who lost the 1916 Democratic Party primary for governor of Florida, then was elected to that office on the Prohibition line. Charles H. Randall of California served three terms in the U.S. House of Representatives. Overall, the party has been a minor factor in American politics even though their cause did triumph for a while with the approval of the 18th Amendment in 1919. Prohibition then was repealed when the 21st Amendment was ratified in 1933.

In general, 1900 was a replay of 1896; the Republican and Democratic presidential candidates were the same, each campaigned the same way, and neither had changed his beliefs, although Bryan did some tempering and adjusting. He emphasized less his free coinage of silver position, hoping to regain those who rejected his monetary position. This tactic had little effect since Bryan's stance was too well known. A second issue, opposition to the establishment of an American empire, did not strike a responsive chord with enough voters to propel the campaign to victory, but it did bring his vehement 1896 opponent Bourke Cockran, a gold Democrat, back into the fold. At the time of the July national convention, Bryan strongly condemned this imperial growth, warning that "a large standing army is not only a pecuniary burden to the people and, if accompanied by compulsory service, a constant source of irritation but it is even a menace to a republican form of government. The army is the personification of force, and militarism will inevitably change the ideas of the people and turn the thoughts of our young men from the arts of peace to the science of war."[16] This was the thinking of a different Bryan than the volunteer colonel of 1898. These 1900 words, though, were more in line with what he was on a deeper level. In this address, he continued by alleging that American overseas expansion was motivated by the desire for profit going into the pockets of a few, but for most people in this country "it would bring expenditure without return and risk without reward."[17]

Bryan then proceeded to stir more controversy by criticizing taxation based on consumption, a debate continuing to resound in political contests today. He argued, "Farmers and laboring men have, as a rule, small incomes, and, under systems which place the tax upon consumption, pay much more than their fair share of the expenses of government."[18] In 1900, most Americans would not accept the argument that the more one made, the larger the percentage that he or she must pay.

The victory over Spain had been quick and at limited cost. Most Americans backed our acquisition of Puerto Rico, the Philippines, Guam, and, in a separate move, Hawaii. By October, Bryan conceded this was not a winning issue and ended his campaign warning of the danger to freedom from trusts—large business combinations.

It would have been difficult for any Democrat to have won in 1900 in view of the advantages the McKinley Administration enjoyed: victory in war, a strong economy, and a well-balanced ticket with the calm, experienced McKinley and the dynamic war hero Roosevelt. In mid–September, the Hearst *New York Morning Journal* reduced its coverage of the presidential campaign, recognizing the poor prospects for Bryan to win. Bryan tried—he was energetic and dynamic as in 1896, keeping a schedule which would overwhelm most people—but Roosevelt surpassed him, giving more speeches and traveling more miles. McKinley campaigned as in 1896, mostly by addressing crowds who travelled to his home in Canton.

As was true from the end of the Civil War until the late 1940s, Democratic Party hopes for winning the presidency began with their control of the Southern states. Southern whites could be counted on to support

Bryan's populism emphasized, probably 1900 (Library of Congress, https://www.loc.gov/item/2003670249/).

those the Democrats nominated and the black vote was solidly Republican. In these states, the black vote was suppressed. Bryan knew this, but he also realized that he had no realistic chance of winning the presidency without the electoral votes of the region, so he kept silent about freedom for black Americans. Roosevelt charged him with hypocrisy because he favored freedom for Filipinos while keeping silent on the blatant repressing of blacks in the South. Bryan did condemn lynchings of blacks and cautiously sought black votes in the North, but he had nothing critical to say about the suppression of blacks in Southern states.

In addition to Roosevelt, other Republicans hit Bryan on his failure to espouse the same freedom for American blacks that he demanded for foreigners. Senator George Hoar of Massachusetts was one of the most vocal on this point. Bryan tried to parse the issue, stating that in the South the situation might change soon whereas in the Philippines no means had been provided for enfranchisement. As it turned out, he was very much in error; in 1907, Filipinos gained the right to elect a national assembly while full voting rights for black Americans still were several decades in the future. There are indications that Bryan had some discomfiture, caught as he was between his Christian conviction that God reaches out to people and accepts them as His children regardless of race and the political reality that he needed the votes of the white-dominated South in order to implement the program he believed the country needed.[19]

The Republicans by no means were color blind, but there was more sentiment in that party during these years favoring more openings for those of African heritage. After the end of the Civil War, those who had been involved with the Confederate States of America, which meant the vast majority of Southern white men, were disenfranchised. Southern state governments, therefore, were dominated by blacks supported by "carpetbaggers," Northerners who had moved in to profit from the Union victory, and "scalawags," Southerners who had been pro Union. Slowly white men regained the vote, a process completed after the 1877 compromise between Rutherford Hayes and the Democrats. Under this arrangement, former Confederates were restored to full citizenship and black civil rights would be guaranteed. The first was done, but the Southern states did not implement the second and the status of blacks there deteriorated markedly. Earlier in the post Civil War years, two black men had been elected to the U.S. Senate from the former Confederate states and 18 to the U.S. House of Representatives.[20] For Southern whites, it now was payback time. Senator Ben Tillman of South Carolina well exemplified the extreme wing of Southern Democrats on race, stating with pride that "in 1876 we shot negroes and stuffed ballot boxes."[21] Republican support for Southern blacks started to slip more in the 1890s as some party leaders wanted to downplay the bitterness between the North and the South, that this would foster better national unity. The hope of many Republicans was that removing federal government domination would end Southern white resentment, bind the country together, and ensure that blacks would not be forced back into a subservient position. They were wrong; decades would pass before one race or the other no longer was subservient.

For the Democrats, the South was solid; the states of the former Confederacy plus Kentucky and Missouri voted for Bryan plus Nevada, Idaho, Montana, and Colorado, giving him 155 electoral votes. The rest of the country preferred McKinley, resulting in his having a commanding win with 292 electoral votes. Voting for McKinley were 7,228,864, 51.64 percent and for Bryan 6,370,932, 45.52 percent. Bryan did worse than in 1896; the breaches still were wide. Still opposing him were conservatives such as Grover Cleveland. Supporting him were some conservative Democrats such as Senator David Hill and Richard Olney, attorney general and secretary of state under Cleveland. More, such as J. Sterling Morton, agreed with Bryan on foreign policy but vehemently opposed his economics. He said: "It is a choice between evils, and I am going to shut my eyes, hold my nose, vote, go home and disinfect myself."[22] Differences between the candidates were sharply drawn, but the intensity level was somewhat lower than in 1896. Still, voter turnout hit 72 percent, the last time so far that the 70 percent level has been surpassed.

Third party enthusiasm was less than it had been in 1892 when the Populists burst into national politics and less than it would be in 1912 when Progressive Party nominee Theodore Roosevelt would finish second. The continued decline of the Populists as a political party brought the enthusiasm level even further down from 1896 when the Populists still were a significant presence before largely folding themselves into the Democratic Party. The Wharton Baker/Ignatius Donnelly ticket attracted only 50,989 votes, a substantial fading from the hope-filled days of 1892 when they seemed on the verge of major party status. Further to the left, Eugene Debs and Job Harriman, the Social Democratic standard bearers, won 87,945 votes. Still further to the left, Joseph F. Malloney, the choice of the Socialist Labor Party, gained 40,943 votes. The strongest third-party finish in 1900 was that of the Prohibition slate of John G. Wooley and Henry B. Metcalf which ended up with 210,864 votes, 1.51 percent of the total.

A dozen years still lay ahead before the Democrats could threaten the Republican domination of the national government.

10

Second Term

The year 1901 opened well for McKinley. As was his practice, he opened the White House to the general public on January 1, shaking 5350 hands in a period of three hours.[1] On January 25, he and Ida celebrated the 30th anniversary of their wedding. Just before that happy event, on January 22, Queen Victoria died, bringing to an end a most remarkable reign which had begun back in 1837. McKinley ordered that the flag at the White House be lowered to half-staff, the first time that this had been done to honor a foreign ruler.[2] This was indicative of the great esteem accorded her as well as the closer Anglo-American relations as both countries focused more on their common heritage and their common interests such as the threat to both, for example, from the aggressive expansion of Germany and Japan. The animosity dating back to the American Revolution and the War of 1812 was being pushed aside by these factors.

The Platt Amendment took effect on March 2. Bearing the name of Senator Orville Platt of Connecticut (not to be confused with Senator Thomas Platt of New York), this legislation was developed in close consultation with McKinley and Elihu Root, the secretary of war then. The Amendment stipulated that Cuba would be independent, but that the United States could intervene "for the preservation of Cuban independence, the maintenance of a government adequate for the protection of life, property and individual liberty."[3] This represented the McKinley Administration's concern about aggressive German expansion and our wanting to be a constructive force keeping Cuba from becoming another Latin American dictatorship. The United States also would acquire a naval base on the island.

McKinley's second inaugural was preceded by a touch of drama which provided an interesting footnote to history. Senator Thomas H. Carter, Republican from Montana, was determined to filibuster a rivers and harbors bill he considered wasteful, preventing its final passage. The inaugural was scheduled for noon in the Senate Chamber. Around midnight Carter got the floor and started talking. He continued until it was time for the proceedings to begin when he stopped, having achieved his purpose of stopping action on the bill.[4] It was, of course, only a short-lived triumph since pork barrel bills such as this do not stay dead.

Inaugural day, March 4, was a dreary, rainy day in Washington. In his address, McKinley set forth the successes of his administration over the past four years. He opened by reminding his listeners that the deficit he inherited at the beginning of his first term had been eliminated and replaced by a surplus.[5] That certainty was true, but to be fair the recovery from the 1893 depression, the "Panic of 1893," had begun during Cleveland's presidency.

Since assuming the presidency, McKinley had modified his protectionist trade position somewhat. He stated that the dramatic increase in American production necessitated more foreign trade. He went on to propose that "for this purpose reciprocal trade arrangements with other nations should in liberal spirit be carefully cultivated and promoted."[6]

He further rejoiced that the bitterness engendered by the Civil War was gone, that a greater sense of national unity now prevailed.[7]

McKinley also reassured his listeners that the policy of his administration was to evacuate Cuba, leaving the country free and peaceful. He did, though, clarify our continued interest in what happened there: "We became sponsors for the pacification of the island, and we remain accountable to the Cubans, no less than to our own country and people, for the reconstruction of Cuba as a free commonwealth on abiding foundations of right, justice, liberty, and assured order."[8]

He proceeded with the reminder that the United States was not engaged in war against the people of the Philippines, that only a portion of them was opposing us, that most of the people there "recognize American sovereignty and welcome it as a guaranty of order and of security for life, property, liberty, freedom of conscience, and the pursuit of happiness."[9]

Shortly thereafter, on March 23, the American position was solidified when the leader of the Philippine independence movement, Emilio Aguinaldo, was captured by a contingent led by Brigadier General Frederick Funston, who had led an adventurous life in the American West, fought with Cuban guerrillas against Spain, then was commissioned in the American army after the war with Spain broke out. Already in the Philippines, he had demonstrated leadership and courage above and beyond the call of duty earning him the Congressional Medal of Honor. Now, with four other American officers and a force of pro–American Filipinos, he seized Aguinaldo in a brilliant operation. The expedition posed as a guerrilla contingent with American prisoners, then overpowered the rebels and captured Aguinaldo. Recognizing the futility of continuing the war, on April 19 Aguinaldo called for Filipinos to stop fighting and to accept "the sovereignty of the United States throughout the entire Archipelago, as I do now, without any reservation whatsoever."[10] By the end of the year, only scattered resistance continued. Aguinaldo was set free and lived out his life in the Philippines, dying in 1964 at almost 95.

Before leaving behind the conflict in the Philippines, there is a rather bizarre episode which ran counter to the usual patriotic soldiering by black Americans. One of them, David Fagan, a 24-year-old corporal in the 24th Infantry Regiment, shipped out for the Philippine campaign in June 1899. During the next several months, he saw action against the guerrillas in central Luzon. On November 17, he deserted and joined the insurrection. The rebel leader, Emilio Aguinaldo, earlier that year had appealed to black soldiers, telling them: "It is without honor that you are spilling your costly blood. Your masters have thrown you into the most iniquitous fight with double purpose—to make you the instrument of their ambition and also your hard work will soon make the extinction of your race. Your friends, the Filipinos, give you this good warning. You must consider your situation and your history."[11]

Fagan served in combat over the next two years, rising in rank to captain in the rebel forces. On December 5, 1901, a Filipino allied with the Americans brought in a head identified as that of Fagan. According to records, Fagan was one of only 20 soldiers, black and white, who deserted during the campaign in the Philippines.[12] This is impressive considering the continuing racial prejudice in the United States and the intense rebel appeals to blacks to abandon a country treating them as second class citizens.

In 1902, the Philippine Organic Act granted limited self-government, providing for a bicameral legislature with the lower house, the Philippine Assembly (later renamed the House of Representatives) elected. The Philippine Autonomy Act of 1916 promised eventual independence. The 1934 Philippine Independence Act called for full independence in 1944. The Japanese conquest of the country in 1942 necessitated a change in schedule until 1946 by which time the Japanese had been defeated, the Philippines freed, and the new country joined the soon to be swelling ranks of those no longer ruled by a colonial power.

William McKinley versus William Jennings Bryan

For McKinley, the capture of Aguinaldo and his subsequent calling for an end to hostilities were welcomed as significant progress in the spread of American order, justice, and freedom. Within a few years, the Filipinos would be electing their own leaders within the American system. Much of the credit for this belongs to William Howard Taft, who was appointed by McKinley as president of the five-man Philippine Commission. He arrived in Manila on June 3, 1900. The next year, the Philippines transitioned from military government to having a civilian administration. On July 4, Taft was sworn in as governor. Another example of McKinley's ability to recruit people of principle and ability, Taft was significant for advancing economic development, education, and in laying the foundation for self-government. He continued to serve as governor into Theodore Roosevelt's administration, returning to the United States in 1904 to succeed Elihu Root as secretary of war.

In May, McKinley launched a six-week speaking tour hitting the South and the Pacific coast states. He set forth his wanting to improve trade through reciprocal agreements on tariff rates with other countries; each side would lower its rates on those items where there was no competition between them. He also intended to take action on egregious trusts, those combinations which did interfere with economic freedom. There is no question that McKinley was committed to free market economics, but he did recognize that there were combinations that were contrary to economic freedom and that government had a role to play in ensuring that this freedom flourished. He believed firmly that trade promoted the peaceful working together of people both within this country and around the world.

On June 11, McKinley announced that he would not be a candidate for a third term, honoring the tradition dating back to George Washington. A potential exception was Ulysses Grant, but a third term for him was shot down by growing awareness of the number of scandals involving people in his administration; he personally was not corrupt, but his political leadership was much inferior to what he had shown in the army during the Civil War. Now, with McKinley's making clear his intention to step down after two terms, a good number of Republicans would be rubbing their chins and calculating their chances for 1904. For now, they would be circumspect since it then was bad form and bad politics to seem too eager too soon.

McKinley had been scheduled to speak in Buffalo at the Pan-American Exposition during his national tour but had cancelled when his wife fell ill while they were on the West Coast. The date was changed to September 5. The Exposition had opened on May 1 and would close on November 2. It occupied 342 acres. In addition to midway entertainment, engineering and technological innovations drew crowds. Lighting was provided by hydroelectric power from Niagara Falls.

On September 5, McKinley addressed a crowd of 50,000. In keeping with the goal of the event, he emphasized the increasing U.S. role in world trade. We would ensure both the protection of the vital economic interests of this country and develop more trade agreements with other countries. He proclaimed that with trade essential to our national prosperity, "we must not repose in fancied security that we can sell everything and buy little or nothing."[13] After completing his address, he toured the grounds, visiting some of the exhibits.

The next day, he visited Niagara Falls, then returned to the Exposition for a reception at the Temple of Music. McKinley's staff, especially George B. Cortelyou, his secretary, were concerned about the problems of protecting the president at this event. The building would be opened to throngs of people who wanted to shake his hand. Cortelyou, who later would be secretary of commerce and labor, postmaster general, and secretary of the treasury under Theodore Roosevelt, did what he could to enhance security. Exposition police were at the doors into the event and Buffalo police detectives patrolled the aisles. Two more Secret Service agents were added to the regular one who normally accompanied the president. Although the 12 artillerymen in full dress uniforms were present primarily for decorative purposes, their being trained soldiers did add to Cortelyou's hopes for protecting the president. McKinley expressed no concern for his safety, being convinced that no one opposed him to the extent of wanting to kill him. Twice Cortelyou had cancelled the Temple of Music event; each time McKinley restored it. Now, on the afternoon of September 5, the end would begin.

At 4:00 o'clock in the afternoon the doors were opened, and the people lined up began filing past McKinley, shaking his hand and briefly speaking to him. Near the front of the line was Leon Czolgosz, the son of Polish immigrants. Born in Detroit in 1873, he had worked at a variety of jobs, always moving on, looking for something not really clear, perhaps not even to himself. As a restless malcontent, he was drawn to left-wing causes and a purpose for his life started to clarify. In May he met Emma Goldman, a leftist anarchist born in 1869 in Lithuania, then part of the Russian Empire. She came to the United States in 1889, rapidly becoming one of the most prominent advocates of revolutionary change. Czolgosz was attracted to her because of the cause they shared and, apparently, attracted to her personally and wanted to impress her. He may also have been a hypochondriac who was convinced that he had not much longer to live and wanted to end his life dramatically. Of course, all of these could have been focusing him on this final dramatic act. He plotted his strike at McKinley carefully, holding back at earlier times over the past couple of days when he could not get close enough to his target and was concerned that people around him in the crowd could interfere with his plan.

Now his chance had come. He was near the front of the line waiting to shake McKinley's hand. His weapon, a .32 caliber Iver Johnson revolver, was covered by a large bandage on his right hand. Seeing the bandaged hand and assuming the man was injured, McKinley reached for Czolgosz's left hand with his left hand. Two shots from the concealed revolver struck McKinley. One bullet did not penetrate, just grazing the president's ribs. The other proved to be fatal. Czolgosz then was grabbed by James Parker, who was just behind him in the line, preventing him from getting off any more shots. Parker, born a slave in 1856 and now working as a waiter in Buffalo, was assisted in subduing Czolgosz by Buffalo detective John Geary and artilleryman Francis O'Brien. They, especially Parker, showed courage and quick thinking.

The bullet which glanced off a rib caused no serious damage. The other penetrated McKinley's stomach, pancreas, and one kidney. The president staggered back and was helped to a chair. Seeing Czolgosz being battered by those responding to the shooting, McKinley admonished those who had subdued and disarmed him to avoid hurting him. He then put his hand on Cortelyou's shoulder and told him to be careful how his wife would be told what happened.[14] Less than 20 minutes later, McKinley was in the emergency medical facility at the Exposition. The medical director there, Dr. Roswell Park, a well-respected surgeon, had been called away by a patient who needed an operation. The most experienced physician on the scene was Dr. Matthew Mann, a gynecologist. He, assisted by three other doctors, prepared the president for emergency surgery. Although an X-ray machine was being demonstrated at the Exposition, it was not used by the operating physicians due to concern that the radiation could be dangerous to the patient. The doctors observed that the bullet had passed through the stomach, but they could not find it. Because they were concerned the president would not survive further probing, they sutured the tears in the stomach, cleaned the area, and finished the procedure at 5:20. The White House physician, Dr. Presley M. Rixey, arrived during the operation and assisted the surgical team. McKinley then was taken to the home of John G. Milburn, president of the Exposition, where he and Ida had been staying.

Initially, everything appeared to have gone well; McKinley's temperature was down, his spirits were good, and on Tuesday, September 10, he was given nourishment by enema. Vice President Roosevelt, who together with other key leaders had hurried to the president's side, now left Buffalo to continue his vacation. He was told that the president seemed past the crisis time and Roosevelt did not want to hang around lest he give the impression that he was waiting in eager anticipation of becoming president himself. Off he went to climb Mount Marcy in northern New York not far from Lake Champlain.

On Thursday, McKinley was feeling well enough to have a breakfast of coffee, toast, and chicken broth. Not long after eating, he experienced discomfort and a racing pulse which the doctors attributed to indigestion. They tried purgatives and digitalis, but his condition worsened. Friday he was worse and again Roosevelt was summoned. A messenger found the vice president on his way down Mount Marcy and he set off again for Buffalo.[15]

McKinley slept through much of Friday. He awoke in the evening and, aware of his worsened condition, now realized that his life on earth was nearing its end. He asked for Ida and Cortelyou to be brought to him. She held his hand and they kissed. Weakly, he said, "It is God's way. His will, not ours, be done." He put his arm around Ida, smiled at her, and, in little more than a whisper, started his favorite hymn, "Nearer, My God to Thee." After only a few words, his strength gave out. He spoke no more, although he was conscious a while longer before slowly fading and taking his last breath at 2:15 a.m. on Saturday, September 14.[16]

Supporter and protégé Charles Dawes arrived about 9:00. McKinley still was conscious, but no longer could speak. Dawes stayed with him until the end. As the president faded, Ida was led away.

Mark Hanna, faithful friend and political lieutenant, arrived after McKinley had slipped into semi-consciousness. Approaching the bed on which the president lay, he was almost overcome by the reality that the end was near. Sorrowfully, almost piteously, he asked, "Mr. President, Mr. President, can't you hear me? Don't you know me?" Getting no response, Hanna harked back to their years of friendship before the

McKinley presidency and begged of him, "William, William, don't you know me?"[17]

The autopsy determined that, as was all too common at the time, gangrene had developed and spread. Understanding of this danger had developed by 1900, but the doctors on the scene had not taken the precautions which later would be standard. As serious as was the damage caused by the bullet, McKinley would have had a good chance to survive had the shooting been several decades in the future.

There was another ironic might-have-been which is more frustrating since it could have saved McKinley's life at the time. Shortly before the Buffalo excursion, the Rev. Casimir Zeglen of Chicago, a Roman Catholic priest, invented a lightweight bulletproof vest with a thin layer of steel plates inside tightly woven silk. Interest was expressed by McKinley's staff, but no action was taken prior to this last trip.[18]

After a brief private service at the Milburn house, McKinley's body was taken back to Washington where it lay in state before being transported back to Canton, Ohio, for the final service and interment. The service was held in the First Methodist Episcopal Church, of which McKinley was a member, with the eulogy delivered by the Rev. C.E. Manchester, pastor. Manchester later said of McKinley, "Another beauty in the character of our President, which was a chaplet of grace about his neck, was that he was a Christian. In the broadest, noblest sense of the word that was true. His confidence in God was strong and unwavering; it held him steady in many a storm, where others were driven before the wind and tossed. He believed in the Fatherhood of God and in his sovereignty. His faith in the Gospel of Christ was deep and abiding."[19]

In 1907, the body was moved a short distance to the McKinley National Memorial. That same year, Ida died and was buried beside her husband.

On September 16, Leon Czolgosz was indicted, and the trial began on September 23. No evidence had been found that he was part of a larger conspiracy, even though there were those who hoped to connect radicals such as Emma Goldman to the murder. Czolgosz refused to cooperate with the lawyers appointed by the court to defend him; as an anarchist, he rejected the jurisdiction of the court. For two days the prosecution presented testimony establishing the defendant's guilt. No defense witnesses were presented, and defense attorney Loran L. Lewis took only about half an hour with his closing argument. The jury deliberated only 34 minutes before returning a guilty verdict. Two days later, they recommended the death penalty. It was duly carried out on October 29 with his electrocution in Auburn, New York.

Often tributes to prominent people after their deaths are effusive rather than sincere, but careful reading of these eulogies can separate genuine admiration from carefully parsed sentences which really don't say much. On September 13, former president Cleveland spoke at a Princeton University service for McKinley, describing him as a man of faith who had demonstrated kindness, generosity, and patriotism. He lauded McKinley as a worthy example for the students to emulate.[20] This was meaningful because Cleveland could be counted on to say what he believed without sugar coating. Many other similar statements in this country and overseas testified to the widespread appreciation for the dead president's character and ability. His favorite hymn, "Nearer, My God to Thee," had a surge of popularity throughout the land.

Back in 1898, in the weeks after the sinking of the Maine, Theodore Roosevelt had considered McKinley weak for not leading the country more decisively to declaring war on Spain, even stating that "McKinley has no more backbone than a chocolate éclair."[21] His opinion of him grew during the subsequent months. They shared many convictions even though their personalities were different and even though as vice president, Roosevelt was not part of McKinley's innermost circle. Still, as Roosevelt looked back on the life of his predecessor, he focused on the good. In his first annual message as president on December 3, 1901, he said of him:

> It is not too much to say that at the time of President McKinley's death he was the most widely loved man in all the United States; while we have never had any public man of his position who has been so wholly free from the bitter animosities incident to public life. His political opponents were the first to bear the heartiest and most generous tribute to the broad kindliness of nature, the sweetness and gentleness of character which so endeared him to his close associates. To a standard of lofty integrity in public life he united the make-up of national character. A gallant soldier in the great war for the Union, he also shone as an example to all our people because of his conduct in the most sacred and intimate of home relations. There could be no personal hatred of him, for he never acted with aught but consideration for the welfare of others. No one could fail to respect him who knew him in public or private life.[22]

Theodore Roosevelt was both honest and opinionated. This tribute was carefully phrased; it does present the thoughts and feelings of the new president who almost immediately became the most prominent American and a figure of world significance. Roosevelt was very different in temperament and personality from his predecessor, but the divergence was less sharp between their policies. Both favored the increase of American power beyond this continent and both saw that the national government had a role to play keeping a healthy balance between capital, labor, and the consuming public. How much further McKinley would have gone had he completed his second term cannot be ascertained. He did take a few steps in the direction of the powerful presidency which would develop in the 20th century. In 1898, he became the first president since Andrew Johnson to campaign actively for congressional seats for his party in elections when the chief executive is not on the ballot. Lewis Gould, in his history of the Republican Party, speculated that in his second term, McKinley probably would have brought lawsuits against the growing trusts and would have moved to build an American canal across Central America.[23] McKinley himself stated of trusts that "there must be a remedy for the evils involved in such organizations."[24] The indications are that the second McKinley term would have taken these directions, but certain knowledge of what might have been lies beyond the range of our minds.

11

Bryan's End as the Dominant Democrat

Still a force in American politics was William Jennings Bryan. His defeat in 1900 did not shatter him, convinced as he was that his campaigns proclaimed what was good and true, positions that most Americans would accept tomorrow if not today. Many of those who supported him, however, fell into despair, unable to comprehend how their righteous cause could fail. One of his followers even compared Bryan to Christ, who also had been rejected by "the worldly Sadducees and aristocratic Pharisees." Bryan continued his crusading, earning a good income on the lecture circuit and building a mansion on 35 acres near Lincoln, Nebraska. He still inspired many people who still shared his vision for what the country should be, but they were not a majority. His weekly newspaper, *The Commoner*, kept his ideas flowing. It grew quickly from eight to 12 pages and by 1902 hit 16 pages, half of which were advertisements. Ad revenue plus subscriptions made it a flourishing enterprise with circulation growing from 18,000 initially to 145,000 in about five years. He paid union wages and required no more than eight hours of work per day from his employees.[1]

The assassination of McKinley and the rise of Theodore Roosevelt to the top of American government and politics presented Bryan with a dramatically different set of circumstances. The new Republican president was a man with the ability to stir crowds to charge the enemy; in this he was at least the equal of Bryan. Ensuring exciting times for those enjoying political drama was Roosevelt's firm conviction that Bryan was a leftist demagogue whose coming to power would be disastrous for freedom and prosperity. Unfortunately for those anticipating what would have been one of the most, if not the most, definitive and entertaining elections in our history, this confrontation never occurred. In 1904, Bryan did not win the Democratic Party nomination and in 1908 when he again was the nominee, Roosevelt did not run for what would have been six months short of three consecutive terms.

Bryan's lecture circuit success did not interfere with his campaigning in 1902 and 1903 for Democratic Party office seekers loyal to his vision. *The Commoner* called for his supporters to establish Democratic clubs which would further his positions. He still had a loyal coterie, but it was battered and weaker as 1904 opened. Recognizing his weakness after two losing presidential campaigns, Bryan faced the prospect of not getting his third consecutive nomination that year. If he could not be the Democratic Party standard bearer himself, most assuredly he did not want to see a successful return by Grover Cleveland. Bryan stated of the former president that "Cleveland represents as no one else does the plutocratic element of the party and is the logical candidate if the party returns to wallow in the mire."[2] Cleveland, his health declining and only a few months left to live, stayed retired in Princeton, New Jersey.

When the Democratic national convention opened in St. Louis on July 6, it was clear that Bryan still was a force, but no longer the dominant force. He showed his familiar dramatic flair with a stem-winder of a speech seconding the nomination of Senator Francis M. Cockrell of Missouri. This quixotic campaign went nowhere, but Bryan did serve notice that he still was around. Conservatives who had stayed in the party—men such as David Hill of New York, Arthur Gorman of Maryland, and John Daniel of Virginia—now had another chance. Their choice for the presidential nomination was Alton Parker, chief justice of the New York Court of Appeals, the highest court in the state, who had bucked the Republican surge by being the only Democrat elected to a state office in 1897. He was one of those conservatives who managed to swallow hard and support Bryan's two runs for the White House. Joseph Pulitzer's *New York World*, the daily newspaper with the largest circulation in the country, supported the Democrat conservatives as being solid Jeffersonians standing between Republican imperialists and Bryan's failed populist crusade.[3] The party platform presented planks attempting to appease the Bryan liberals. The support for labor and opposition to trusts were close to what was set forth in the 1900 platform. Although Parker stated clearly that he supported the gold standard, the platform punted on the issue, stating nothing on the monetary controversy. This was hardly a display of conviction and courage, but the hope was that the silence would keep the Bryan liberals on board. If a political party is not united on philosophy and issues, it must have a leader who can attract people across the divide in order to win or the opposition party must be inept. Neither of these was true in 1904.

Learning of this back at his home in New York, Parker, honest and determined as ever, telegraphed William F. Sheehan, who led the New York delegation at the convention, that since the platform said nothing about the gold standard, the convention delegates should understand and accept that our monetary system is and must remain gold backed: "I regard the gold standard as firmly and irrevocably established, and shall act accordingly if the action of the convention shall be ratified by the people. As the platform is silent on the subject, my view should be made known to the convention, and if it is proved to be unsatisfactory to the majority, I request you to decline the nomination before adjournment."[4] Although the platform remained silent on the matter, the convention accepted Parker's terms. Roosevelt commended Parker for being so forthright.[5]

A footnote to the Democratic Party presidential nomination contest that year was the decision of William Randolph Hearst, one of the most powerful and richest newspaper magnates, to throw his hat in the ring, his political ambitions now peaking. Elected to the U.S. House of Representatives in 1902, Hearst saw 1904 as the year when the White House could be his. He had hoped that Bryan would endorse him before the convention. That did not happen. Bryan had not given up his own ambitions; if not this year, perhaps in 1908. In addition, Hearst was liberal enough on domestic issues, but he diverged sharply from Bryan in that he supported American overseas expansion. Hearst arrived at the convention with about one-fourth of the delegates pledged to him. Nothing came of his hoped-for alliance with Bryan which might deadlock the convention and give Hearst an opening. On the first ballot, Parker had 667 votes, just nine short of the requisite two-thirds majority, to Hearst's 204. With Parker so close, delegates now shifted to him making him the nominee without a second ballot. Hearst endorsed the party ticket and dreamed of 1908 or 1912, but, after careful reflection, stayed out of future direct forays into the arena.[6]

There was an element of calculation motivating Bryan's actions at the convention. He recognized the difficulties involved in challenging Theodore Roosevelt whose status as a war hero and reputation as a reformer had been reinforced by the strong economy plus the continued growth of the United States as a world power. For Bryan, 1904 did not look to be a good year. If a Democrat from the conservative wing of the party were nominated and lost in the general election, Bryan's return as the party standard bearer in 1908 would be welcomed.

With Parker the nominee, the convention then chose as his running mate Senator Henry Gassaway Davis of West Virginia, a coal and lumber magnate. At 81 years of age, he is the oldest person to date on a major party ticket.

Bryan's campaigning for the Parker/Davis ticket burnished his reputation as a loyal Democrat without any downside since the election of that ticket was not likely. Roosevelt's election to a full term of his own was a virtual certainty; looking ahead to 1908, Bryan would be remembered as a man who put his party ahead of his personal disappointment at being passed over at the convention. Timewise, Bryan pushed the envelope by announcing 10 days before the election his intention to change dramatically the party of Grover Cleveland and Alton Parker, organizing it "along radical lines."[7]

No matter what they did, the Democrats were facing the reality that 1904 would not be a good year. For most Americans, the economy was going well, and the international prestige of the country was higher. Even though the Democrats still were more free trade oriented than the Republicans, overall the differences between the parties and their nominees that year were less than in the last two national elections and less than they would be in most future contests. Parker did call for Philippine independence but did not specify when. Although an energetic man, he did not mount an energetic campaign, there being few substantial differences between himself and Roosevelt. Personally honest, but a dull speaker, Parker could do little to stop the landslide bearing down on him. Theodore Roosevelt had solidified his reputation as an honest, dynamic leader who was in firm control of his administration. The Republican Old Guard were not enthusiastic about him but did appreciate his strength with most voters. When the votes had been counted, Roosevelt had won the most one-sided election since Andrew Jackson had defeated Henry Clay in 1832. He had 7,628,785 votes, 57.4 percent of the total to Parker's 5,084,442, 37.6 percent of the votes cast. Eugene Debs of the Socialist Labor Party was chosen by 402,460 voters, followed by Silas C. Swallow, the Prohibition Party choice with 259,256, and Thomas Watson of the Populist Party who attracted only 114,753 votes.

In September 1905, Bryan, his wife, and two of their children sailed from San Francisco on a trip around the world. To finance the journey and to keep his name before the public, he wrote weekly articles on the places they visited, people they met, religion, and politics. They were published by the Hearst newspapers and by his own *The Commoner*. On the trip, he met with such foreign dignitaries as the emperor of Japan and King Edward VII of the United Kingdom.

Back in the United States, Bryan laid the groundwork for his return to the presidential arena campaigning for his allies in the 1906 election, speaking to still supportive audiences across the country, and making money with his voice more than with his pen. The Chautauqua circuit was a prime venue for Bryan. Taking its name from Chautauqua Lake in western New York where summer educational and cultural programs began being held in 1874, the Chautauqua circuit featured prominent speakers in different locations, most often in tents. The programs were extraordinarily popular, bringing in such luminaries as Taft, Eugene Debs, and Samuel Gompers. The speaker heard more frequently than all was William Jennings Bryan. His standard fee was $250 per lecture plus half of the proceeds over $500; he averaged $2000 per week.[8]

As the 1908 election drew near, Bryan evinced a shift farther to the political left. While in Europe, he had expressed high praise for the German socialists and supported the progressive income and inheritance taxes of the British Liberal Party. Now, leading up to the 1908 election in the United States, he called for government ownership of the railroads.[9]

There was little doubt that Bryan would lead the Democratic Party in the 1908 election. Although he again dominated the Democratic Party as he had before 1904, he no longer was the handsome figure of the 1896 campaign; the ambition, determination, and the voice still were there, but by now he was mostly bald and carrying too much weight. The more conservative elements were discredited politically, having made a partial comeback in 1904, nominating their candidate, then leading the party into the November electoral catastrophe. Nor was there any liberal who could challenge Bryan seriously. At that time, Woodrow Wilson was president of Princeton University and had not yet migrated as far to the left as he soon would. He lamented that there appeared to be no Democratic leader who could challenge Bryan's appeal to so many party members.[10] Grover Cleveland, nearing the end of his life, also lamented the likelihood that the Democrats again would nominate Bryan. He did not live to see that day, dying shortly before the party convened.

There also was little doubt concerning the Republican Party nominee. Theodore Roosevelt had served three and a half years of McKinley's second term. When elected to a full term of his own in 1904, he pledged

Bryan at the 1908 Democratic National Convention (Library of Congress, https://www.loc.gov/item/2001697078/).

not to run in 1908. Although he came to regret having promised that, he considered himself obligated to keep his word, so announced his backing William Howard Taft as his successor in 1908. Taft had served as a U.S. Circuit Court of Appeals judge, as governor-general of the Philippines, and as secretary of war. Years later, he would be chief justice of the United

States Supreme Court, the only person to have been both president and chief justice. There were other Republicans with White House dreams, such as Vice President Fairbanks, Speaker of the House of Representatives Cannon, and Senator Foraker of Ohio, but there was no prospect for anyone to challenge successfully Roosevelt's choice. At the national convention held in Chicago, Taft easily won the presidential nomination on the first ballot. Representative James Sherman of New York was chosen as his running mate.

Two weeks later in Denver, the Democrats nominated the ticket of Bryan and John W. Kern of Indiana. Kern was a successful attorney and popular orator prominent in Democratic Party politics in this normally Republican state; only three times since Lincoln won the presidency in 1860 had the state voted to elect a Democrat to that office. He did serve as a state senator and as Indianapolis city solicitor but lost two gubernatorial elections and a U.S. Senate try before winning the nomination for vice president. In spite of this less than impressive electoral record, he was chosen due to the friendship with Bryan. He did win a seat in the U.S. Senate in 1910.

As usual, Bryan entered into the campaign season full of optimism; he had little regard for Taft who never had undergone the rigors of running for office himself. This time, Bryan decided to downplay the silver issue which had catapulted him to the top of the Democratic Party in 1896, but which was opposed by a majority of Americans. This year too he chose not to bring imperialism into the campaign since the acquisition of overseas territories was accepted by the majority of Americans, even welcomed. He chose instead to emphasize that the election was a clear choice between government devoted to the people and government controlled by big business. This was a tactical mistake since Roosevelt, while certainly not as left-wing as Bryan, had acted vigorously to break-up economic combinations in restraint of trade. Bryan was attacking the Republicans where they were strong and where he could not present the voters with a dramatic difference. Roosevelt reminded the electorate that while the Democratic Party platform called for punishing those corporations guilty of acting in restraint of trade, his administration had accomplished that.[11] Taft pledged to continue the Roosevelt policies.

Bryan still had trouble connecting with urban workers and gaining their votes, although Samuel Gompers did support him. This endorsement resulted from Bryan's getting an anti-injunction plank in the platform. The labor vote was far from monolithic and Bryan, with his Midwest, small town roots, never did figure out how to appeal successfully to this segment of the populace. Labor never would be fully comfortable with Bryan.

As if he did not have enough problems, a new one rose up to plague Bryan. His campaign treasurer, Governor Charles Haskell of Oklahoma, had had secret dealings with Standard Oil. This was revealed by William Randolph Hearst, no fan of Bryan's. Haskell resigned as campaign treasurer. This hurt Bryan even though he personally was not involved in any wrongdoing.

Bryan, as expected, campaigned vigorously, leading to Republican worries that public opinion might be shifting in his direction. Taft now in mid–September increased his pace. He was no Theodore Roosevelt, as few were, reading his speeches. He was, though, a pleasant, smiling man who conveyed intelligence and good will. The key factors were the general prosperity and his pledge to continue the Roosevelt program.

Now, as the November election neared, Bryan again had the worry about antagonizing Southern whites if he were to support civil rights for blacks. The Democrats needed the Southern white vote in order to carry Southern states and have a chance to win the presidency. Again Bryan, although uncomfortable, hesitated, equivocated, and stayed on the fence.

When the votes were counted, Bryan had suffered the worst of his three defeats. Taft received 51.6 percent of the popular vote and 321 electoral votes. The Bryan totals were 43.1 percent and 162. Somewhat hopeful for the Democratic Party was their electing governors in five states where Bryan lost to Taft. Furthermore, party candidates for governor ran ahead of Bryan in New York and Illinois.[12] The Democrats gained one seat in the Senate, but still trailed substantially, holding 32 seats while 59 were in Republican hands. In the House of Representatives, the Republicans lost three seats, but still led 219–172.

The minor parties were not a significant factor this year. The Socialist nominee, Eugene Debs, did get 420,820 votes followed by Eugene W. Chafin, the Prohibition Party nominee, who polled 252,683 votes. They were the only ones to top 100,000. Voting for Thomas L. Hisgen of the Independence Party were 83,562 people. Thomas E. Watson was the last presidential candidate of the once up-and-coming Populists; his vote total was only 28,131. August Gillhaus of the Socialist Labor was the choice of 13,825 individuals.[13]

Periodically in our history fears of the Roman Catholic Church as a foreign entity have flared. Since the pope is both the spiritual leader of the Roman Catholic Church worldwide and the temporal leader of the

Vatican, recognized then and now as an independent country, there was the view held by some that members of that church in the United States owed their primary allegiance to a foreign ruler. Actually, some Roman Catholics did so believe, although most separated the two, accepting papal authority in spiritual matters while being loyal Americans rejecting the jurisdiction of the pope as a political ruler. Cardinal James Gibbons of Baltimore and Archbishop John Ireland of St. Paul were key leaders of this position known as "Americanism." Historian David O'Brien wrote of this stance that "religious freedom, separation of Church and state, and religious pluralism, the three basic elements of this new religious culture, were bound to shape a new form of public Catholicism."[14]

The Vatican and American Roman Catholics had appreciated that the McKinley and Roosevelt Administrations had not interfered with the freedom of the Filipino Catholics to retain their faith. Taft, as governor-general of the Philippines, had gone to the Vatican to negotiate the sale of 410,000 acres of Philippine land owned by monastic orders to the United States government. This earned Taft praise at a White House dinner in 1904 from the apostolic delegate who commended him for his "admirable equity and prudence" and that the church would flourish under American rule.[15]

Although Roman Catholics were a minority of the American population, they had constituted the largest denomination in the country since 1850.[16] In the election of 1908, indications were that Bryan might have received more Catholic votes than any other candidate and that publications of that church preferred him over his rivals. Still, a number of Bryan's supporters blamed his loss on a conspiratorial combination of the Roman Catholic Church and big business.[17] For them, this was a preferable alternative to believing that most Americans simply did not agree with Bryan.

Even though there now no longer appeared to be any realistic prospect for a Bryan presidency, by no means would he fade into being a figure of the past. He was still convinced that his beliefs were right and that they would triumph later even though rejected now; a significant number of Americans continued to support him. Additionally, he still enjoyed the battle and earned his living speaking and writing. Outside of his not being a likely presidential nominee again, he still was the same man in terms of his core convictions.

Now that he no longer sought votes for himself, Bryan's prohibition convictions rose to the surface. He never had been a drinker of alcoholic beverages, never had supported their manufacture or consumption, but had avoided denouncing them. Many of his supporters, such as those of Irish, German, and Italian origins, enjoyed their drinks; he could not afford to antagonize them. No longer a candidate for office, he came out foursquare for prohibition. The cause had a lot of other prominent people endorsing it such as novelists Upton Sinclair and Jack London, the latter of whom considered running for office on the Prohibition Party line.

In the 1910 election, the Democrats showed more strength than they had since 1892. They gained the House of Representatives and elected governors in the key states of New York, Ohio, and Indiana, but of particular significance was Woodrow Wilson's winning the governorship of New Jersey. Having achieved a reputation as a scholar and president of Princeton University, he now shot into the front rank of prospective presidential contenders in 1912. Taft had failed to provide strong and effective leadership as president, lowering party morale and facing it with the prospect of a split. Roosevelt was convinced that his former protégé had to be replaced, that this necessity would overrule his pledge not to run again after leaving office in March 1909. This conviction that running in 1912 was not a violation of his word was clinched by the intervening Taft term. Democratic morale was high as they sensed that the political wind had shifted.

Bryan had been clear that he was not seeking a fourth nomination, but his interest in the 1912 national convention still was intense because of his ongoing love of the political arena, his dedication to principles he considered right, and, once the Republicans split, his seeing this as a Democratic Party year.

Bryan was hired by Pulitzer's *The New York World* to cover both the Republican and Democratic conventions. An incident at the Republican convention showed that his sense of humor reinforced his recognition that his time had passed. When he entered the press box, another reporter said to him: "If you don't look out, the Baltimore convention [the Democrats would convene there in a few days] will nominate you for President." Bryan responded with self-deprecating humor: "Young man, do you suppose that I'm going to run for President just to pull the Republican Party out of a hole?"[18] There would be very little additional good humor as the Republican convention continued.

The Republicans convened first, gathering in Chicago beginning on June 18. Most of the delegates had been chosen by state conventions and/or caucuses controlled by the party establishment which did not want Roosevelt as the presidential nominee again since he was so independent of their control and was more supportive of governmental activism than they. That year 12 states chose their delegates in direct primary elections: California, Illinois, Maryland, Massachusetts, Nebraska, New Jersey, North Dakota, Ohio, Oregon, Pennsylvania, South Dakota, and Wisconsin.[19] Roosevelt dominated these states, losing Massachusetts due to the power there of Senator Henry Cabot Lodge, old friend and political ally of Roosevelt's who this time could not endorse his candidacy. He believed that it would be better for the country, the Republican Party and the ex-president himself for this run not to take place; a strong second Taft term would be best. In addition, Senator Robert La Follette of Wisconsin, a maverick not part of the Republican mainstream, carried two states. He and Roosevelt agreed on much, but La Follette had his own ambitions and ran his own race. Roosevelt, in spite of their areas of commonality, had qualms about La Follette's soundness, saying of him, "He is, however, an extremist, and has the touch of fanaticism which makes a man at times heedless of means in attaining his ends."[20]

Roosevelt's winning nine of 12 primary elections was an impressive beginning for his quest to be president. At the end of the primary season, he had won 1,157,397 popular votes and 278 delegates. Trailing him were Taft, who garnered 761,716 popular votes and 48 delegates, and La Follette in third with, respectively, 351,043 and 36.[21] A total of 1078 delegates would be at the convention with 540 needed to win.

Careful analyses of the Republican convention this year have concluded that had the delegate selection process been fair and honest, Roosevelt at least could have prevented a first ballot Taft victory and could have won the nomination on the second,[22] but this was not to be. The intensity of the contest for delegates resulted in disputed returns from the convention and/or caucus states. The delegate selection process here often got murkier than in the states which held primary elections where the votes clearly could be counted. Where there was no primary, competing meetings could claim to be the official, legitimate Republican Party. This had to be sorted out now at the convention. Since the Republican National Committee which would adjudicate the disputes was controlled by supporters of Taft, the awarding of delegates caused few surprises, but much consternation. Of the 254 contested positions, 235 were given to Taft and 19 to Roosevelt. This clinched the nomination for Taft and precipitated a standing aside from the formal voting by most Roosevelt backers. For the nomination, Taft received 561 votes, Roosevelt 107, La Follette 41 while 344 delegates expressed their disgust with the whole process by refusing to vote.[23] Most of the Roosevelt supporters now walked out of the convention to form a new party although some, such as Elihu Root, stayed with Taft out of loyalty to the Republican Party.

This was good news for the Democrats. Bryan acerbically proclaimed: "When the Republicans fall out, honest men come into their own."[24] This gloating was premature since the Democrats were about to begin one of the most contentious conventions in their history which would go through a record 46 ballots before finally agreeing on a presidential nominee. A key difference was that the Democrats would put all their squabbles aside once the ticket had been chosen and would work to elect it. A good deal of drama, however, would precede this coming together.

As the convention opened in Baltimore on June 25, the strongest presidential contender was Speaker of the House James "Champ" Clark of Missouri. Also with delegate strength were Oscar Underwood of Alabama, Chairman of the House Ways and Means Committee and Governor Judson Harmon of Ohio. A new face stirring a good deal of interest was Woodrow Wilson who came out of an academic background as a professor and president of Princeton University, then won election as the governor of New Jersey in 1910.

Bryan still was a force in the Democratic Party even if he no longer dominated it. Initially he endorsed Clark who had favored him in previous years, even though he now had some qualms about the firmness of Clark's commitment to principle. Bryan was deeply disturbed by the support just given Clark by Tammany, an organization Bryan, with good reason, considered corrupt. He now was gratified by the substantial majority of delegates who voted for his motion that the convention was "opposed to the nomination of any candidate for President who is the representative of or under obligation to J. Pierpont Morgan, Thomas F. Ryan, August Belmont or any other member of the privilege-hunting or favor-seeking class."[25] This vote probably reflected more the philosophical tenor of the delegates than the continued mastery of the party by Bryan.

The Democrats now had a few primaries which, unlike those held by the Republicans, did not exhibit a clear preference by the party faithful. Clark, backed this year by William Randolph Hearst, won primaries in California, Illinois, Massachusetts, and Maryland. Wilson was on top in New Jersey, Wisconsin, South Dakota, and Oregon.

On the second day of the convention, the voting began. Clark led the first ballot with 440¼ delegates calling for his nomination. He was followed by Wilson with 324, Harmon with 148, Underwood with 117¼ and the rest of the votes going to minor candidates, including one for Bryan.[26] Clearly substantial obstacles had to be overcome before the party would have a ticket.

For nine more ballots the deadlock continued before a dramatic break in the Harmon ranks appeared to bring the party within sight of having their nominee. There now was a shift of 90 New York delegates from Harmon to Clark, giving him a majority, which almost always meant that very soon the requisite two-thirds margin would be his and he would be the party nominee. This year would be different; Wilson and Underwood would not yield, and the balloting continued with Clark still not over the finish line.

Now as the 14th ballot approached, Bryan once again moved to center stage. In spite of his doubts about Clark, Bryan and the Nebraska delegation had continued to support his campaign. At this stage, suspecting that a deal had been made between Clark and Tammany, Bryan rose to announce his switching his vote to Wilson. This was bitterly resented by many at the convention, but his announcement was key to stopping the Clark momentum and starting the shift toward Wilson. Bryan was aging— hair receding, stomach expanding—and he bore the stigma of leading the Democrats to defeat three times, yet the charismatic persona was still there to thrill audiences even though the number of people captivated by him, while still large, had shrunk. He was a figure of power, but no longer could a speech by him stampede a convention as in 1896. On the 28th ballot, Wilson gained the lead, but still was short of the two-thirds mark. Finally, on the 46th ballot, the opposition to him gave way and Wilson became the party standard bearer. Selected as his running mate was Governor Thomas Marshall of Indiana, best remembered for his remark "What this country needs is a good 5-cent cigar." This statement did not mean that he was a facetious idiot, but rather demonstrated his disgust with a long-winded senator's pompously setting forth his beliefs concerning what was needed in the United States.

On August 5, the Theodore Roosevelt dissidents would meet in the same building where the Republicans had convened in June. This convention drew together a fascinating aggregation of people excited by the prospects for a crusade led by a man who generated energy and enthusiasm as few figures in our history have done. This was the first major party convention with women delegates. When Jane Addams seconded Roosevelt's nomination for president, this also marked a first at a major party convention. Obviously, woman suffrage was a popular issue here.

Also present were black delegates, but not from the Deep South since Roosevelt believed that he could win Southern white votes if he avoided raising the race issue. His conviction was that if by doing so now he won in November, then he would be in the position to enhance racial justice. As president, he had been a moderate reformer who had opened up some opportunities for blacks to work in the federal government. Also, in 1901 he had entertained Booker T. Washington at the White House, something for which he was vilified by Southern newspapers and politicians and did not repeat. Principled and courageous Roosevelt may have been, but political calculations sometimes asserted themselves. Still, his racial views were more enlightened than those of most major party leaders during this time of our history. After the death of Washington in 1915, Roosevelt wrote of him, "It is not hyperbole to say that Booker T. Washington was a great American. For twenty years before his death he had been the most useful, as well as the most distinguished, member of his race in the world, and one of the most useful, as well as one of the most distinguished, of American citizens of any race."[27] Because of his need for the vote from Southern states, Wilson lagged behind Roosevelt and the Republican Party on the racial progress front.

In his two-hour long address to the convention, Roosevelt called for political revival, supporting primary elections, the popular election of United States senators who then were chosen by state legislatures, the vote for women, and full disclosure of campaign funding. He closed with the rousing "We stand at Armageddon, and we battle for the Lord."[28] The next day, he was nominated for president by acclamation as was his running mate Governor Hiram Johnson of California.

No election since that of 1860 had presented the voters with so much electoral strength outside the two-party system. The established parties still were there—the Republicans with Taft and the Democrats with Wilson. Now, though, the Progressive Party led by Roosevelt had burst on the scene creating the prospect for the first major restructuring of the party system since the mid–1850s when the Whigs faded and the Republicans rose. And, although not as dramatic a force, the Socialist Party led by Eugene Debs would hit their high water mark this year.[29]

The Taft Administration had undertaken more anti-trust actions than that of Roosevelt, but overall, the president represented and campaigned on conservative, limited government principles. Clearly, he occupied the right wing of the political spectrum in 1912. Clearly, too, Eugene Debs held the left flank. They represented an important segment of the voting public, but the major contest would pit the two candidates between them—Roosevelt and Wilson.

Both of these men believed in vigorous, active government though they differed concerning the underlying reasons for this activism and the means to be used. Wilson condemned Roosevelt for being soft on monopolies, for wanting to accept them and regulate them; he wanted to eliminate them through legislation and government directed competition. Wilson embraced the position of his friend and later U.S. Supreme Court Justice Louis Brandeis that the "difference in the economic policy of the [Democratic and Progressive] parties is fundamental and irreconcilable. It is the difference between industrial liberty and industrial absolutism, tempered by governmental (that is, party) supervision."[30] Roosevelt and Wilson advocated increasing the size and scope of government well beyond what had been the norm in the post Civil War United States. Roosevelt was more concerned with Wilson than with Taft, hence his determination to challenge Wilson for the liberal political market. A difference between them was that Roosevelt looked to control big business, whereas Wilson wanted to break them up.

Taft conducted the rather restrained campaign that had been standard for most incumbents while Roosevelt, Wilson, and Debs covered the country with the vigor more familiar to political observers of the present. The greatest drama was provided by, as might be expected, Theodore Roosevelt. On October 14 in Milwaukee, he was wounded in an attempted assassination by John Schrank, a deranged immigrant from Germany. Providentially the .38 caliber bullet first had to penetrate the 50 doubled-over pages of Roosevelt's speech, then his metal glasses case before entering his chest. Although it did break a rib, thanks to the obstacles it encountered, the bullet did not reach any vital organs, stopping less than an inch from his heart. He insisted on giving his scheduled speech, talking for about an hour. Vividly demonstrated were Roosevelt's courage and determination along with his showmanship. The audience was informed of his being wounded and he showed them his bloody shirt. Only after finishing his address did he go to the hospital in Milwaukee for emergency treatment, then moved on to Mercy Hospital in Chicago. The doctors there decided that there were fewer chances of complications of the bullet if it were left in place rather than attempting to remove it. He would suffer no problems from it during the remaining years of his life.[31] Out of respect for Roosevelt, the other candidates curtailed their campaigning until he was back on his feet.

William McKinley versus William Jennings Bryan

To the surprise of few, the Republican split brought Woodrow Wilson to the White House. On election day, November 5, he received 6,286,820 votes, 42 percent of the total cast, and 435 electoral votes from 40 states. Roosevelt was second with 4,126,020 supporting him, 27 percent of the aggregate, and 88 electoral votes from six states. Taft finished third, the choice of 3,483,972 people, 23 percent of the turnout, and won only two states. Eugene Debs finished with 901,255 votes, 6 percent of those casting ballots. This would be the strongest showing for the Socialist Party. Wilson was only the second Democrat to win the presidency since James Buchanan in 1856. The other Democrat, Grover Cleveland, who won in 1884 and in 1892, actually was more of a solid conservative than his Republican opponents. Wilson was the most liberal American president up to 1933 and the Franklin Delano Roosevelt Administration. Of course, had the Republicans not split, his victory was most unlikely.

12

Last Years

Even after he had won the presidency, Wilson continued to court Bryan, who might not dominate the Democratic Party as he once did, but who still was a revered figure to a significant number of its members. Wilson asked him to join the cabinet as secretary of state. Although not the steppingstone to the presidency it had been in the early decades of the republic, this still was the premier post in the administration. For Wilson, this appointment was a political necessity, but certain realities made it unlikely that this would be a successful, long lasting relationship. Bryan was independent, used to being in command, and convinced that he was right. He did work at being a loyal subordinate, but that was not easy for him. To compound the problem, in spite of appreciating Bryan's political skill, Wilson had only limited regard for Bryan's intellect or for his administrative abilities. Clearly storms lay ahead.

Initially, the relationship between the two men worked well as Bryan negotiated bilateral treaties calling for countries to submit disputes to an international tribunal, holding off armed conflict for at least a year. Thirty countries so agreed, including the major European powers except Germany and Austria-Hungary.[1] Also during Bryan's tenure at the state department, the United States got involved in Mexican and Caribbean interventions, with the laudable desire to promote freedom and peace. This the administration, especially Bryan, found to be an elusive goal, not taking sufficiently into account that there are ruthless, unscrupulous people who will lie, cheat, and resort to violence if they can so gain power. As an example of optimistic naiveté, Bryan saw the Mexican revolutionary bandit Pancho Villa as a true man of the people who wanted laudable reforms to promote their well-being.[2]

Increasingly Bryan was out of step with the rising generation of new Democratic Party leaders. Eleanor Roosevelt, writing of the impact he had made on her, commented that "William Jennings Bryan, secretary of state,

President Woodrow Wilson (left) and Secretary of State Bryan in 1913 (Library of Congress, https://www.loc.gov/item/2004668354/.)

was a well-known pacifist. I was always fond of Mrs. Bryan, but in spite of my admiration for Mr. Bryan's powers of oratory there were certain things that did not appeal to me at this time."[3] In spite of this rather restrained and diplomatic language; it is obvious that Bryan had not made a very favorable impression on her. Her words were indicative of the view now held of him by Democratic Party insiders. One of the sad realities for Bryan was his now being a figure of the past at an age when most people in politics are peaking.

The outbreak of World War I in August 1914 would create conflict between Bryan and Wilson serious enough to cause Bryan's resignation. Both men opposed the war and wanted the United States to remain neutral. In spite of his having been a colonel commanding the 3rd Nebraska volunteer regiment during the Spanish-American War, a unit which never left the United States, Bryan fundamentally was a pacifist. This conviction was stronger now than in 1898, perhaps because of his having grown more firm in that belief, perhaps because there was more political support now for the United States to stay on the sidelines. Each was moralistic, each Presbyterian, although Bryan had a firmer Biblical foundation for his faith. They would diverge too in the foreign policy positions which grew from that faith. Wilson saw the Allies, especially the British, as bearing less responsibility for the outbreak of the war than the Central Powers, especially Germany. Bryan did try to stay neutral, but the naval domination of the British led him to criticize them more. Perhaps his complaining about the British more came from his fear that the Germans were more ruthless and, therefore, had to be appeased more. At any rate, the sinking of the British liner *Lusitania* by a German submarine off the coast of Ireland on May 7, 1915, brought the Wilson-Bryan differences to a boiling point. A total of 1201 people died of whom 128 were Americans. A massive mood of revulsion against Germany swept through the United States. Wilson issued a strong note condemning the German action. Bryan believed the ship could have been carrying some munitions, which it probably was although it primarily was a civilian passenger liner, and he wanted the United States to be neutral in word as well as in deed. At a June 1 cabinet meeting, Bryan found himself very much in the minority and accused the others of favoring the Allies. This they did, along with most Americans, although there was little support for this country to enter the war. Wilson rebuked Bryan but did not call for his resignation. The president wanted to avoid the internal party conflict that could result from firing him. By now, relations between Wilson and Bryan were frigid. The president and his supporters eagerly anticipated his departure. No longer himself wanting to be part of this administration, on June 8 he resigned.[4]

When the 1916 Democratic national convention met in St. Louis, for the first time in 20 years Bryan was not a delegate or the nominee, but he was called upon to speak, which he did to good effect; as usual, the delegates were enthused by his words. During the fall, he campaigned effectively for Wilson who defeated Republican Charles Evans Hughes in one of the closest presidential elections in our history. Wilson appreciated Bryan's help in several key states but did not want him as part of the administration. Bryan continued to oppose the movement of the country toward the Allied cause and strongly objected to our entry into the war in April 1917, but loyally supported his country once the decision was made, although he did not wear a uniform this time as he had done 19 years previously.

Two other causes he also supported vigorously and with greater success were prohibition and the vote for women. Bryan long had opposed the manufacture, sale, and consumption of alcoholic beverages. The movement gathered momentum during World War I with the idea of conserving resources and sacrificing for victory augmenting the old familiar arguments. The supporters celebrated victory with the ratification of the 18th Amendment on January 16, 1919, which stipulated, "After one year from the ratification of this article the manufacture, sale, or transportation of intoxicating liquors within, the importation thereof into, or the exportation thereof from the United States and all territory subject to the jurisdiction thereof for beverage purposes is hereby prohibited."

Bryan long had been convinced that women were morally superior to men, that society would benefit as their status grew. In 1916, he now openly supported suffrage, arguing that it would lessen crime and reduce the likelihood of war. The movement, which had been gathering strength since the end of the Civil War in 1865, won nationally with the ratification of the 19th Amendment on August 18, 1920. It proclaimed: "The right of citizens of the United States to vote shall not be denied or abridged by the United States or by any state on account of sex."

At the end of World War I, he, along with Wilson, called for the United Sates to help organize and join the new League of Nations. Since Wilson was unwilling to compromise with Republicans on the terms of joining, the United States never became part of it. Bryan did call in vain for the United States to have more votes in the organization than did small countries and for only Congress to be able to commit the country to war. In spite of not gaining all that he wanted, Bryan did support Senate ratification of joining the League and disagreed with Wilson's refusal to compromise.[5] The president insisted that Senate Democrats vote against ratification rather than accept anything less than total victory. Most Senators favored American involvement, but the combination of Wilson loyalists who went along with his demands and those who never liked the idea of the League in the first place, doomed chances for ratification. Twice, in November 1919 and in March 1920, the combination of Wilsonian stubbornness and isolationist sentiment kept the United States out of the League.

In 1920, there was some talk of Bryan's again leading the Democratic Party. Wilson had served two terms, suffered a severe cerebral hemorrhage, and had lost favor with most voters. In spite of his health decline and regardless of the two-term tradition, he had shown some interest in running again, but for the reasons just stated, his fellow Democrats quickly made clear that Wilson as president and Party leader now was a figure of the past. Leading prospects to replace him were Secretary of the Treasury William Gibbs McAdoo, who also was Wilson's son-in-law, and the tough anti-communist Attorney General A. Mitchell Palmer. Wilson did not endorse anyone for the nomination he no longer could have. The convention deadlocked until the 44th ballot when a compromise candidate, Governor James M. Cox of Ohio, was chosen with Assistant Secretary of the Navy Franklin Delano Roosevelt as his running mate. Roosevelt, fifth cousin of Theodore Roosevelt, at 38 years of age was regarded as one of the most promising young figures in the Democratic fold. He would go no higher this year, though, since the Cox/Roosevelt ticket went down to ignominious defeat as the country overwhelmingly elected Republican Senator Warren Harding of Ohio and Governor Calvin Coolidge of Massachusetts. The Republicans won 60.4 percent of the popular vote and 404 Electoral College votes while the Cox/Roosevelt ticket was well behind with 34.2 percent of the popular vote and 127 Electoral College votes. The country had returned to the Republican voting pattern which would continue until 1932 when the Great Depression and Franklin Delano Roosevelt shattered the pattern.

Harding died in 1923 just as reports of scandals in his administration were surfacing, but potential problems for the Republican Party in the 1924 election were squelched by Coolidge's integrity, his firm handling of corruption, and the continuing good economy.

The brief moment earlier in 1920 when the idea of another Bryan presidential run had attracted some attention had faded. Even though there now was not even a faint prospect for this, he still continued into the 1920s as an influential man with a popular following. This standing of his would be strained by his speaking out on a very controversial issue at the 1924 Democratic national convention which met at Madison Square Garden in New York.

The Ku Klux Klan rose after the Civil War as an underground white vigilante force since Southern white men who had supported the Confederacy, which meant most of them, were barred from voting and holding office. In some states, this continued into the late 1870s. Once these white men regained control, blacks lost their new-found influence and the KKK was not needed. The organization revived in the 1920s proclaiming Christian patriotism. This, though, was a smokescreen for its old opposition to blacks plus now Roman Catholics, Jews, and immigrants. Especially in his presidential runs, Bryan had shied away from advocating civil rights for blacks. Wanting to avoid causing the Democrats problems winning Southern states in the upcoming election, he opposed here at the convention an anti–Klan resolution which lost by one vote. His stance caused Bryan a lot of discomfort as he tried to reconcile his anti-resolution advocacy with his favoring civil rights for all Americans.

The Democratic convention was deadlocked for 102 ballots between Governor Al Smith of New York and William Gibbs McAdoo, still one of the most powerful figures in the party. Bryan supported McAdoo. Finally, on the 103rd ballot, the convention turned to John W. Davis, a Wall Street lawyer who had served as ambassador to the United Kingdom. This, as did Alton Parker's nomination in 1904, marked a partial shift away from the left-of-center control of the party dating back to the Bryan revolution of 1896. Both were only partial defeats for the left and definitely were short-lived. At least until the present, the Democratic Party never returned to the limited government, private sector-oriented days of Grover Cleveland. Depending on one's beliefs, Bryan deserves a good amount of credit or a good amount of blame for this change. As an attempt to create some enthusiasm from the Democratic Party left, Bryan's brother Charles, governor of Nebraska, was nominated for vice president on the first ballot. The Democrats were worried about their left flank since Senator Robert La Follette of Wisconsin, a liberal Republican, was running for president using the Progressive Party label. Charles agreed with his older brother on populist politics but did not share the Christianity which was so much the core of his being. In spite of having little interest in religion and rarely attending church, Charles loyally supported and directed the three Bryan presidential runs. Now, after those three losses and the election of Woodrow Wilson in 1912, it was evident that William Jennings Bryan would not win election to the White House, opening the door for Charles to begin his own political career. Over almost 30 years, he would blaze a remarkably persistent record marked by statewide victories, winning two-year terms as governor in 1922 and again in 1930 and 1932, which, however, were overshadowed by even more losses in races for both governor and U.S. senator. Charles died in 1945.

Looking back on 1924, there was little that any Democrat could have done to head off a Republican victory. Harding had died in 1923 and Coolidge had established himself as an honest and capable president, presiding over a flourishing economy. The division between Davis and Bryan and the La Follette candidacy just made a bad situation worse. Actually, both the Bryan brothers were closer to La Follette than they were to Davis. There has been speculation that Charles, realizing that the Democrats could not win the presidency in the November election, hoped that the

12. *Last Years*

La Follette independent candidacy would ensure that no one gained a majority of the electoral vote, throwing the presidential and vice presidential choices to Congress where he would have had a better chance at power. This is possible, but it cannot be proven.

The strong economy plus Coolidge's reputation for political ability and honesty would have been a massive hurdle for the Democrats to overcome even without the siphoning away of votes by La Follette. Coolidge garnered 15,700,000 votes, 54 percent of the total, and 382 electoral votes. Davis was chosen by 8,400,000 voters, only 28.8 percent of those cast, and 136 electoral votes. La Follette mounted one of the strongest third-party challenges in our history, 4,800,000 votes amounting to 16.8 percent. He won only his home state of Wisconsin, good for 13 electoral votes.

Bryan's speeches on Christian and cultural matters still were popular and lucrative for him. One last moment in the spotlight lay ahead. Certainly, his politics still were left-of-center—government ownership of railroads, telephone and telegraph companies, high taxes on the productive—but it was Bryan's Christian faith which would be the focal point of his last crusade.

During the 1920s, the conflict between those adhering to Christianity as the foundation of Western Civilization and those wanting human reason as the ultimate criterion intensified. One of the most prominent controversies concerned evolution. Those adhering to the Bible as divine revelation believe that God created everything, that evolutionary change takes place within species, but that lower species do not evolve into higher species. For many others, Charles Darwin's theory that lower species do evolve upward is true. In Tennessee a law was passed making it "unlawful for any teacher in any of the Universities, Normals and all other public schools of the state which are supported in whole or in part by the public funds of the state, to teach any theory that denies the story of the Divine Creation of man as taught in the Bible, and to teach instead that man has descended from a lower order of animals."[6] The American Civil Liberties Union, founded just a few years previously in 1920, entered the case determined that the law be declared unconstitutional. Recruited to break the law and bring about this challenge was John Scopes, a recent graduate of the University of Kansas who was teaching science and coaching football at Dayton High School.

When Bryan was invited to join the prosecution team, he enthusiastically accepted. Once this was known, Clarence Darrow, then probably the most prominent attorney in the country, jumped at the opportunity to lead the defense. Back in 1924, he had made many enemies and a lot of money defending Nathan Leopold and Richard Loeb, two university students from wealthy families who had killed 14-year-old Bobby Franks to demonstrate their brilliance by committing a perfect crime. They were caught and their families engaged Darrow. He was the one who demonstrated brilliance by getting them life imprisonment instead of the death penalty. It is one of history's ironies that Bryan spoke at Scopes' high school graduation in 1919.[7]

The trial, formally the *State of Tennessee v. John Thomas Scopes*, lasted for 12 sweltering days in July 1925. National attention was great; this was the first trial to be broadcast on radio—WGN in Chicago. Bryan argued that the legislature was the place to argue the wisdom of the law, not the courtroom. Defense attorney Dudley Field Malone of the American Civil Liberties Union lauded the Bible for its theology and teachings on morality, but that it should not be looked to for science. Bryan by no means opposed science but stated that the Bible is a higher source of truth, that its teachings had not been negated by science. Darrow affirmed his conviction that scientific evidence is superior to Bible teachings.

Bryan accepted being cross-examined by Darrow on the teachings of the Bible. A man of intelligence, but not a Bible scholar, the overconfident Bryan by no means was at his best in this confrontation. At one time, Darrow had supported Bryan politically, but now the focus was on the Bible and the agnostic Darrow scorned Bryan's faith. He launched his offensive, challenging his former mentor to explain the Genesis accounts of Jonah's being swallowed by a great fish and how Joshua made the sun to stand still. Bryan affirmed his faith in the Bible, but he was not a scholar who could counter Darrow and reconcile Christian faith with true science. When called upon to state the date of the Great Flood also recorded in Genesis, Bryan responded that he had never calculated it. Darrow continued to push, asking him what he thought, to which Bryan replied: "I do not think about things I don't think about." Seeing this rather inane response as an opening for a quick strike, Darrow hit him with "Do you think about things you do think about?" Bryan's answer, "Well, sometimes,"[8] moved the mostly pro–Bryan audience to laughter.

Darrow pushed Bryan by inquiring whether he believed that God had created everything in six days, wanting to trap him between the Genesis account and scientific evidence on the age of the earth. Since the word day is used in Scripture to mean the hours of light, a 24-hour period, and an era of indefinite length, Bryan had no trouble pointing that out to Darrow and then affirming his belief in the likelihood of a long period of time in creation.

Darrow used his considerable abilities to expose Bryan as an unlettered rube, as a man whose lack of learning would be evident to all. Overall, Darrow bested him rhetorically, but the battle was by no means a rout. To those who believe as did Darrow, Bryan's answers made no sense. For those who believed the Bible, the image of Bryan is considerably brighter.

When the trial began anew the next morning, the judge ordered the exchange between Bryan and Darrow be expunged from the trial record as not germane to the matter before the court. This disappointed Bryan who believed that had he cross-examined Darrow, he could have reversed the setback; by no means did he consider his cause lost. The month before the trial, he had written a well-reasoned exposition of the Christian stance, arguing that the voters of Tennessee, through their legislature and boards of education, have the right to set stipulations for schools, such as prohibiting a teacher from instructing students that monarchies are the only good governments.[9] Bryan proceeded to set forth his conviction that it is equally logical to prohibit people from being employed in public schools and teaching that the Bible is wrong: "That is the Tennessee case. Evolution disputes the Bible record of man's creation, and the logic of the evolution eliminates as false the miracles of the Bible, including the virgin birth and the bodily resurrection of Christ. Christians are compelled to build their own colleges in which to teach Christianity; why not require agnostics and atheists to build their own colleges if they want to teach agnosticism or atheism?"[10]

He further elucidated his position, affirming advances in medicine, transportation, and communication, that people are better off because of science. He then returned to his objection that the evolutionary theories of Darwin remained unproven:

> Christianity welcomes truth from whatever source it comes, and is not afraid that any real truth from any source can interfere with the divine truth that comes by inspiration from God Himself. It is not scientific truth to which Christians object, for true science is classified knowledge, and nothing therefore can be scientific unless it is true.
>
> Evolution is not truth; it is merely an hypothesis....[11]

Writing of Bryan, H.L. Mencken, journalist, critic, editor of *American Mercury*, and all-around curmudgeon, stated, "It was hard to believe, watching him at Dayton, that he had traveled, that he had been received in civilized societies, that he had been a high officer of state. He seemed only a poor clod like those around him, deluded by a childish theology, full of an almost pathological hatred of all learning, all human dignity, all beauty, all fine and noble things. He was a peasant come home to the barnyard."[12] Mencken was an elitist who disliked Bryan's espousal of democracy and especially rejected his Christian profession.

Since there was no doubt that Scopes had violated the state law, he was found guilty and fined $100. The state supreme court upheld the law under which he was tried but overturned his conviction on a technicality; the fine should have been determined by the jury rather than by the judge. The Tennessee law formally was abolished in 1967 by the legislature. Scopes moved on to graduate study in geology at the University of Chicago and a career in oil and gas until his retirement in 1963. He died in 1970.

Bryan had a considerably shorter time to live after the end of the trial on Monday, July 20. On the following Sunday, he attended church in Dayton, gave a prayer, ate a hearty dinner, and lay down for a nap to refresh himself for a sermon that evening. Shortly after lying down, he died. Apparently, his being an overweight diabetic plus the strain of the trial and the enervating heat were too much for his aging body. No autopsy was performed.

Bryan's body was taken by train to Washington, D.C., where a viewing was held at the New York Avenue Presbyterian Church. The burial was at Arlington National Cemetery, something to which he was entitled having served as a colonel in the army during the war with Spain. It is intriguing that he chose this location in view of his later developed near pacifism. One can wonder whether a part of Bryan yearned for the broader acceptance and acclaim given past American heroes, such as Theodore Roosevelt, who had so served. Talker that he was, he appeared so open, his opinions stated so firmly that it can be surprising to uncover a part of him hidden from view. Often those who have served in the armed forces look back nostalgically on this time in their lives with fond memories of the sense of purpose, the dedication to a cause, the camaraderie, and the disciplined structure of which they were a part. Speculation can be an enjoyable pastime, especially for those who love history, but no definitive answers concerning this choice were left behind by Bryan in his writings, nor did his wife, other family members, or friends shed any light on the matter.

Mary survived her husband by only a few years, dying in 1931. She completed *The Memoirs of William Jennings Bryan by Himself and His*

12. Last Years

Wife, Mary Baird Bryan. The title is a final reminder that she was very much his partner, but always the primary focus was on his career. That came before any consideration for her personal interests.

The first of the Bryan's three children, Ruth, was born in 1885 and proceeded to lead an adventurous life. In 1903, she married artist William Homer Leavitt who was painting a portrait of her father. The marriage ended in 1909 when she divorced him for "incompatibility of temper and non-support."[13] The next year, she married Reginald Owen, an officer in the British army. During World War I, she did relief work in England and in Egypt, the latter post getting her near her husband who was stationed there.

Ruth's trailblazing continued into the decades between the wars. She produced and directed a movie, *Scheherazade*, which was not distributed. So far, no copy of the film has been found and the reason for its not being shown is not known.

In 1928, after the death of her husband, she was elected to the United States House of Representatives from Florida, her district stretching down the east coast of that state from Jacksonville to Key West. After winning a second term in 1930, Ruth lost in the 1932 Democratic Party primary. A prohibition supporter, as her father was, she lost to an advocate of the repeal movement which was gathering strength and soon would triumph nationally. The next year, her friendship with Eleanor Roosevelt helped gain her selection as the United States minister to Denmark and Iceland (at that time, the designation "ambassador" was not used for our diplomats assigned to smaller countries). She was the first American woman to serve in this capacity. In 1936, she married Borge Rohde, a captain in the Danish royal guard, and resigned her post.

Ruth ended her career in public service as a delegate to the 1945 San Francisco Conference which set up the United Nations and later as an alternate delegate to the U.N. General Assembly. She died in 1954.

William Jr., born in 1889, graduated from the University of Arizona and from Georgetown University Law School. Living first in Arizona, he served as an assistant United States attorney and on the Arizona State University Board of Regents. Moving to California in 1921, he achieved success as a lawyer and continued his civic and political activity. William Jr. actively assisted his father during the Scopes trial. He died in 1978.

The youngest of the three children, Grace, was born in 1891. She too engaged in public speaking and started but did not finish a biography of her father. She was hampered by poor health and an unhappy marriage. She died in 1945.

13

Relevance for Today

If McKinley and Bryan could have gone to sleep in 1900 and awakened today, what would be the political prospects for each in the political arena? How would they fit in with their political parties now? Undoubtedly some prominent figures of the past would have major problems today. John Adams, for example, believed that voters should have qualifications beyond being citizens who have lived a certain number of years. He certainly would have difficulty today convincing people to limit the franchise. James Madison would be unlikely to succeed today because of his small stature—he was 5'4" tall and weighed only 100 pounds—and his weak speaking voice. By 1900, McKinley, Bryan, and other prominent political figures did not espouse the franchise limitations of Adams and others of the Federalist Party. Furthermore, neither McKinley nor Bryan had the physical limitations of Madison. It is likely that both could adjust and do well in the 21st-century political fields of combat. McKinley's Christian faith, balanced budget, sound money, and strong foreign policy stands would fit in well with most Republicans. Bryan, however, would find the Democratic Party of today a difficult fit. His economic policy stances would be applauded; his calls for more taxation, more spending, and the nationalization of some businesses would be well supported. Conversely, his strong Biblical faith would find limited support from 21st-century Democrats. It would be much more in accord with the large evangelical Christian wing of the Republican Party. They, though, would not accept his big government liberalism. Bryan would have no problem being applauded by large numbers of people for his religious and political/economic pronouncements; the problem is that they are in different political parties.

Most Americans today either support both cultural and economic conservatism or they are for both cultural and economic liberalism. Some Americans are economic conservatives and cultural liberals. Some others, as did Bryan, espouse cultural conservatism and economic liberalism. He would find it extraordinarily difficult to win control of the Democratic Party today, let alone win a presidential election.

Both McKinley and Bryan were intelligent, strong-willed men who shared Christian convictions rooted in the Bible. Each was a believer, McKinley Methodist, Bryan Presbyterian, albeit neither was a deep Scriptural scholar. Bryan was not an adherent of traditional Presbyterian belief that God absolutely chooses the elect, that others are passed by. He firmly believed in the Second Coming of Christ, but did not enter into the controversies between premillennialists, post-millennialists, and amillennialists who differ on details concerning Christ's return. Bryan's spiritual beliefs are better known thanks to the Scopes Trial. McKinley's statements of faith, numerous as they are, generally have been overshadowed by the dramatic events of his terms in office and the paucity of his writings. Each was a faithful family man about whom no scandals arose.

Bryan's racial attitude would present him with a major headache today were he to throw his hat into the presidential ring. He was torn by his sense that Christianity precluded his believing in white racial supremacy, yet his practical side recognized that the 11 former Confederate states had almost half of the electoral votes needed to win the presidency. White supremacy was a key article of faith for Southern Democrats. Were he to disagree with them on this, his hope for victory would vanish. Still, his racial views seemed more deeply rooted than rising only from pragmatic political concerns. In his autobiography which was published in 1925, Bryan wrote, "I was born a member of the greatest of all races—the Caucasian Race."[1] That statement would be condemned by both Democrats and Republicans today, dooming the speaker to life on the fringes of American politics.

Differences arose between them concerning the political and economic principles which grow out of that faith. McKinley believed that the greatest national prosperity and individual well-being would come from a private sector economy with limited government involvement. The government would preserve order and stability protecting the freedom and opportunity for people to rise or not to rise based on their ambition, drive, and ability. Bryan believed in a much more active government role in controlling the economy. He seemed to assume that people preferred security to freedom of opportunity. Certainly many do, but progress comes from people willing to take risks, who eschew following the path of those who want to be taken care of by others.

William McKinley versus William Jennings Bryan

William McKinley may not have been charismatic as was Bryan, but he did speak well and knew the issues and his beliefs, with the caveat that it took him some time to firm up his monetary policy stance. As the issue heated up going into the 1896 campaign, he came to see that the gold standard position was both sounder economics and better politics than his former bimetallism. His support for the Gold Standard Act of 1900 was vital to its passage. He also showed skill working behind the scenes to persuade people on the fence for one reason or another to join him. A good many Americans still saw value in inflating the money supply through silver or paper and there was political pressure from these people on wavering members of Congress. McKinley's demonstration of leadership was impressive in the success of the sound money cause.

By the end of his first term and as his second term began, McKinley had tempered his support of high tariffs, coming to realize that protectionism can hamper international trade and thereby damage our economy. He was far from being a free trader, but also far from being an automatic supporter of tariff walls. He believed that we needed to modify our policy on imports if we expected other countries to accept our exports.

McKinley did not favor increasing taxation and he believed that the government must control spending, not engaging in deficit financing unless confronted by an emergency on the scale of the Civil War. The way out of a major depression, such as that of 1893, is not through spending more than revenue. The major depressions which hit in 1893 and 1920 ended without the massive federal government deficit spending and controls which characterized the Hoover and Franklin Delano Roosevelt policies to combat the depression which began in 1929, policies which worsened it and prolonged it.

Although McKinley did recognize that by the late 1890s the United States needed a stronger government than previously, he by no means was the big government chief executive that Wilson and Franklin Delano Roosevelt would be. McKinley's limited government and sound money policies plus his willingness to assert American power overseas would fit in with most Republicans of the present. Government obviously is bigger, more expensive, and more intrusive today and the gold standard is no more. Yet the principles of limited government and sound money still are powerful. McKinley would have plenty of allies today who do not believe that more government spending means more prosperity and that simply increasing the money supply would improve the economy. He also moderated his earlier protectionist stance on trade, recognizing that this country cannot expect to export without being willing to import and in the last few years of his life he spoke out more on the reality that two-way trade benefits both parties; we cannot expect to export if we refuse to import. He referred to another benefit of international trade in a speech he delivered in San Francisco when he asserted that "there is nothing in this world that brings people so close together as commerce."[2] This too would fit in with most Republicans today who espouse a position between free trade and absolute protectionism. McKinley could have some problems in the political arena today because of his not being a dynamic, exciting speaker; he much preferred to use a calm appeal to reason. There were, though, times when he did demonstrate that he knew how to stir the feelings of the public. Here too, he most likely would succeed in the political combat of today.

Bryan's winning the presidency probably would have been bad for the future success of the Democratic Party since his personal charisma was not matched by administrative skill. An ineffective Bryan Administration would have opened the door to future electoral success by the Republican Party, a situation quite different from the McKinley record which led to a continuation of Republican party control of Washington.

The two men further differed on the expansion of the United States beyond North America. Bryan was leery of this spreading of American power. Initially McKinley too was not a devotee of this policy but changed his view as he recognized the reality that if we did not acquire these territories, another country would; freedom for the Philippines, Hawaii, Guam, and Puerto Rico was not an option. They would be American or part of another empire—German, Japanese, or British. Again, it must be remembered that Hawaii, Guam, and Puerto Rico have chosen freely to be part of the United States. Before World War II, the Philippines had a substantial amount of self-government and had been promised full independence. This independence was delayed by the Japanese conquest but was granted in 1946. The Filipinos were unique among Asiatic subjects of foreign powers in that they fought alongside us as loyal and effective allies. In retrospect, the McKinley policies come across as good both for the United States and for the territories we acquired.

As a leader, McKinley was more effective than was Bryan in uniting his party and in projecting a positive image to the electorate. Bryan certainly had an enthusiastic style, but he spent much of his time warning of the people's enemies, especially the industrial East. He did enthuse many voters, but he alarmed and turned away more. It is necessary to identify enemies and what is wrong in the country, but the primary focus should be on what is good, uplifting, and uniting. Both parties had dissatisfied segments—the gold Democrats and the silver Republicans—but McKinley and the Republicans were better at minimizing their own rifts and at reaching out to the other party's dissidents.

The questions which divided people in the 1890s still roil the waters today. Will monetary inflation increase prosperity? What role should the United States play beyond our borders? How much should the government control the behavior of individuals in order to avoid the opposite extremes of regulating so little that chaotic collapse ensues and regulating to such an extent that freedom is destroyed? Should the government redistribute wealth through taxing the productive and giving to those with less ability and/or drive?

Most Americans then advocated sound money which kept its value. They further accepted the reality that the United States had grown to such an extent that it did have a constructive role to play beyond North America. Finally, most advocated limited regulation and that the government should not undertake the redistribution of wealth. The same values continue dominant today, although those who advocate more regulation and redistribution are stronger now than in the 1890s. Still, most of our citizens do recognize the danger that high tax rates discourage economic growth and generous benefit programs reduce incentives to work. This debate still enlivens political contests.

The debate continues also concerning the extent to which McKinley controlled his administration and the extent to which he was controlled by stronger personalities. Historian Samuel Eliot Morison shrugged him off as "a kindly soul in a spineless body."[3] Also, during the weeks before McKinley gave up on a settlement short of war, an impatient Theodore Roosevelt said that he "has no more backbone than a chocolate éclair."[4] Roosevelt later pulled back from this opinion as he got to know both McKinley and the presidency better. There were a good number of Washington insiders whose opinion of the man increased as they got to know him. McKinley overall was well regarded during his presidency and for some years later. Then, with the rise of the imperial presidency and with more attention going to political figures with more flair, he faded, especially losing ground with the rise of the dynamic, colorful Theodore Roosevelt. His favoring limited government more than most of those who occupied the White House after him was a negative with most historians of the 20th century.

Again, a key difficulty in evaluating McKinley is that he left behind few written insights concerning his policy decisions. He did not write books as did Roosevelt and his letters reveal little in depth, but strong and capable men who knew him well were impressed by his abilities. Charles Gates Dawes, a very successful lawyer and businessman, showed his organizational and leadership skills in the 1896 McKinley winning campaign. Only 31 years old at the time, he was considered too young to join the cabinet as secretary of the treasury, so did accept appointment as comptroller of the currency, a post which he filled very effectively. Personally wealthy, he did not need the position and spent most of his life in the private sector. His opinion of McKinley, therefore, rings true. In his *A Journal of the McKinley Years*, Dawes wrote of the president's beliefs and positive qualities:

> He impliedly assumes for the future an excess of income over expenditures under present and future revenue laws, and urges that no greenbacks hereafter redeemed in gold shall be paid out again except in return for gold.... He also recommends that banks be allowed to issue notes to par of U.S. bonds now on deposit. Had a long talk with him on this subject. I feel that with his usual ability and keenness of perception as to the "best possible" he is going to take the proper position.[5]

In a memorial service at Princeton University, former president Grover Cleveland praised McKinley as a man of faith who was kind, generous, and a patriotic American. He further used the service as an opportunity to call for Americans to follow McKinley's example and "to meet any call of patriotic duty in any time of our country's danger and need."[6]

Alvin S. Felzenberg has rated the American presidents through Clinton on character, vision, competence, economic policy, preserving and extending liberty, and defense, national security, and foreign policy. He omitted William Henry Harrison and James Garfield since they were chief executives for too short a time to weigh fairly and accurately where they would have ended up had they served longer. As a point of interest, Abraham Lincoln scored highest followed by George Washington and, tied for third place, Ronald Reagan and Theodore Roosevelt. The lowest ranked president was James Buchanan. Only slightly better were Franklin Pierce and Andrew Johnson. Tied one place above them were John Tyler, Herbert Hoover, and Richard Nixon.

William McKinley versus William Jennings Bryan

Felzenberg considered McKinley one of our better presidents, in a tie for seventh place along with Zachary Taylor, Ulysses Grant, Harry Truman, and John Kennedy. He gave McKinley top scores of five for character and defense, national security, and foreign policy, then fours for competence and economic policy, a three for vision, and a two for preserving and extending liberty.[7]

Felzenberg probably is correct in his evaluation of McKinley, but the 25th president most likely will continue to be elusive for historians. Evaluations of him will range from those who believe he was at worst a decent, well-meaning man not up to the job of president, a man who was influenced and led by stronger personalities, to those who credit him with command of his administration and with patiently leading the country where he wanted it to go. Over the years since his assassination, rankings of presidents have categorized McKinley as average or above average; none placed him among the great or the near great on the one hand or stigmatized him as a failure or below average.[8]

Walter A. McDougall, in his study of the presidents published by *National Review* on October 27, 1967, diverged somewhat from Felzenberg, classifying seven as great: Washington, Jefferson, Lincoln, Theodore Roosevelt, Franklin Delano Roosevelt, Eisenhower, and Reagan. Felzenberg and McDougall were in general accord on those in the great group, except Jefferson; Felzenberg put him in 14th place. As failures, McDougall labeled: William Henry Harrison, Tyler, Taylor, Buchanan, Andrew Johnson, Grant, Wilson, Hoover, Lyndon Johnson, and Carter. There were no attention-grabbing differences here, although Felzenberg did have a slightly higher placing for Lyndon Johnson.[9] The variation in their views of McKinley are quite pronounced with McDougall putting him in the below average slot. His reasons are interesting, showing his opposition to the expansionist policies of the McKinley Administration:

> William McKinley—Below Average: A very tough call, since he was an honorable man whose term came to be identified with the Spanish-American War and acquisition of colonies in 1898, neither of which he especially wanted. Most damning is his decision to annex the Philippines, which landed the Army in a bloody colonial war and launched the United States on its twentieth-century career as a self-righteous crusader. Suffice it to say that Woodrow Wilson *approved* of all that he did and could not wait to get his hands on the enhanced power of the presidency.[10]

McDougall's opposition to American overseas expansion clearly was a significant reason for his placing McKinley lower than did Felzenberg.

13. Relevance for Today

In 1996, Arthur Schlesinger, Jr., organized an evaluation of the presidency by a mostly liberal panel of historians and political scientists among whom were Doris Kearns Goodwin, James MacGregor Burns, Alan Brinkley, Henry Graff, and Eric Foner. Also part of the group were former governor of New York George Pataki and former United States Senator Paul Simon of Illinois. Six categories were available for their classification of the presidents: great, near great, high average, low average, below average, and failure. McKinley ended up in the high average grouping.

In 1997, the Intercollegiate Studies Institute brought together 38 scholars to the right of the Schlesinger aggregation. Included among them were Donald Kagan, Forrest McDonald, Harvey Mansfield, Martin Anderson, Larry Arnn, Richard Brookhiser, George Carey, and Burton Folsom. In the name of honest disclosure rather than egocentricity, the name of John M. Pafford also was among them. This panel also categorized McKinley as one of our high average chief executives. At that time, I personally considered McKinley average. Having studied him more, I now rate him high average.

As can be seen by comparing the side by side survey results, the panels agreed in most cases concerning the ranking of presidents through Taft. Then, as the era of big government as a principle rather than as a response to a crisis took root, the sharp differences in the two sets of scholars doing the evaluating becomes evident. The Schlesinger Survey gives higher positions to those presidents favoring bigger government as the key criterion for placement in the upper echelons. The ISI survey takes a more conservative/libertarian stance in determining the placement of them.

The controversy over how to view some of our past chief executives still is very much alive, and it is not likely to end as long as people have the liberty to think freely and to express these thoughts without fear of reprisal. Of particular note are the sharp differences between the two surveys in the placement of Ronald Reagan, Calvin Coolidge and John Kennedy. *See table next page.*

It is not likely that McKinley's ranking in the average to high average range will change. He was not a dynamic leader who excited the feelings of people and he preferred to influence events from behind the scenes. There is general agreement that he was a Christian man, honest, well meaning as well as being politically adept. The controversy about him is focused on his abilities, on the extent to which he was a leader who controlled his

William McKinley versus William Jennings Bryan

	Schlesinger Survey	*ISI Survey*
GREAT	Washington, Lincoln, F.D. Roosevelt	Washington, Lincoln
NEAR GREAT	Jefferson, Jackson, Polk, T. Roosevelt, Wilson, Truman	Jefferson, Jackson, Reagan, T. Roosevelt, F.D. Roosevelt, Eisenhower
HIGH AVERAGE	Monroe, Cleveland, McKinley, Eisenhower, Kennedy, L.B. Johnson, J. Adams	J. Adams, J.Q. Adams, Cleveland, McKinley, Taft, Coolidge, Truman, Polk, Monroe
LOW AVERAGE	Madison, J.Q. Adams, Van Buren, Hayes, Arthur, B. Harrison, Taft, Ford, Carter, Reagan, Bush, Clinton	Madison, Van Buren, Ford, B. Harrison, Hayes, Garfield, Arthur, Bush
BELOW AVERAGE	Tyler, Taylor, Fillmore, Coolidge	Tyler, Fillmore, Wilson, Kennedy, Nixon, Hoover
FAILURE	Pierce, Buchanan, A. Johnson, Grant, Harding, Hoover, Nixon	Buchanan, Grant, Harding, L.B. Johnson, Carter, Clinton, Pierce, A. Johnson[11]

administration. There are those who, agreeing about his exemplary personal character, see him as a man who was led too much by others to warrant rating him higher.

There are, though, realities which should be kept in mind. It is indisputable that the prosperity and power of the United States grew during the McKinley years. While it is true that when a country is in good shape, there are factors other than the occupant of the White House deserving credit, it is equally true that the responsibility for a country in decline will be laid squarely on the administration in office.

Final Thoughts

It is interesting to speculate how McKinley and Bryan would fit in today with their political parties. McKinley's Christian faith would be welcomed by the largest segment of the current Republican Party. The key difference he would note were he to zip through the years from his time to ours would be that American culture in the 21st century does not have the same degree of adherence to those cultural standards which characterized his time. Then there was more of a general acceptance of and support for those values. For example, there were fewer challenges to Christianity and to the traditional family. People today have to consider carefully the point at which supporting the freedom for individuals not only to express ideas freely, but also to act on them weakens our country by reducing societal stability and cohesion.

When it comes to analyzing where Bryan would be in the politics of today, more problems arise than was true of McKinley. His Christian theological and cultural beliefs would be out of step with the majority of Democrats today. The past 50 years have seen profound changes in that party concerning these matters. These convictions of his would find a welcome home with conservative Republicans today. However, his wanting to increase the size and scope of government would alienate them while appealing to liberal Democrats. So, he would not fit in well with either party today. Perhaps he instead would lead a new political alliance of cultural conservatives and political liberals. There does not seem to be, though, a large segment of the population so oriented.

If McKinley had not been assassinated and had served out his second term, it is likely that Theodore Roosevelt would have been elected in 1904 and reelected in 1908. The 1912 split of the Republican Party would not have occurred and Woodrow Wilson would not have won the White House that year. Could World War I have been prevented by a more assertive United States? Without that war, would Communism and Fascism have risen to positions of power from which they inflicted as much misery on so many? Further speculation concerning how history might have been changed had McKinley served two full terms lie beyond the scope of an historical biography, although it does provide the basis for an enjoyable foray into counterfactual history.

William McKinley left behind a country stronger and more prosperous than it had been when he first took the oath of office back on March 4, 1897. He was a man of principle, an adept politician, and a capable administrator who should be remembered well by each new generation as it inherits this country.

Chapter Notes

Chapter 1

1. H. Wayne Morgan, *William McKinley and His America* (Syracuse: Syracuse University Press, 1963), p. 16.

2. Tom Chaffin, *Pathfinder: John Charles Fremont and the Course of American Empire* (New York: Hill and Wang, 2002), pp. 472–474.

3. Morgan, *William McKinley and His America*, p. 23.

4. J.F.C. Fuller, *Decisive Battles of the U.S.A.* (New York: Thomas Yoseloff, 1942), p. 206.

5. Morgan, *William McKinley and His America*, p. 25.

6. David Herbert Donald, *Lincoln* (New York: Simon & Schuster, 1995), pp. 354, 362–364, 377–379. Todd Brewster, *Lincoln's Gamble: The Tumultuous Six Months that Gave America the Emancipation Proclamation and Changed the Course of the Civil War* (New York: Scribner, 2014), pp. 245–249.

7. Geoffrey Perret, *Ulysses S. Grant: Soldier and President* (New York: Random House, 1997), p. 173.

8. Shelby Foote, *The Civil War: A Narrative*, vol. 2: *Fredericksburg to Meridian* (New York: Vintage Books), p. 580.

9. Geoffrey Perret, *Lincoln's War: The Untold Story of America's Greatest President as Commander in Chief* (New York: Random House, 2004), p. 391.

10. Harry Barnard, *Rutherford B. Hayes and His America* (New York: Bobbs-Merrill, 1954), p. 219.

11. Charles Bracelen Flood, *1864: Lincoln at the Gates of History* (New York: Simon & Schuster, 2009), p. 338.

12. Morgan, *William McKinley and His America*, p. 30.

13. *Ibid.*, p. 33.

14. Hans L. Trefousse, *Rutherford Hayes* (New York: Times Books, Henry Holt, 2002), pp. 45–62.

15. Jean Edward Smith, *Grant* (New York: Simon & Schuster, 2001), pp. 458–461.

16. Morgan, *William McKinley and His America*, pp. 47–49, 12.

17. Trefousse, *Rutherford B. Hayes*, pp. 61–66.

18. Michael A. Bellesiles, *1877: America's Year of Living Violently* (New York: The New Press, 2010), p. 35.

19. *Ibid.*

20. Trefousse, *Rutherford B. Hayes*, pp. 82–83; Smith, *Grant*, p. 598.

21. Morgan, *William McKinley and His America*, p. 58.

22. Charles W. Calhoun, *Benjamin Harrison* (New York: Times Books, Henry Holt, 2005), p. 141.

23. Ronald C. White, Jr., *A. Lincoln: A Biography* (New York: Random House, 2009), p. 192.

24. http://immigrationtounitedstates. org/advocacy-organizations-and-movements/, American Protective Association, pp. 1–3.

Chapter 2

1. Michael Kazin, *A Godly Hero: The Life of William Jennings Bryan* (New York: Alfred A. Knopf, 2006), p. 7.

2. *Ibid.*, pp. 12–13.

3. *Ibid.*, pp. 13–14.

4. William Jennings Bryan and Mary Baird Bryan, *The Memoirs of William Jennings Bryan* (Chicago: John C. Winston, 1925), pp. 248–249.

5. Jules Witcover, *Party of the People: A History of the Democrats* (New York: Random House, 2003), p. 269.

6. *Ibid.*

7. Joseph Nathan Kane, *Facts about the Presidents* (New York: Ace Books, 1976), pp. 650–651.

8. Kazin, *A Godly Hero*, pp. 33–36.

9. Kane, *Facts About the Presidents*, pp. 253–254.

10. Kazin, *A Godly Hero*, pp. 41–43.

Chapter 3

1. Grover Cleveland, *Grover Cleveland: Addresses, State Papers and Letters*, Albert Ellery Bergh, ed. (New York: Sun Dial Classics, 1909), p. 381.

2. Morgan, *William McKinley and His America*, p. 225.

3. *Ibid.*, pp. 215–216.

4. Wikipedia, "Silver Threads Among the Gold," http://en.wikipedia.org/wiki/Silver_Threads_Among_the_Gold.

5. Michael J. Connolly, *I Make Politics My Recreation: Vice President Garret A. Hobart and Nineteenth Century Republican Business Politics* (Newark: New Jersey Historical Society, 2010) p. 27.

6. David Magie, *Life of Garret Augustus Hobart: Twenty-fourth Vice-President of the United States* (New York: G.P. Putnam's Sons, 1910), p. 279.

7. Witcover, *Party of the People: A History of the Democrats*, p. 275.

8. William J. Bryan, *The First Battle: A Story of the Campaign of 1896* (Chicago: W. B. Conkey, 1896), p. 208.

9. Quoted in John M. Pafford, *The Forgotten Conservative: Rediscovering Grover Cleveland* (Washington, D.C.: Regnery History, 2013), p. 121.

10. American Rhetoric: Online Speech Bank, William Jennings Bryan "A Cross of Gold," http://www.americanrhetoric.com/speeches/williamjenningsbryan1896dnc.htm.

11. *Ibid.*

12. *Ibid.*

13. *Ibid.*

14. *Ibid.*

15. *Ibid.*

16. Bryan, *The First Battle*, p. 228.

17. See Wikipedia page 9: http://en.wikipedia.org/wiki/1896_Democratic_National_Convention.

18. Grover Cleveland, *Letters of Grover Cleveland*, Allan Nevins, ed. (Boston: Houghton Mifflin, 1933), p. 456.

19. Morgan, *William McKinley and His America*, pp. 241–242.

20. *Ibid.*, p. 241.

21. Bryan, *The First Battle*, pp. 276–277.

22. http://projects.vassar.edu/1896democrats.html.

23. Bryan, *The First Battle*, pp. 178–187.

24. Edward P. Kohn, *Hot Time in the Old Town: The Great Heat Wave of 1896 and the Making of Theodore Roosevelt* (New York: Basic Books, 2010), p. 174.

25. *Ibid.*, pp. 53–55.

26. *Ibid.*, p. 167.

27. *Ibid.*, p. 228.

28. *Ibid.*, p. 230.

29. Edmund Morris, *The Rise of Theodore Roosevelt* (New York: The Modern Library, 2001), p. 355.

30. Kazin, *A Godly Hero*, pp. 67–68, 321n.64.

31. Morgan, *William McKinley and His America*, p. 233.

32. Theodore Roosevelt, *Campaigns and Controversies*, vol. XIV: *The Works of Theodore Roosevelt* (New York: Charles Scribner's Sons, 1926), p. 258.

33. Theodore Roosevelt, *The Selected Letters of Theodore Roosevelt*, H. W. Brands, ed. (New York: Cooper Square Press, 2001), p. 124.

34. Theodore Roosevelt, *Campaigns and Controversies*, p. 256.

35. Kane, *Facts About the President*, p. 202.

36. *Ibid.*

37. Morgan, *William McKinley and His America*, p. 246.

38. Kazin, *A Godly Hero*, p. 81.

39. *Ibid.*, pp. xviii–xix.

40. *Ibid.*, pp. 81–82.

41. James Ford Rhodes, *The McKinley and Roosevelt Administrations, 1897–*

1909 (New York: Macmillan, 1922), p. 45.

42. Pafford, *The Forgotten Conservative*, pp. 127–128.

Chapter 4

1. C. Bernard Ruffin, *Profiles of Faith: The Religious Beliefs of Eminent Americans* (Ligouri, MO: Ligouri/Triumph, 1997), p. 223.

2. William McKinley, *Speeches and Addresses of William McKinley* (New York: Doubleday and McClure, 1900), p. 2.

3. *Ibid.*, p. 3.

4. *Ibid.*, pp. 4–5.

5. *Ibid.*, pp. 5–6.

6. Morgan, *William McKinley and His America*, pp. 251–253.

7. Michael Blow, *A Ship to Remember: The Maine and the Spanish-American War* (New York: William Morrow, 1992), pp. 71–72.

8. David Rockefeller, *Memoirs* (New York: Random House, 2002), p. 11.

9. Jean Strouse, *Morgan: American Financier* (New York: Random House, 1999), pp. 344, 348, 350.

10. Vincent Curcio, *Henry Ford* (New York: Oxford University Press, 2013), pp. 22–24.

11. Douglas Brinkley, *Wheels for the World: Henry Ford, His Company, and a Century of Progress 1903–2003* (New York: Viking, 2003), p. 31.

12. Fred Howard, *Wilbur and Orville, A Biography of the Wright Brothers* (New York: Alfred A. Knopf, 1987), pp. 125, 129–131.

13. Tevi Troy, *What Jefferson Read, Ike Watched, and Obama Tweeted* (Washington, D.C.: Regnery, 2013), pp. 60, 62.

14. Brodsky, *Grover Cleveland*, p. 165.

15. Larry Madaras and James M. SoRelle, eds., *Reconstruction to the Present*, vol. 11: *Clashing Views on Controversial Issues in American History* (Guilford, CT: McGraw-Hill/Dushkin, 2001), p. 75.

16. *Ibid.*, p. 111.

17. Morgan, *William McKinley and His America*, p. 280.

18. *Ibid.*, p. 281.

19. *Ibid.*, p. 289.

Chapter 5

1. G.J.A. O'Toole, *The Spanish War: An American Epic—1898* (New York: W. W. Norton, 1984), pp. 57–58.

2. Paul Grondahl, *I Rose Like a Rocket: The Political Education of Theodore Roosevelt* (New York: Free Press, 2004), pp. 244–246.

3. Nathan Miller, *The U.S. Navy: A History*, 3d ed. (Annapolis: Naval Institute Press, 1997), p. 155; Stephen Howarth, *A History of the United States Navy, 1775–1998* (Norman: University of Oklahoma Press, 1999), p. 288.

4. George Dewey, *Autobiography of George Dewey Admiral of the Navy* (New York: Charles Scribner's Sons, 1913), pp. 168–169.

5. Morris, *The Rise of Theodore Roosevelt*, pp. 586–587.

6. *Ibid.*, p. 602.

7. O'Toole, *The Spanish War: An American Epic—1898*, p. 22.

8. Ivan Musicant, *Empire by Default: The Spanish-American War and the Dawn of the American Century* (New York: Henry Holt, 1998), pp. 90–91, 122.

9. David Traxel, *1898: The Birth of the American Century* (New York: Alfred A. Knopf, 1998), p. 99.

10. O'Toole, *The Spanish War: An American Epic—1898*, p. 122.

11. Musicant, *Empire by Default*, p. 279.

Chapter 6

1. O'Toole, *The Spanish War: An American Epic—1898*, pp. 28–29.

2. Blow, *A Ship to Remember: The Maine and the Spanish-American War*, pp. 114–115, 410–411.

3. O'Toole, *The Spanish War: An American Epic*, p. 127.

4. Morris, *The Rise of Theodore Roosevelt*, pp. 604–605.

5. *Ibid.*

6. Blow, *A Ship to Remember*, pp. 155–156.

7. Morris, *The Rise of Theodore Roosevelt*, pp. 606–607.

8. *Ibid.*, p. 608.

9. McKinley, *Speeches and Addresses of William McKinley*, p. 135.
10. Patrick W. Carey, *Catholics in America: A History* (Westport, CT: Praeger, 2004), p. 64.
11. Morris, *The Rise of Theodore Roosevelt*, p. 614.
12. Morgan, *William McKinley and His America*, pp. 290–291.
13. Theodore Roosevelt, *The Rough Riders*, vol. XI: *The Works of Theodore Roosevelt* (New York: Charles Scribner's Sons, 1926), p. 6.
14. *Ibid.*, p. 14.
15. Arthur Herman, *To Rule the Waves: How the British Shaped the Modern World* (New York: Harper Perennial, 2005), pp. 462–463.
16. *Ibid.*, p. 476.
17. Musicant, *Empire By Default*, pp. 201–202.
18. Fuller, *Decisive Battles of the U.S.A.*, p. 337.
19. *Ibid.*, pp. 202–203, 207.
20. Musicant, *Empire By Default*, p. 228.
21. Dewey, *Autobiography of George Dewey Admiral of the Navy*, pp. 222–223; Musicant, *Empire By Default*, p. 228.
22. David J. Silbey, *A War of Frontier and Empire: The Philippine-American War, 1899–1902* (New York: Hill and Wang, 2007), pp. 13–16.
23. Musicant, *Empire By Default*, p. 197.
24. Dewey, *Autobiography of George Dewey Admiral of the Navy*, pp. 246–247.
25. O'Toole, *The Spanish War: An American Epic—1898*, p. 250.
26. Musicant, *Empire By Default*, p. 547.
27. Silbey, *A War of Frontier and Empire: The Philippine-American War, 1899–1902*, p. 44.
28. Dewey, *Autobiography of George Dewey Admiral of the Navy*, pp. 254–256.
29. *Ibid.*, pp. 262–267.
30. John C. G. Rohl, *Kaiser Wilhelm II, 1859–1941: A Concise Life*, Sheila De Billaigue, trans. (Cambridge: Cambridge University Press, 2014), pp. 78–79.
31. Fuller, *Decisive Battles of the U.S.A.*, p. 336.
32. *Ibid.*

33. H. Paul Jeffers, *Colonel Roosevelt: Theodore Roosevelt Goes to War, 1897–1898* (New York: John Wiley and Sons, 1996), pp. 181–182.
34. Virgil Carrington Jones, *Roosevelt's Rough Riders* (Garden City, NY: Doubleday, 1971), p. 60.
35. Jerome Tuccille, *The Roughest Riders: The Untold Story of the Black Soldiers in the Spanish-American War* (Chicago: Chicago Review Press Incorporated, 2015), p. 6.
36. *Ibid.*, p. 191.
37. Theodore Roosevelt, *The Rough Riders*, vol. XI, *The Works of Theodore Roosevelt* (New York: Charles Scribner's Sons, 1926), p. 52.
38. Fuller, *Decisive Battles of the U.S.A.*, p. 350.
39. John McCain and Mack Salter, *Thirteen Soldiers: A Personal History of Americans at War* (New York: Simon & Schuster, 2014), p. 156.
40. Gail Buckley, *American Patriots: The Story of Blacks in the Military from the Revolution to Desert Storm* (New York: Random House Trade Paperbacks, 2002), pp. 120–121.
41. Jerome Tuecille, *The Roughest Riders: Untold Stories of the Black Soldiers in the Spanish-American War* (Chicago: Chicago Review Press, 2015), p. 250.
42. Buckley, *American Patriots*, p. 198.
43. *Ibid.*
44. O'Toole, *The Spanish War: An American Epic—1898*, p. 293.
45. Fuller, *Decisive Battles of the U.S.A.*, p. 335.
46. Walter La Feber, *The American Search for Opportunity*, vol. 11 of *The Cambridge History of American Foreign Relations* (New York: Cambridge University Press, 1993), p. 146.
47. O'Toole, *The Spanish War: An American Epic—1898*, pp. 345–346.
48. *Ibid.*, p. 346.
49. *Ibid.*, p. 348.
50. *Ibid.*, p. 350.
51. *Ibid.*
52. Theodore Roosevelt, *The Rough Riders*, pp. 165–166.
53. *Ibid.*, p. 168.
54. Morris, *The Rise of Theodore Roosevelt*, pp. 659–662.

Chapter 7

1. McKinley, *Speeches and Addresses of William McKinley*, pp. 186–187.
2. *Ibid.*, p. 191.
3. Ralph F. Young, *Dissent in America: The Voices That Shaped a Nation* (New York: Pearson Longman, 2006), p. 361.
4. *Ibid.*
5. John Ford Rhodes, *The McKinley and Roosevelt Administrations 1897–1909* (New York: Macmillan, 1922), pp. 101–102.
6. Harry Ricketts, *Rudyard Kipling: A Life* (New York: Carroll and Graff, 1997), p. 233.
7. *Ibid.*, pp. 234–235.
8. Kazin, *A Godly Hero*, pp. 86–87.
9. *Ibid.*, p. 88.
10. *Ibid.*, p. 89.
11. *Ibid.*, p. 90.

Chapter 8

1. Grover Cleveland, *Addresses, State Papers, and Letters*, pp. 353–354.
2. John Lukacs, *The Passing of the Modern Age* (New York: Harper Torchbooks, 1970), p. 85.
3. McKinley, *Speeches and Addresses of William McKinley*, p. 166.
4. *Ibid.*, p. 168.
5. *Ibid.*, p. 177.
6. *Ibid.*, p. 178.

Chapter 9

1. Allen Churchill, *Remember When: A Loving Look at Days Gone By—1900–1942* (New York: Golden Press, 1967), p. 16.
2. Paul Johnson, *A History of the American People* (New York: HarperCollins, 1997), p. 585.
3. Alexis de Tocqueville, *Democracy in America*, Harvey C. Mansfield and Delba Winthrop, trans. and eds. (Chicago: University of Chicago Press, 2000), pp. 395–396.
4. Maurice Matloff, ed., *American Military History*, vol. 1 *1775–1902* (Conshohocken, PA: Combined Books, 1996), p. 340.

5. *Ibid.*, pp. 341–342.
6. *Ibid.*
7. Morris, *The Rise of Theodore Roosevelt*, p. 723.
8. *Ibid.*, p. 724.
9. *Ibid.*, pp. 725–726.
10. *Ibid.*, pp. 726–728.
11. Bryan, *The Memoirs of William Jennings Bryan*, p. 125.
12. Kazin, *A Godly Hero*, p. 106.
13. *Ibid.*, pp. 102–103.
14. Julian E. Zelizer, ed., *The American Congress: The Building of Democracy* (Boston: Houghton Mifflin, 2004), p. 254.
15. James Chace, *1912. Wilson, Roosevelt, Taft and Debs—the Election that Changed the Country* (New York: Simon & Schuster, 2004), p. 85.
16. Ralph F. Young, *Dissent in America: The Voices that Shaped a Nation* (New York: Pearson Longman, 2006), p. 364.
17. *Ibid.*, p. 368.
18. *Ibid.*
19. Kazin, *A Godly Hero*, pp. 93–94.
20. Zelizer, ed., *The American Congress: The Building of Democracy*, p. 254.
21. *Ibid.*, p. 255.
22. R. Hal Williams, *Years of Decision: American Politics in the 1890s* (New York: John Wiley and Sons, 1978), p. 154.

Chapter 10

1. R. Hal Williams, *Years of Decision*, p. 155.
2. Tony Rennell, *Last Days of Glory: The Death of Queen Victoria* (New York: St. Martin Press, 2000), p. 198.
3. Rhodes, *The McKinley and Roosevelt Administrations 1897–1909*, p. 180.
4. Paul F. Boller, Jr., *Presidential Inaugurations* (New York: Harcourt, 2001), pp. 231–232.
5. http://www.bartleby.com/124/pres41.html, p. 2.
6. *Ibid.*
7. *Ibid.*, p. 3.
8. *Ibid.*, pp. 5–6.
9. *Ibid.*, p. 7.
10. David Howard Bain, *Sitting In Darkness: Americans in the Philippines* (Boston: Houghton Mifflin, 1984), pp. 99–101, 367.
11. Buckley, *American Patriots*, p. 157.

12. *Ibid.*, p. 158.

13. Williams, *Years of Decision*, p. 157.

14. Margaret Leech, *In the Days of McKinley* (Norwalk, CT: The Easton Press, 1986), pp. 595–596.

15. *Ibid.*, pp. 598–600.

16. *Ibid.*, p. 601.

17. Morgan, *William McKinley and His America*, p. 524.

18. Rick Beyer, *The Greatest Presidential Stories Never Told: 100 Tales From History to Astonish, Bewilder and Stupefy* (New York: HarperCollins, 2007), p. 120.

19. Louis Albert Banks, *The Religious Life of Famous Americans* (Boston: American Tract Society, 1904), pp. 69–70.

20. Grover Cleveland, *Addresses, State Papers and Letters*, Albert Ellery Bergh, ed. (New York: Sun Dial Classics, 1909), p. 414.

21. Rhodes, *The McKinley and Roosevelt Administrations, 1897–1909*, p. 57.

22. Roosevelt, *State Papers as Governor and President*, vol. XV: *The Works of Theodore Roosevelt*, pp. 81–82.

23. Gould, *Grand Old Party: A History of the Republicans*, p. 136.

24. *Ibid.*, p. 132.

17. Kazin, *A Godly Hero*, pp. 165–167.

18. Morris, *Colonel Roosevelt*, pp. 207–208.

19. James Chase, *1912: Wilson, Roosevelt, Taft and Debs: The Election That Changed the Country* (New York: Simon & Schuster, 2004), p. 110.

20. H. W. Brands, *T.R.: The Last Romantic* (New York: Basic Books, 1997), p. 683.

21. Chase, *1912*, p. 113.

22. Paul F. Boller, Jr., *Presidential Campaigns* (New York: Oxford University Press, 1984), p. 192; Morris, *Colonel Roosevelt*, pp. 191–193, 200.

23. Chace, *1912*, p. 122.

24. *Ibid.*, p. 125.

25. Witcover, *Party of the People*, p. 306.

26. *Ibid.*, p. 307.

27. Roosevelt, *The Works of Theodore Roosevelt*, vol. XI: *The Rough Riders and Men of Action*, p. 273.

28. Brands, *TR: The Last Romantic*, p. 719.

29. James Chace, *1912* (New York: Simon & Schuster, 2004), p. 167.

30. *Ibid.*, pp. 195–196.

31. *Ibid.*, pp. 230–233.

Chapter 11

1. Kazin, *A Godly Hero*, pp. 111–112.

2. Witcover, *Party of the People*, pp. 292–293.

3. Kazin, *A Godly Hero*, p. 113.

4. Morris, *Theodore Rex*, p. 342.

5. *Ibid.*

6. David Nasaw, *The Chief: The Life of William Randolph Hearst* (Boston: Houghton Mifflin, 2000), pp. 181–183.

7. Witcover, *Party of the People*, p. 294.

8. Kazin, *A Godly Hero*, pp. 131–132.

9. *Ibid.*, p. 146.

10. *Ibid.*, p. 153.

11. Goodwin, *The Bully Pulpit*, p. 554.

12. Witcover, *Party of the People*, p. 297.

13. Kazin, *A Godly Hero*, p. 164.

14. Chester Gillis, *Roman Catholicism in America* (New York: Columbia University Press, 1999), p. 66.

15. Kazin, *A Godly Hero*, p. 166.

16. Gillis, *Roman Catholicism in America*, p. 60.

Chapter 12

1. Kazin, *A Godly Hero*, pp. 217–218.

2. *Ibid.*, p. 231.

3. Eleanor Roosevelt, *The Autobiography of Eleanor Roosevelt* (New York: Harper and Brothers, 1961), p. 82.

4. Kazan, *A Godly Hero*, pp. 235–238.

5. *Ibid.*, pp. 259–260.

6. Geoffrey Perrett, *America in the Twenties: A History* (New York: Simon & Schuster, 1982), p. 199.

7. Kazin, *A Godly Hero*, p. 287.

8. Sadakat Kadri, *The Trial: A History from Socrates to O.J. Simpson* (New York: Random House, 2005), pp. 282–283.

9. Bryan, *The Memoirs of William Jennings Bryan*, pp. 526–527.

10. *Ibid.*, p. 527.

11. *Ibid.*, p. 532.

12. Terry Teachout, *The Skeptic: A Life of H.L. Mencken* (New York: HarperCollins, 2002), p. 220.

13. Kazin, *A Godly Hero*, p. 171.

Chapter 13

1. Bryan, *The Memoirs of William Jennings Bryan*, p. 10.

2. R. Hal Williams, *Years of Decision: American Politics in the 1890s*, p. 156.

3. Samuel Eliot Morison, *The Oxford History of the American People* (New York: Oxford University Press, 1965), p. 799.

4. Evan Thomas, *The War Lovers: Roosevelt, Lodge, Hearst, and the Rush to Empire, 1898* (New York: Little, Brown, 2010), p. 224.

5. Charles G. Dawes, *A Journal of the McKinley Years* (Chicago: The Lakeside Press, 1950), p. 129.

6. Cleveland, *Addresses, State Papers and Letters*, p. 283.

7. Arthur S. Felzenberg, *The Leaders We Deserved (And a Few We Didn't): Rethinking the Presidential Rating Game* (New York: Basic Books, 2008), p. 378.

8. Robert W. Merry, *Where They Stand* (New York: Simon & Schuster, 2012), pp. 244–245.

9. Walter A. McDougall, "Rating the Presidents," *National Review*, October 27, 1967, pp. 32–36.

10. *Ibid.*, p. 34.

11. *The Weekly Standard*, September 29, 1997, p. 23.

Bibliography

Primary Sources

Bryan, William Jennings. *The First Battle: A Story of the Campaign of 1896.* Chicago: W. B. Conkey, 1896.
_____, and Mary Baird Bryan. *The Memoirs of William Jennings Bryan.* Chicago: John C. Winston, 1895.
Cleveland, Grover. *Addresses, State Papers and Letters.* Albert Ellery Bergh, ed. New York: Sun Dial Classics, 1909.
_____. *Letters of Grover Cleveland.* Allan Nevins, ed. Boston: Houghton Mifflin, 1933.
Dawes, Charles G. *A Journal of the McKinley Years.* Chicago: The Lakeside Press, 1950.
Dewey, George. *Autobiography of George Dewey Admiral of the Navy.* New York: Charles Scribner's Sons, 1913.
Douglass, Frederick. *The Life and Times of Frederick Douglass.* New York: Doubleday and McClure, 1900.
McKinley, William. *Speeches and Addresses of William McKinley.* New York: Doubleday and McClure, 1900.
Rockefeller, David. *Memoirs.* New York: Random House, 2000.
Roosevelt, Eleanor. *The Autobiography of Eleanor Roosevelt.* New York: Harper and Brothers, 1961.
Roosevelt, Theodore. *An Autobiography,* vol. XX of *Ibid.*
_____. *Campaigns and Controversies,* vol. XIV of *Ibid.*
_____. *The Rough Riders,* vol. XI of *The Works of Theodore Roosevelt.* New York: Charles Scribner's Sons, 1926.
_____. *The Selected Letters of Theodore Roosevelt.* H. W. Brands, ed. New York: Cooper Square Press, 2001.

Secondary Sources

Anthony, Carl Sferraza. *First Ladies: The Saga of the Presidents' Wives and Their Power 1789–1961.* New York: William Morrow, 1990.
Auchincloss, Louis. *Theodore Roosevelt.* New York: Times Books, 2001.
Barnard, Harry. *Rutherford B. Hayes and His America.* New York: Bobbs-Merrill, 1954.
Bellesiles, Michael. *1877: America's Year of Living Violently.* New York: The New Press, 2010.
Blow, Michael. *A Ship to Remember: The Maine and the Spanish-American War.* New York: William Morrow, 1997.
Boller, Paul E., Jr. *Presidential Campaigns.* New York: Oxford University Press, 1984.
Bradford, James E., ed. *Crucible of Empire: The Spanish-American War and Its Aftermath.* Annapolis: Naval Institute Press, 1993.

Bibliography

Bradley, James. *The Imperial Cruise: A Secret History of Empire and War.* New York: Little, Brown, 2009.

Brands, H.W. *T.R.: The Last Romantic.* New York: Basic Books, 1997.

Brinkley, Douglas. *Wheels for the World: Henry Ford, His Company, and a Century of Progress 1903–2003.* New York: Viking, 2003.

Brodsky, Alyn. *Grover Cleveland: A Study in Character.* New York: St. Martin's Press, 2000.

Buckley, Gail. *American Patriots: The Story of Blacks in the Military from the Revolution to Desert Storm.* New York: Random House Paperbacks, 2002.

Cadenhead, J.E., Jr. *Theodore Roosevelt: The Paradox of Progressivism.* Woodbury, NY: Barron's Educational Series, 1974.

Calhoun, Charles W. *Benjamin Harrison.* New York: Times Books, 2005.

Carey, Patrick W. *Catholics in America: A History.* Westport, CT: Praeger, 2004.

Cashman, Sean Dennis. *America in the Gilded Age: From the Death of Lincoln to the Rise of Theodore Roosevelt.* New York: New York University Press, 1984.

Chace, James. *1912. Wilson, Roosevelt, Taft and Debs—the Election that Changed the Country.* New York: Simon & Schuster, 2004.

Chafin, Tom. *Pathfinder: John Charles Fremont and the Course of American Empire.* New York: Hill and Wang, 2002.

Churchill, Allen. *Remember When: A Loving Look at Days Gone By—1900–1942.* New York: Golden Press, 1967.

Connolly, Michael J. *I Make Politics My Recreation: Vice President Garret A. Hobart and Nineteenth Century Republican Business Politics.* Newark: New Jersey Historical Society, 2010.

Curcio, Vincent. *Henry Ford.* New York: Oxford University Press, 2013.

Dalton, Kathleen. *Theodore Roosevelt: A Strenuous Life.* New York: Alfred A. Knopf, 2002.

Denison, John V., ed. *Reassessing the Presidency: The Rise of the Executive State and the Decline of Freedom.* Auburn: Ludwig von Mises Institute, 2001.

DeRose, Chris. *The Presidents: Six American Presidents and the Civil War That Divided Them.* Guilford, CT: Lyons Press, 2014.

Donald, David Herbert. *Lincoln.* New York: Simon & Schuster, 1995.

Dumond, Dwight Lowell. *Roosevelt to Roosevelt: The United States in the Twentieth Century.* New York: Henry Holt, 1937.

Felzenberg, Arthur S. *The Leaders We Deserved (and a Few We Didn't): Rethinking the Presidential Rating Game.* New York: Basic Books, 2008.

Foote, Shelby. *Fredericksburg to Meridian,* vol. 2 of *The Civil War: A Narrative.* New York: Vintage Books, 1963.

Fuller, J.F.C. *Decisive Battles of the U.S.A.* New York: Thomas Yoseloff, 1942.

Gillis, Chester. *Roman Catholicism in America.* New York: Columbia University Press, 1999.

Goodwin, Doris Kearns. *The Bully Pulpit: Theodore Roosevelt, William Howard Taft, and the Golden Age of Journalism.* New York: Simon & Schuster, 2013.

Gould, Lewis L. *Grand Old Party: A History of the Republicans.* New York: Random House, 2003.

Graf, Henry F. *Grover Cleveland.* New York: Times Books, 2002.

Green, Robert P., Jr. *Historic U.S. Court Cases: An Encyclopedia,* 2d ed. John W. Johnson, ed. New York: Routledge, 2001.

Grondahl, Paul. *I Rose Like a Rocket: The Political Education of Theodore Roosevelt.* New York: Free Press, 2004.

Harpine, William D. *From the Front Porch to the Front Page: McKinley and Bryan in the 1896 Presidential Campaign.* College Station: Texas A & M University Press, 2005.

Healy, Gene. *The Cult of the Presidency: America's Dangerous Devotion to Executive Power.* Washington, D.C.: Cato Institute, 2008.

Hoffer, Peter Charles, Williamjames Hull Hoffer, and N.E.H. Hull. *The Supreme Court: An Essential History.* Lawrence: University of Kansas Press, 2007.

Bibliography

Howard, Fred. *Wilbur and Orville: A Biography of the Wright Brothers.* New York: Alfred A. Knopf, 1987.

Howard, Robert P. *Mostly Good and Competent Men,* 2d ed. Springfield, IL: The Institute of Public Affairs, 1988.

Howarth, Stephen. *A History of the United States Navy, 1775–1998.* Norman: University of Oklahoma Press, 1999.

Huggins, Nathan Irvin. *Slave and Citizen: The Life of Frederick Douglass.* Boston: Little, Brown, 1980.

Jeffers, H. Paul. *Colonel Roosevelt: Theodore Roosevelt Goes to War, 1897–1898.* New York: John Wiley and Sons, 1996.

_____. *An Honest President: The Life and Presidencies of Grover Cleveland.* New York: HarperCollins, 2000.

Johnson, Paul. *A History of the American People.* New York: HarperCollins, 1997.

Jones, Stanley, *The Presidential Election of 1896.* Madison: University of Wisconsin Press, 1964.

Jones, Virgil Carrington. *Roosevelt's Rough Riders.* Garden City, NY: Doubleday, 1971.

Kadri, Sadaket. *The Trial: A History from Socrates to O.J. Simpson.* New York: Random House, 2005.

Kazin, Michael. *A Godly Hero: The Life of William Jennings Bryan.* New York: Alfred A. Knopf, 2006.

Kohn, Edward P. *Hot Time in the Old Town: The Great Wave of 1896 and the Making of Theodore Roosevelt.* New York: Basic Books, 2010.

LaFeber, Walter. *The American Search for Opportunity,* vol. II: *The Cambridge History of Foreign Relations.* New York: Cambridge University Press, 1993.

Linn, Brian McAllister. *The Philippine War 1899–1902.* Lawrence: University Press of Kansas, 2000.

Lukacs, John. *The Passing of the Modern Age.* New York: Harper Torchbooks, 1970.

Magie, David. *Life of Garrett Augustus Hobart: Twenty-Fourth Vice President of the United States.* New York: G.P. Putnam's Sons, 1910.

Matloff, Maurice, ed. *American Military History,* vol. 1: *1775–1902.* Conshohocken, PA: Combined Books, 1990.

May, Ernest R. *Imperial Democracy: The Emergence of America as a Great Power.* New York: Harper Torchbooks, 1961.

McCain, John, and Mack Salter. *Thirteen Soldiers: A Personal History of Americans at War.* New York: Simon & Schuster, 2014.

McCutcheon, Marc. *The Writer's Guide to Everyday Life in the 1800s.* Cincinnati: Writer's Digest Books, 1993.

McElroy, Robert. *Grover Cleveland: The Man and the Statesman.* New York: Harper and Brothers, 1923.

McFeely, William S. *Frederick Douglass.* New York: W.W. Norton, 1991.

McGurrin, James. *Bourke Cockran: A Free Lance in American Politics.* New York: Charles Scribner's Sons, 1948.

Merrill, Horace Samuel. *Bourbon Leader: Grover Cleveland and the Democratic Party.* Boston: Little, Brown, 1957.

Merry, Robert W. *President McKinley: Architect of the American Century.* New York: Simon & Schuster, 2017.

Miller, Nathan. *The U.S. Navy: A History,* 3d ed. Annapolis: Naval Institute Press, 1997.

Miller, Scott. *The President and the Assassin: McKinley, Terror, and Empire at the Dawn of the American Century.* New York: Random House, 2011.

Morgan, H. Wayne. *William McKinley and His America.* Syracuse: Syracuse University Press, 1963.

Morris, Edmund. *The Rise of Theodore Roosevelt.* New York: Coward, McCann and Geoghegan, 1979.

_____. *Theodore Rex.* New York: Random House, 2001.

Bibliography

Musicant, Ivan. *Empire by Default: The Spanish-American War and the Dawn of the American Century*. New York: Henry Holt, 1998.

Nasaw, David. *The Chief: The Life of William Randolph Hearst*. Boston: Houghton Mifflin, 2000.

Nevins, Robert J. *Grover Cleveland: A Study in Courage*. New York: Dodd, Mead, 1932.

Norrell, Robert J. *Up from Slavery: The Life of Booker T. Washington*. Cambridge: The Belknap Press of Harvard University, 2009.

O'Toole, G.J.A. *The Spanish War: An American Epic—1898*. New York: W.W. Norton, 1984.

Pafford, John M. *The Forgotten Conservative: Rediscovering Grover Cleveland*. Washington, D.C.: Regnery History, 2013.

Perret, Geoffrey. *Lincoln's Way: The Untold Story of America's Greatest President as Commander in Chief*. New York: Random House, 1997.

_____. *Ulysses S. Grant: Soldier and President*. New York: Random House, 1997.

Rauchway, Eric. *Murdering McKinley: The Making of Theodore Roosevelt's America*. New York: Hill and Wang, 2003.

Reed, Lawrence W. *A Lesson in History: The Silver Panic of 1893*. Irvington-on-Hudson, NY: The Foundation for Economic Education, 1993.

Rhodes, James Ford. *The McKinley and Roosevelt Administration, 1897–1909*. New York: Macmillan, 1922.

Ricketts, Harry. *Rudyard Kipling: A Life*. New York: Carroll and Graf, 1997.

Roberts, Andrew. "The Whale Against the Wolf" in Robert Cowley, ed. *What If? Eminent Historians Imagine What Might Have Been*. New York: G.P. Putnam's Sons, 2003.

Rohl, John C.G. *Kaiser Wilhelm II, 1859–1941: A Concise Life*. Sheila DeBellaigue, trans. Cambridge: Cambridge University Press, 2014.

Ruffin, C. Bernard. *Profiles of Faith: The Religious Beliefs of Eminent Americans*. Ligouri, MO: Ligouri/Triumph, 1997.

Salvatore, Nick. *Eugene V. Debs: Citizen and Socialist*. Urbana: University of Illinois Press, 1987.

Schlesinger, Arthur M. *The Imperial Presidency*. Boston: Houghton Mifflin, 1973.

Schweikart, Larry, and Michael Allen. *A Patriot's History of the United States: From Columbus's Great Discovery to the War on Terror*. New York: Sentinel, 2004.

Shenkman, Richard. *Presidential Ambition: How the Presidents Gained Power, Kept Power, and Got Things Done*. New York: HarperCollins, 1999.

Silbey, David J. *A War of Frontier and Empire: The Philippine–American War, 1899–1902*. New York: Hill and Wang, 2007.

Siler, Julia Flynn. *Lost Kingdom: Hawaii's Lost Queen, the Sugar Kings, and America's First Imperial Adventure*. New York: Atlantic Monthly Press, 2012.

Smith, Page. *The Rise of Industrial America*, vol. 6 of *A People's History of the Post-Reconstruction Era*. New York: McGraw-Hill, 1984.

Smock, Raymond W. *Booker T. Washington: Black Leadership in the Age of Jim Crow*. Chicago: Ivan R. Dee, 2009.

Strouse, Jean. *Morgan: American Financier*. New York: Random House, 1999.

Tocqueville, Alexis de. *Democracy in America*. Harvey C. Mansfield and Delba Winthrop, trans. and eds. Chicago: University of Chicago Press, 2000.

Traxel, David. *Crusader Nation: United States in Peace and the Great War, 1898–1920*. New York: Alfred A. Knopf, 2006.

_____. *1898: The Birth of the American Century*. New York: Alfred A. Knopf, 1998.

Trefouse, Hans L. *Rutherford Hayes*. New York: Times Books, 2000.

Truman, Margaret. *First Ladies*. New York: Random House, 1994.

Tugwell, Rexford G. *Grover Cleveland*. New York: Macmillan, 1968.

Wead, Doug. *All the Presidents' Children: Triumph and Tragedy in the Lives of America's First Families*. New York: Atria Books, 2003.

Whalen, Thomas J. *A Higher Purpose: Profiles in Presidential Courage*. Chicago: Iran R. Dee, 2007.

Bibliography

Williams, R Hal. *Realigning America: McKinley, Bryan, and the Remarkable Election of 1896*. Lawrence University Press of Kansas, 2010.

_____. *Years of Decision: American Politics in the 1890s*. New York: John Wiley and Sons, 1978.

Witcover, Jules. *The American Vice Presidency: From Irrelevance to Power*. Washington, D.C.: Smithsonian Books, 2014.

_____. *Party of the People: A History of the Democrats*. New York: Random House, 2003.

Zinn, Howard. *A People's History of the United States 1492–Present*. New York: Harper-Collins, 1995.

Index

Index

Index

Index

Index

Index

Index

Vilas, William 38
Villa, Pancho 149
Vizcaya (Spanish ship) 85, 91

Wainwright, Richard 75
Wake Island 97–98
Wallace, Jonathan H. 24
Wanton, George 91
Warwick, John G. 24
Washington, Booker T. 107, 146
Washington, George 31, 126
Watson, Thomas 43, 136, 140
Weaver, James 29–30, 43–44, 47
Western Civilization 101–102, 155
Weyler, Valeriano 69, 72–73, 77
Wheeler, Joseph 87
Wheeler, William 22
Whig Party 146
White House 92
Whitney, William C. 37

Wilderness, Battle of the 14
Wildman, Rousenville 83
Williams, Oscar 83
Wilson, James 57
Wilson, Woodrow 6, 137, 142, 144–153
Winchester 16
women's suffrage 63, 152
Wood, Leonard 79, 89
Wooley, John 118, 122
World War I 150–152
Wright brothers (Orville and Wilbur) 61

x-ray machine 128

Young, Cy 109
Young, Samuel B.M. 87

Zafiro (U.S. ship) 81
Zeglen, Casimir 130